URBAN LIFE AND URBAN LANDSCAPE SERIES

BOSS COX'S CINCINNATI

Urban Politics in the Progressive Era

ZANE L. MILLER

With an
Introduction by
HOWARD P. CHUDACOFF

OHIO STATE UNIVERSITY PRESS
Columbus

Introduction copyright © 2000 by The Ohio State University.
First Ohio State University Press edition published 2000.

    Library of Congress Cataloging-in-Publication Data

Miller, Zane L.
    Boss Cox's Cincinnati : urban politics in the Progressive Era / Zane L.
Miller ; with an introduction by Howard P. Chudacoff.—1st Ohio State
University Press ed.
        p. cm. — (Urban life and urban landscape series)
    Originally published: New York : Oxford University Press, 1968. (The
Urban life in America series). With new introd.
    Includes bibliographical references and index.
    ISBN 0-8142-0861-4 (alk. paper) — ISBN 0-8142-5064-5 (pbk. : alk.
paper)
        1. Cincinnati (Ohio)—Politics and government.   2. Cox, George
Barnsdale, 1853–1916.   I. Title.   II. Series.

JS738 .M5 2000
320.9771′78—dc21   00-032647

Cover design by David Drummond.
Printed in the United States.

9 8 7 6 5 4 3 2 1

*To my mother and
the memory of my father*

Contents

Introduction

In 1968, when Oxford University Press published *Boss Cox's Cincinnati* in its Urban Life in America series, edited by Richard C. Wade, the number of scholars teaching and researching American urban history would probably have filled only a few booths in an inner-city diner. To be sure, amateur historians of varying competence had been producing urban biographies, survey chronicles of individual cities, for almost a century, and a few social and cultural historians such as Arthur M. Schlesinger, Carl Bridenbaugh, Bayrd Still, and Constance McLaughlin Green had written studies that focused on urban life.[1] Yet the academic-based study of urbanization was still in its infant—or at least, childhood—stage. Only in the previous few years had Wade's *The Urban Frontier* (1959) and Sam Bass Warner's *Streetcar Suburbs* (1962) sparked genuine interest in the field. Wade had overturned Frederick Jackson Turner, an icon of American historiography, by contending that cities spearheaded, rather than climaxed, settlement of the frontier, and Warner had created his own waves by showing that outward settlement into the suburbs had resulted from myriad private decisions made by individual families.[2]

No sooner had these books broken new paths than a rush of momentous events in the decade of the 1960s transformed historical scholarship as well as American politics and society. Intensification of the civil rights movement, with its mass demonstrations and federal legislation, and a new public focus on poverty, including urban poverty, during the presidential administration of John F. Kennedy pushed cities and their inhabitants into the scholarly limelight. Then, beginning in 1964, the eruption of violence that shook urban areas in every region of the country provoked social analysts, historians among them, to ask new questions about the organization of cities and how conditions had evolved into their current and, to some, distressing state. By the 1970s scores of academics were identifying themselves as urban historians, and courses on urban history sprouted in colleges and universities across the country. In 1975 the *Journal of Urban History* began publication, and several years later the Urban History Association was formed with Richard Wade as its first president.

Zane Miller helped form the vanguard of young historians whom Wade inspired in the graduate history program at the University of Chicago. Launched from Wade's graduate seminar on urban history, this group explored a gamut of topics in their dissertations, ranging from boss politics to law enforcement, education, race relations, social mobility, saloons, and the Ku Klux Klan. It was no surprise, then, that once Miller completed his dissertation on the political and social history of Cincinnati in the Progressive Era, Wade recruited the manuscript for a series of monographs he was editing for Oxford University Press. *Boss Cox's Cincinnati* became the fifth volume in the Urban Life in America series, and it made an instant impact. Writing in the *Journal of American History*, Frederick Jaher labeled the book "a superior study which presents an informed and useful examination of political movements and social issues and organizations."[3] Another reviewer called Miller's work "a masterful case study of urban politics in the progressive era,"[4] and the *New York Times Book Review* described it as an "absorbing, informative work," adding that "our understanding of contemporary urban problems would be considerably enriched if a comparable history existed of every major city."[5]

As happens with many landmark studies, *Boss Cox's Cincinnati* came about by accident. An Ohioan who grew up not far from Cin-

cinnati, Zane Miller entered graduate study at the University of Chicago without any specific plans for a doctoral dissertation or even
the intention of specializing in American urban history. He had developed an interest in what then was called "civics" in junior high
school and had written a master's thesis in history at Miami University (Ohio), where he also had received his bachelor's degree. His
adviser, an alumnus of the University of Chicago, urged Miller to
apply to that school for further study. In graduate school he took the
equivalent of an M.A. in U.S. history and devoted most of his Ph.D.
course work to the study of modern British history, early modern
European history, and English and European historiography. His
only contact with urban American history came through a research
assistantship with Bessie Louise Smith, who was then compiling her
multivolume history of Chicago.

When the time arrived for him to identify a dissertation topic,
Miller mentioned a vague interest in urban politics to the department chair, who referred him to Richard Wade, then a new faculty
member at the university. Wade had recently written an influential
essay in which he outlined a model of urban politics between the
1870s and 1940s based upon a dialogue between a city's inner and
outer regions, the inner region characterized by the boss politics and
immigrant working-class neighborhoods, the outer the home of reform and native, middle-class voters. These two forces, said Wade,
contested with each other for control of the metropolis, with the
inner city interested mainly in patronage and personal service while
the outer city strove for moral uplift, economic efficiency, and government by experts.[6] This scheme seemed especially applicable to
the Progressive Era of the late nineteenth and early twentieth centu-
ries, when bossism and reform contended most vigorously for control of city governments. Wade told Miller that there were valuable
documentary sources on this era at the Cincinnati Historical Society
and other local archives and coaxed (or pushed) him into doing a
study of George B. Cox, a boss who oversaw Cincinnati's politics and
general development between 1880 and 1913.

Miller began his research influenced by Wade's model of the center versus the periphery, which seemed to coincide in Cincinnati

with regions Miller called the Circle and the Hilltops. But as his investigation of Cincinnati progressed, Miller discovered a separate band of territory between the inner and outer city, one that Wade, influenced by theory developed early in the twentieth century by the Chicago School of Sociology, identified as the "zone of emergence" and that Miller eventually designated in his study as the "Zone."[7] Here, economically mobile middle-class and well-paid working-class families resided and often provided the balance of power in the contest between core and periphery for political offices and influence. As Miller developed his study and transformed it into a book, he made the interaction and shifting coalitions among Cincinnati's three districts the keys to understanding Boss Cox's rise, his ability to sustain and regain control as opponents continually tried to outmaneuver him, and his ultimate removal from power in 1913.

George B. Cox emerges in this book as a shrewd, fascinating, and enigmatic character. In many ways a stereotypical political boss with his saloonkeeper background, his base in a working-class ward, and his autocratic hold over his organization, Cox also confounds the conventional model. With a sensitive eye to personality and coalition building, Miller corrects the stereotype by positing a more realistic model, showing Cox to be a skilled mediator between Cincinnati's social and economic factions, one who balanced diverging interests among different geographical regions by making both the reform interests and the personal-liberty interests feel that he could be on their side. Cincinnati was not really Boss Cox's; rather, the city traversed a challenging period of its history with the aid of George Cox's ability to satisfy groups whose antipathies and cultural differences might have paralyzed progress. This was an era when backroom deals and endorsements meant something; Cox knew how to make those deals and negotiate those endorsements.

A particular observation in *Boss Cox's Cincinnati* has persisted in arousing controversy. In his concluding paragraph, Miller states that "residence rather than race, religion, or ethnicity provides the touchstone to the city's social and political experience" (p. 241). Such an assumption follows logically from the complex characteristics and political experiences of Cincinnati's Circle, Zone, and Hilltops which

Miller has analyzed so thoroughly. For example, he presents a fascinating examination of the ways that different interest groups in the
three different regions were disposed toward providing the city with
transportation, electricity, gas, telephone, and other services. Moreover, when it came to issues such as education and law enforcement,
Miller's analysis moves beyond a simple identification of attempts by
the Hilltops and Zone regions to "discipline the Circle" with social
control by showing that expanding urban services involved earnest
efforts at helping Circle residents cope with urban life. Miller's in-
sights into these issues provoked intense discussion about motivation
and culture several decades ago. Readers today may wish to deter-
mine for themselves to what extent residence is a proxy for some
other characteristics or group of characteristics, such as social class
or some mixture of ethnic and religious culture. Miller provides in-
triguing clues, as pertinent now as they were when he wrote his
book.

Zane Miller retired in the fall of 1999 from a remarkable career
of more than three decades as a faculty member at the University
of Cincinnati. A list of his publications since *Boss Cox's Cincinnati*
fills several pages, and the undergraduate and graduate students
whom he has influenced have distinguished themselves in a variety
of fields as well as in academia. He has maintained his interest in
Cincinnati in much of his scholarship, writing numerous books and
articles about the Queen City's neighborhoods, institutions, residents (including its immigrants and African Americans), and, of
course, its politics. In addition, he has stimulated his peers with in-
sightful "think" pieces on the public interest, city planning, and the
meaning of community. No doubt, more high-quality scholarship lies
ahead as he continues his research. Moreover, Miller has epitomized
the term *active historian* with his myriad activities in local political
and public service organizations. Finally, as editor of the Ohio State
University Press Urban Life and Urban Landscape series and as
president of the Urban History Association in 1991, Zane Miller has
boosted the field of American urban history to new heights from
where he first started, with Richard Wade and the Urban Life in
America series. Republication of *Boss Cox's Cincinnati* thus offers

readers not only a new opportunity to reexamine one of the pioneer
works in American urban history but also a well-deserved tribute to
an inspiring scholar and teacher.

HOWARD P. CHUDACOFF

Brown University

NOTES

1. Arthur Meier Schlesinger, *The Rise of the City, 1978–1989* (New
   York: Macmillan, 1933; rpt. Columbus: Ohio State University Press,
   1999); Carl Bridenbaugh, *Cities in the Wilderness: Urban Life in
   America, 1625–1742* (New York: The Ronald Press, 1955); Bayrd Still,
   Milwaukee: The History of a City (Madison: State Historical Society
   of Wisconsin, 1948); Constance McLaughlin Green, *Holyoke, Massachusetts: A Case of the Industrial Revolution in America* (New Haven:
   Yale University Press, 1939).
2. Richard C. Wade, *The Urban Frontier: The Rise of Western Cities,
   1790–1830* (Cambridge, Mass.: Harvard University Press, 1959); Sam
   Bass Warner, Jr., *Streetcar Suburbs: The Process of Urban Growth in
   Boston, 1870–1900* (Cambridge, Mass.: Harvard University Press,
   1962).
3. Review in *Journal of American History* 55 (March 1969): 883.
4. Louis Leonard Tucker in *The Historian* 32 (1970): 509.
5. W. V. Shannon, in the *New York Times Book Review*, February 9,
   1969, p. 6.
6. Richard C. Wade, "Urbanization," in *The Comparative Approach to
   American History*, ed. C. Vann Woodward (New York: Basic Books,
   1968), pp. 187–205. See also Wade's foreword to *Boss Cox's Cincinnati*, p. xvii–xix.
7. The center-periphery scheme was influenced by the theory of con-
   centric-ring development most prominently discussed by Ernest W.
   Burgess in "The Growth of the City: An Introduction to a Research
   Project," in Robert E. Park, Ernest W. Burgess, and Roderick D.
   McKenzie, *The City* (Chicago: University of Chicago Press, 1925),
   pp. 47–62. The term *zone of emergence* derives from a study of Boston
   undertaken by residents at the South End Settlement House in the
   1910s. Robert A. Woods supervised the study, which was written by
   Albert J. Kennedy. It remained in typescript until 1962, when the
   Joint Center for Urban Studies of the Massachusetts Institute of
   Technology and Harvard University published it with a preface by
   Sam Bass Warner, Jr.

Tables

Maps

Tables

Foreword

The extraordinary growth of cities in the nineteenth century transformed the physical environment of most Americans and altered the shape of national development. In this urban explosion are to be found the roots of our metropolitan life—both its extraordinary affluence and comfort and its persistent problems. The whole range of contemporary questions stemmed from the destruction of the compact historic city and the appearance of the expansive modern metropolis. The special agent of this revolution was a change in urban transportation. The introduction of rapid mass transit made it possible for the city to spread beyond its earlier confines, thus permitting people to live some distance from where they worked or shopped. The horse-drawn street railway, the cable car and trolley car, the subway and elevated railway, and finally the automobile encouraged also the constant creation of new communities at the outer edges of municipal boundaries.

The new city was quite different from the old city. Rather than compact, it was sprawling; the mixture of land uses, residential and commercial and industrial, gave way to the specialized and somewhat segregated functions characteristic of the modern metropolis. At the center of the new urban complex was the old city, now constantly reshaped to serve an ever-increasing population. On the periphery, "the cool green rim" as one observer described it, pleasant residential communities sprang up. Between was the transitory zone where industrial and commercial installations shared the ground with older homes and apartments. And the entire structure was always in motion. Old downtown areas were made and remade, established neighborhoods declined and sometimes disappeared, factories and warehouses moved out from the congested core, and suburban communities sprang up beyond city limits. To the first generation of Americans living through this transformation the whole process was baffling. There were no guide posts which could explain the change; no precedents on which to draw; no ready programs to meet pressing problems.

Hence American cities had somehow to contrive some order out of the confusion, some predictability out of uncontrolled expansion, some discipline out of the chaos. A part of this adjustment took place outside of public policy in the myriad decisions made by private individuals and associations. Business leaders, labor unions, settlement houses, church groups, professional societies, ethnic organizations, and others, developed their own programs to meet the new conditions.

But the most significant response came through political channels and governmental activity. And within the public framework two traditions developed. One was the boss system with its emphasis on patronage and personal favoritism; the other was reform activity with its reliance on experts and disinterested service. Yet the roots of the new municipal politics lay deeper. For each side represented not only a political response but also the aims and ambitions of different sections of the new and divided city. The boss fed on the problems and predicaments of the old congested center of the city while reform committees grew on the fears and anxieties of the new residential neighborhoods. Though the contested issues were often limited and apparently discreet, the stakes in the long run were nothing less than the control of the future of the metropolis. Beneath the complicated maneuvering and reshuffling of factions was the search for viable and permanent coalitions which could give some order and shape to the modern city.

This study by Zane Miller is the first comprehensive study of reform and machine in this broad context. By the detailed analysis of a single city, he reveals both the convulsive consequences of the emergence of the new metropolis and the attempt by reformers and bosses to come to grips with it. In so doing, he goes well beyond the conventional views of urban politics with their emphasis on ethnicity, political organization, status and class and adds a residential dimension. The notion of the periphery and the center is satisfying because it organizes these other elements without excluding them, thus providing a more persuasive synthesis than other approaches.

In many ways, Cincinnati is a fortunate choice for the development of this theme. Founded in 1794, it grew rapidly in the first half of the nineteenth century. Hence it developed established institutions before the urban revolution transformed its shape and the texture of its life. Moreover, almost from the beginning it had a cosmopolitan population comprised of large numbers of Germans, Irish, and Negroes. In addition, its strategic location in the Ohio Valley made it a regional center rather than a mere provincial town. And, though a later historian might entitle his urban biography *The Serene Cincinnatians,* it had, in fact, a long history of disorder and conflict. Added to this was a local topography which sharpened the definition of residential areas as the city spread out from its old center into the surrounding countryside. Finally, historical chance has been kind to Cincinnati, leaving a rich deposit of sources and documentation which enable the scholar to reconstruct this critical period in the city's development. Professor Miller has fully exploited these opportunities to present a compelling and arresting analysis of the politics of an emerging modern city.

RICHARD C. WADE

Chicago, Ill.
July 1968

Preface

This book is, in the conventional sense, neither a biography of a boss nor an analysis of a machine. It seeks rather to re-create in one town the opening of a remarkable era in the history of urbanization in America, a period in which the explosion of the physical proportions of cities launched a desperate yet confident quest for a new urban discipline. Daniel H. Burnham, the Chicago planner, caught the spirit of the search. "Make no little plans," he wrote in 1912, "they have no magic to stir men's blood. Make big plans; aim high in hope and work. . . . Let your watchword be order and your beacon beauty." Boss Cox's Cincinnati shared that exuberance.

Hopefully, too, this volume will help overcome the appalling neglect and widespread misunderstanding of our urban past. Now, when many Americans are troubled by our cities, we badly need liberation from ancient myths and clichés, and new perspectives on our long experience with urban life.

I have compiled vast debts. Fellowships from the University of Chicago and the Social Science Research Council and assistantships with Professor Bessie Louise Pierce furnished me the resources to spend two years in Cincinnati before moving to that city. Private individuals and public officials, with three exceptions, gladly opened records to me and submitted cheerfully to time-consuming interviews. My colleagues and students at Northwestern and the University of Cincinnati listened genially and disagreed graciously and helpfully. Professor Richard C. Wade advised, criticized, and encouraged with wisdom and tact. In addition, Professor Wade first alerted me to the political significance of the periphery-center division, an idea which he has been developing in a general way for several years, and which can be found in its latest form in his essay "Urbanization" in C. Vann Woodward (ed.), *The Comparative Approach to American History* (New York and London, 1968), pp. 187–205. Roger Lotchin, a tenacious interrogator, spent many long evenings discussing the project with me. My wife, Janet, typed, read proof, untangled footnotes, advised on indexing, grounded errant ideas, and earned rent money with skill, patience, and efficiency. Members of my family gave vital assistance at critical stages in the long process of developing the manuscript. Stylistic crudities and errors in fact, judgment, and interpretation I have achieved single-handedly.

Z.L.M.

Cincinnati, Ohio
July 1968

BOSS COX'S CINCINNATI

I

THE NEW CITY, 1880–1914

The city has a government of its own, and it is to a certain extent free. It is obliged however to pay tribute and acknowledge a sort of allegiance to the people who inhabit the mountainous region surrounding the city. The people who inhabit these mountains are a very arrogant race, and have ground the people of the city down to almost complete subjection. . . . As a result of this, the inhabitants of the mountains become very rich and build beautiful residences. I am told however that the people of the city grumble very much at this oppression and will probably soon rise in revolt.*

Cincinnati in the 1850's occupied six square miles of land cradled in a gentle southern bend of the Ohio River. The city lay in a natural basin flanked on three sides by hills rising abruptly to an average height of about 300 feet. From the northeast, Deer Creek Valley, narrow and precipitous, provided a natural entrance to the Basin. The major northern route in and out of the city, however, was Mill Creek Valley on the west. Varying from one-mile to one-mile-and-a-half wide, it was bounded on its western side by a ridge of hills which formed the third side of the amphitheater. The Miami and Erie Canal ran parallel to Mill Creek Valley on its eastern edge. At a point halfway down the Basin the canal swerved eastward, dividing the city into equal halves. The two halves of the Basin formed a plateau, which dipped gently 100 feet into the marshy "bottoms" of Mill Creek on the west, and, on the south, 40 feet to the one-half-mile-broad terrace, which stretched along the Ohio River in front

* Charles T. Greve, "Extracts from a Letter of an Asiatic Traveller in America, October 31, 1885," Charles T. Greve Literary Papers, Cincinnati Historical Society.

of the city. The river, at low water, lay some 57 feet below the crest of this terrace.

The bulk of the city's commercial and manufacturing establishments rested on the bank and terrace along the Ohio River. The retail and financial districts occupied the rear of the terrace and the central sections of the first three or four streets of the Basin proper. Cincinnati's two fashionable residential districts lay at the eastern and western edges of this area. Beyond this central sector of the city was a broad circle in which most of the city's native-born white Protestant population lived.

Still farther out, on the periphery of the city among small shops and factories, lived the submerged classes. Irish and Negroes shared the Ohio river bottoms with wholesale houses and factories. In the extreme southeastern section of the Basin a small group of more prosperous Negroes claimed McAllister Street. Above the canal and at the foot of the northern hills the Germans congregated in a district dubbed "Over-the-Rhine." The Mill Creek bottoms, including much of that portion within the city limits, lay vacant, considered too marshy for either industrial or residential use.

Most of the mid-nineteenth century commuters lived in villages, six to twelve miles distant from the city, built up along the turnpikes and railroads in the valleys. These men, like the few with residences on the hilltops, held positions in the city that permitted them a flexible schedule.

The hilltops and suburban villages, nonetheless, were regarded as the future sites of the homes of most of the city's population. Rising real estate values in the Basin and the relative cheapness of land atop the hills made the outlying districts tempting. "There is," one observer noted in 1851, "a class of citizens, whose business is in Cincinnati, but who propose to live outside its corporate limits, either to escape taxation . . . or in the expectation that the increasing facilities of railroads will enable them to reach their workshops, stores, or other places of employment at as early an hour as necessary." As a result, "shrewd and wealthy citizens" began buying and plotting outlying land despite the fact that much of it required grading, leveling, and filling.[1]

By 1870, a noticeable population increase in the residential hill-top districts had occurred. But the socio-economic level of its inhabitants had not changed and the migration had not yet attained flood proportions. In 1874 the businessmen who had organized the Queen City Club selected a site for a clubhouse in the heart of the Basin, where at least nine-tenths of its members lived within walking distance. Cincinnati, despite the Basin's twelve-mile circumference, remained essentially a "walking city." Men and women seldom had to go beyond the immediate neighborhood for their daily needs. The slow-moving, horse-powered streetcar system which laced the city carried them on more distant journeys. Men lived close to their jobs and women shopped in neighborhood stores. The hilltops remained, for the most part, the sanctuary of charitable and educational institutions, cemeteries, and wealthy citizens.

By the standards of the day this "walking city" in the West ranked as an important urban center. In 1850 it stood sixth in the hierarchy of cities in the United States, first among the cities west of the Alleghenies, and fourth nationally in manufacturing. In the years after 1850, however, Cincinnati faltered and by 1880 no longer reigned as Queen City of the West.

Because of Cincinnati's failure to master the challenge of urban competition between 1850 and 1914, many contemporaries con-

Table 1

POPULATION GROWTH, 1850–1910*

Date	Population	Per Cent Increase
1850	115,435	
1860	161,044	39.5
1870	216,239	34.3
1880	225,139	18.0
1890	296,908	16.4
1900	325,902	9.8
1910	363,591	11.6

* United States Bureau of the Census, *Thirteenth Census of the United States Taken in the Year 1910, Vol. I, Population, 1910, General Report and Analysis* (Washington, D.C., 1913), pp. 80, 81.

cluded that the city was "in a . . . trance," showing neither "evidence of life nor of decay or decomposition." [2] Yet it continued to grow at a gradual, though declining, rate.

More remarkable, however, was the enlargement of the city's physical boundaries. From six square miles in 1850, it expanded to 22.22 square miles in 1880. A spate of annexations in the subsequent thirty years pushed its size to 35.27 square miles in 1900 and to 50.26 square miles in 1910.[3] Population growth, the increasing importance of industry in the city's economy, a successful annexation policy, but most of all, technological innovations in the means of intracity transportation, constituted the dynamics behind this urban explosion.

Before 1867, Cincinnati's suburban development had followed the path of least resistance along the steam railroads which entered the city through the river valleys. The appearance of substantial residential suburbs on the hilltops occurred only after the introduction of the inclined plane, a steam-powered device that raised the horse-drawn streetcars up the sharp grades of the hillsides and led to the rapid expansion of the street railway system. Introduced in the 1850s, it had over 76 miles of track by 1880. The conversion of this system to cables and then electricity between 1880 and 1900 provided the means for the completion of the invasion of the highlands.

Electrically powered streetcars possessed the double virtue of speed and power—speed with which to cover increasingly longer distances in relatively short periods of time, and power with which to ascend the steepest grades. At the same time, continuing industrialization jammed the Ohio River, Mill Creek, and Deer Creek Valley bottoms with factories and the railroad facilities which serviced them, thus intensifying the outward pressure of urban growth. By 1912 the city had 222 miles of track.

Generally, the migration of industry and people out of the Basin proceeded in two waves. The first, beginning about 1867, continued until slowed by the depression in 1893. The second was raised by the winds of prosperity at the end of the decade, only to subside with the economic calm which set in about 1907.

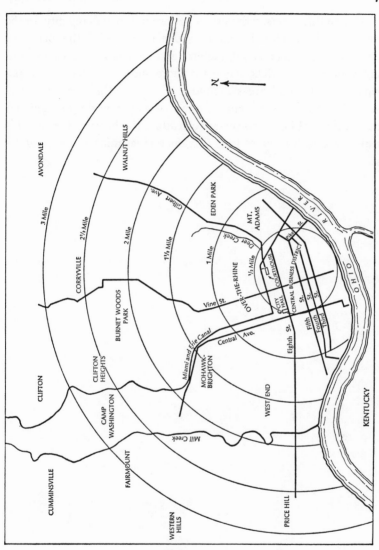

1. Cincinnati, 1875

The exodus reversed the urban pattern of the walking city. In the new, mobilized city the submerged classes shared the Basin, or core, with the commercial, factory, and "downtown" business and entertainment districts, while the more successful fled to the peripheral residential areas around and beyond the new industrial sites.[4] The modes of life and structure of society in this divided and outwardly mobile urban society constitute the heart of Cincinnati's experience in the age of Boss Cox, municipal reform, and progressivism.

1

The Circle

In 1897 a visitor to Cincinnati's riverfront stopped at the corner of
Front Street and Broadway and entered the Spencer House, the
city's most elegant hotel during the Civil War. He was shocked to
find the "stairs and floor[s] . . . covered with filth and dirt . . .
the walls . . . black with smoke and mildew and the atmosphere
. . . thick and sickening with the odors of . . . decaying filth." [1]
The degeneration of the once-fashionable hotel into a disreputable
flophouse dramatized the changes which had overtaken the area.

Once the very heart of the city, this section was, by 1890, occupied largely by factories, railway terminals, and warehouses. Scattered among these buildings were other flophouses, one "a perfect
fire-trap," another with "great cracks in the walls, caused by the
high water, and liable to collapse," and the most notorious of all,
the "Silver Moon . . . favorable to disease, vice and vermin."
Third Street, "the Wall Street of Cincinnati" in the 1890's and the
sole vestige of the riverfront's past importance, ran along the terrace just below the Basin. [2]

While the flophouses and jobbers remained on the terrace, the
banks, insurance companies, and brokers of Third Street, along
with most of the factories, retreated before increasingly severe

9

floods and the invasion of railroads and warehouses. After the turn of the century little of value remained. Most of the manufacturers edged up the Mill Creek Valley toward the residential West End while others spilled out of the lower Deer Creek bottoms onto Broadway and Sycamore. The financiers completed their relocation shortly after the turn of the century. In 1904, one observer noted that Third Street "looks squalid and dismal these days. . . . The pavement is grimy and greasy. . . . Rent signs, removal signs, lease signs, were so numerous that they left a somber impression." [3]

The general exodus of finance and industry from the Ohio River bottoms was not an isolated development. Rather it constituted part of a process of adjustment to centripetal forces that were concentrating certain kinds of businesses in a relatively small area of the Basin north of the old central riverfront. The financial district, for instance, moved but one block north, to a point halfway between Race and Main streets on Fourth. This placed it conveniently near Fountain Square, on Fifth between Vine and Walnut, where the street railways entering the Basin from surrounding suburbs came together.

The continued extension of rapid transit plus the inauguration of telephone service accelerated this trend. In 1905, more than $3,000,000 was invested in new buildings, alterations, and renovations within a ten-block circle centered on Fountain Square. Five new ten- and fifteen-story office buildings went up, and the area also attracted large department stores, hotels and restaurants, as well as specialty shops. The "club district" developed around Eighth, Ninth, Elm, and Race streets, a few blocks northwest of Fountain Square. Real estate prices near the new core soared, but property values and economic activity in the peripheral residential districts of the Basin sagged as small businesses moved from those neighborhoods.

A variety of special services catering to the after-dark activities of the city's growing and increasingly dispersed population sprang up on the fringes of the central ten-block core. The "tenderloin" emerged on the western edge of the Basin. "On both sides of Longworth and George streets," the Reverend John Howard Melish told

the Evangelical Alliance, "nearly every house is used openly for
immoral purposes, with the madams' names upon the doors." [4] Although the red-light district was located in a Negro neighborhood
—where "vice, crime and beastiality hold high carnival and where
ignorance is as dense as it is among the dwarfs of Central Africa"—
the entrepreneuers of the tenderloin served all colors and classes.[5]
One immigrant musician, for example, played for "an all-night ca-
rousal" in one of the "aristocratic bawdy-houses" on Longworth
which "some big butter and egg men put on for their visiting customers. Everything was free. Everybody got gloriously soused,
including the ladies, their gentlemen callers, the cello, guitar, violin
and flute." [6]

Another and more respectable entertainment district lay north of
Fountain Square, extending up Vine from about Court Street
across the canal and into the Over-the-Rhine district. When the lid
was not on, this section offered a gaudy array of saloons, restaurants, shooting galleries, arcades, gambling dens, and dance halls.
Theaters began to locate there in the 1880's, a development quick-
ened by the growth of burlesque in the beer gardens which had
flourished in the Over-the-Rhine district just after the Civil War. By
1900 only two or three beer gardens remained, the rest having
evacuated to the cooler hilltops within easy reach of the new rapid
transit lines.

Upper Vine Street, however, continued to attract out-of-town visitors, suburbanites, politicians, show people, and a motley crowd of
sports, drawn in part by the contrived German flavor. To old residents it was a deplorable change. The section now had "all the
tarnished tinsel of a Bohemianism with the trimmings of a gutter
and the morals of a sewer," and was no longer a place "where one
could take wife, sister or sweetheart and feel secure in the knowledge that not one obnoxious word would profane their ears." [7]

The tawdriness of the Over-the-Rhine district enhanced the dis-
array which characterized the Basin. All who came to the center of
the city struggled through streets increasingly clogged with streetcars, hackneys, omnibuses, carts, carriages, wagons and, after 1900,
automobiles. Hay and horse markets intensified the traffic problem

and added to the filthiness of the area, as did the "ridiculous . . . old-fashioned and unsanitary" public markets where food was sold on "rotten, dirty, open cobblestoned street[s]." [8] Hogs, sheep, and cattle were driven through thoroughfares to slaughterhouses, "obstructing the roadways and traffic of vehicles, and filling the atmosphere with noxious odors." [9] Men and boys unable or unwilling to quit the "spitting habit" made railway stations "unbelievably repulsive" and stained sidewalks, streetcars, and the floors of public buildings with tobacco.[10] Downtown merchants and residents swept dirt onto sidewalks and dumped refuse into the streets. Pedestrians had to "step over or wade through slimy water which is run off roofs, from washtubs and yards . . . into the gutter. On a warm day the stench in some places would knock a horse down." [11]

Steamboats, railroad engines, factories, office buildings, homes, and tenements burned bituminous coal which hung a black veil of smoke over the city. In 1908 a chemist estimated that 172 tons of dirt per square mile fell on the Basin monthly. It smudged furniture, carpets, and household goods and damaged merchandise. "Cleanliness in either person or in dress," reported one visitor, "is almost an impossibility. Hands and faces become grimy, and clean collars and light-hued garments are perceptibly coated with . . . soot." Clothes hung out to dry took on "a permanent yellow hue." [12]

Fires, caused in part by the age and defective construction of business houses and residences, also plagued the area. In 1912, Cincinnati's per capita fire loss of $5.24 was exceeded by only five cities with over 100,000 population, and conditions in the "dangerous congested district" were inviting "a conflagration, such as has occurred in most of the large cities, and which will come, sooner or later, unless preparations are made to prevent the same." [13]

Neither the dirt and disorder, however, nor the gradual expansion of the central business and entertainment sections drove out all the residents of the Basin. A significant portion of the metropolis's population remained around its edge in the area which marked the periphery of the old walking city. This belt formed a great circle beginning at the freight yards in the Deer Creek bottoms, stretch-

ing southward under the brow of Mt. Adams, and curving along
the Ohio riverfront and up the eastern slope of Mill Creek Valley to
the Mohawk-Brighton district in the northwest corner of the Basin,
a section which had served as a haven for German immigrants for
half a century. The Over-the-Rhine district, connecting Mohawk-
Brighton to the Deer Creek yards, completed the district.

The Circle's population was diverse, composed chiefly of recent
arrivals in Cincinnati. They constituted an incongruous crowd of
Negroes and whites from the South plus a diminishing complement
of Irish and German immigrants. In addition, "Russian" Jews began
to arrive along with lesser contingents of Italians in the 1880's.
After 1900 more Italians and a sprinkling of Austrians, Hungarians,
Roumanians, Greeks, Turks, and Syrians added to the ethnic heterogeneity.[14]

The newcomers tended to cluster into colonies. Negroes gathered
in "Bucktown" east of Broadway around Sixth and Seventh streets
and on Rat Row and Sausage Row in the Ohio River bottoms. Sicil-
ians and Syrians shared the lower East End with Irish and Southern whites. A band of Genoans established themselves in the lower
West End next door to "Little Bucktown" on West Fifth and Sixth,
close to a small colony of Levantine Jews. Two Jewish "ghettos"
sprang up, one Russian and the other Roumanian and Austro-Hungarian, the latter spreading into the heavily German Mohawk-
Brighton and Over-the-Rhine districts, where Greeks and Hungarians already resided. Germans continued to live in virtually every
section of the Circle except those of heavy Negro concentration.

Distinct though these colonies were, no invincible barriers separated them. A story by a reporter sent to question the women of
Bucktown about their habit of "sill warming"—leaning on their el-
bows in the window and watching the streets below—suggests the
tedium and tension which characterized Circle life and illustrates
the commingling. One of the first women he approached was Mrs.
Rooney, who told him, " 'God knows, it's little I have. Me husband
goes on excursions an' the like, but devil a wan do Oi sie.' " When
asked her reasons for the practice, Mrs. Mulaney asserted that she
looked " 'to get the news' " and to watch " 'dem durty Nager bees,' "

Table 2

FOREIGN-BORN POPULATION OF CINCINNATI: 1890, 1900, 1910*

Northwest Europe:

	England	Scotland	Wales	Ireland	Germany	Norway	Sweden
1910	1,872	458	177	6,224	28,426	37	114
1900	2,201	461	240	9,114	38,308	12	111
1890	2,951	621	328	12,323	49,415	9	99

	Denmark	Netherlands	Belgium	Luxemburg	France	Switzerland
1910	79	322	24	1	665	696
1900	49	369	38	1	748	657
1890	41	360	22	1	890	587

Southern and Eastern Europe:

	Portugal	Spain	Italy	Russia	Finland	Austria	Hungary
1910	8	20	2,245	4,999	10	1,638	6,344
1900	1	6	917	2,320	1	752	208
1890	4	16	738	978	—	417	120

	Roumania	Bulgaria, Servia, & Montenegro	Greece	Turkey in Europe	Turkey in Asia	Other Europe
1910	454	184	180	280	245	4
1900	4	—	53	6	—	39
1890	—	—	19	14	—	306

* United States Bureau of the Census, *Thirteenth Census of the United States Taken in the Year 1910, Vol. I, Population, 1910, General Report and Analysis* (Washington, D.C., 1913), pp. 854–55.

while Mrs. Jefferson Jackson maintained that her object was to "'keep an eye on dem Irish Mulraney kids an' dere ole oomen.'"[15]

A survey of the Circle's "foreign" population in 1912 not only concluded that "the Negroes and Irish are everywhere together" but also emphasized the residential mixing of all groups. "Cincinnati's foreign populations intermingle very freely. To be sure, they have their little groups, but they are not quite so marked as in other cities. . . . [I]n one single block were found Americans, Germans, Hungarians, Greeks, Italians and Irish." The investigator regarded this as "a redeeming feature" in the city's "great foreign problem."

... In those cities in which foreigners ... are mixed together, the English language becomes the common medium of intercourse for them all, and they break ... more easily from their old-country customs and habits." [16]

Poverty was the common denominator among these peoples. The Circle, as one contemporary bluntly put it, contained "a multitude of men and women of low brain power and general inefficiency, even among those native born." They were "hands rather than heads" which could "do nothing in particular." [17] Generally they held the meanest, poorest paying, and most irregular jobs. Most of them worked within walking distance of their homes to avoid the extra expense of carfare.

The industrial workers held positions primarily in the boot and shoe, clothing, and tobacco factories located in the Basin, or in the tanneries, meat-packing plants, and soap-making establishments in the lower Mill Creek Valley. Common laborers toiled in the streets for the traction or gas company, served as draymen, hackmen, and teamsters, or loaded and unloaded the boats and trains in the commercial districts. The women not engaged in factory work or sweatshops took in washing at a dollar a day or became midwives.

Circle children of school age spent an estimated 23 per cent of their spare time drifting "from one deadening occupation to another." Most employed in industry worked for shoe, paper box, and candy firms. Many delivered messages and ran errands, "a notoriously blind alley occupation," while others shined shoes or hawked papers. In the summer the late sports editions kept newsboys on the streets as late as nine o'clock. Some of them stayed downtown "begging, selling chewing gum, shoe strings or lead pencils ... hanging about five cent theaters and flitting from place to place generally absorbed in the evil features of the city's life." [18]

Not all Circle inhabitants, however, were workers. Each group produced a coterie of small businessmen serving a clientele close to their home neighborhoods. Some opened restaurants, saloons, houses of prostitution, and mortuaries, all designed for Circle inhabitants. According to one old resident, Central Avenue from Fifth Street to Mohawk, a distance of about a mile, was lined with shops, "small one man affairs, operated by the owner, with perhaps one assistant."

A furniture store at Fifth and Central Avenue got the parade off to a good start and was followed by pawn shops, a book store, groceries, barber shops, shoe stores, dry goods stores, cigar stores, and a host of others plentifully seasoned with saloons.[19]

Although, as one social worker believed, "the trolley-car, the telephone, [and] the department store . . . make the peddler anything but indispensable," these mobilized businessmen swarmed over the Basin.[20] Enterprising Circle dwellers sold fruits, nuts, old clothes and rags, creating a cacophonous din in the streets. The Negro hominy man, with his cry of "hominy hot," the pretzel, sauerkraut, and cheese men, the bell-ringing scissors-grinder, and the coal peddler and the rag vendor with the "spavined horse," provided entertainment as well as necessities, dispensing "gossip and anecdotes" with their wares.[21]

Others escaped the streets and small stores, becoming copyists, accountants, salesgirls, stenographers, or typists in downtown firms. The few equipped with an adequate education, often acquired before coming to Cincinnati, entered the professions. They preached, taught school, practised medicine or the law, and performed or taught music.

These occupations could be found in every group in the Circle with the possible exception of the Southerners. But certain elements tended to specialize. Negroes and Irish contributed more than their share to the city's common labor and personal and domestic service force, though Negroes seldom appeared in the semiskilled industries. Germans and southern and eastern Europeans gravitated to the small business and professional fields.[22]

Under the spur of stiff competition, all labored long hours, sometimes seven days a week. Yet they lived precariously. A flood or ice block on the Ohio, seasonal lay-offs in the factories, the extra hardships of winter, a depression or extended illness, reduced them to desperate need and drove them to soup lines and private or public relief agencies. For the less successful this insecurity was augmented by ignorance of how to live economically in the city. As an Associated Charities report put it, "they must be shown how to buy, how to cook, how to make the home attractive, how to find employment." [23] Many of them, "utterly friendless and discouraged," succumbed to " 'verdammte Bedürfnislosigheit'—the damnable absence of want or desire," and grew indifferent "to their own elevation." [24] And one social worker speculated that "the neurotic and temperamental condition of these unfortunates . . . incapacitates them as effectively as real physical disability." [25]

Irregular and low incomes, of course, made home ownership a rarity in the Circle. In 1900 there were 73,519 dwellings in Cincinnati's thirty-one wards, an average of 2371 per ward. In none of the eight lying wholly or in part within the Circle did more than 144 families own homes free of debt. These same wards also contained the fewest houses encumbered by debt.[26]

Not surprisingly, housing in the Circle was among the most crowded in Cincinnati. In 1890, for example, the city averaged nearly nine persons per dwelling. The wards lying within the Circle all exceeded that figure. In 1910, too, the nine wards with the lowest home-ownership rating also exceeded the city average of seven persons per dwelling.[27]

The wretched living conditions in the congested wards appalled outsiders. Shantytown was probably the worst. Located at the mouth of Mill Creek, "the great open city sewer, foul and stifling during the warm season," its squatters "huddled together in their miserable shacks and eked out a . . . barbaric existence." There was just one privy and the nearest water was a quarter-mile away. The inhabitants dumped ashes, garbage, and waste wherever convenient, and a "great unsightly rubbish heap, a junk pile with cans of stagnant, foul smelling water" mouldered at the community's front door.[28] Conditions in the East End slums were not much better. People could be found living in "dreary rat holes," ten, fifteen, and thirty feet underground, which were small, dark, unventilated, wet, dreary dungeons." [29]

Most of the people of the Circle, however, lived in three- or four-story brick structures arranged for three or more families. Indeed,

Cincinnati was one of the few American cities in which the multi-story tenement was common. In these, whether block apartment buildings or converted single-family houses, the chief evils were dark halls, damp, ill-ventilated, gloomy rooms, and a pervasive absence of adequate water supply and drainage, privies, catchbasins, and outdoor toilets. Some were grievously overcrowded, and most dated from the Civil War period or earlier, a fact which played a crucial part in creating the deplorable conditions.

> The remarkably congested center [of the city] was built before people realized that . . . cesspools and privies are entirely out of place at the center of a large city, and before the extensive manufacture of plumbing materials and devices. . . . Tenants have made sinks out of sheet metal boxes fastened to the outside of window sills, emptying their contents into downspouts and onto roofs. Water closets have been installed where they freeze regularly and are out of use the greatest part of the cold weather.[30]

There were no "dumb-bell" tenements in the Circle. Those constructed specifically as apartment buildings were square or rectangular. Many had an open court in the center, providing not only "breathing space" but also a convenient garbage dump for the families of the compound. Water had to be carried to the apartments from the court, an unpleasant task because "Ferguson's Park" was generally "filled with foul odor; for in the center of it a half dozen outhouses are built in circular form."[31] By 1912, an estimated 44 per cent of the city's population lived in apartments and conversions, most of them within the Circle, giving Cincinnati the largest proportion of people living in tenements of any city its size in the United States.[32]

Under these conditions death and contagious diseases flourished. Children under five and Negroes were hardest hit. But the "White Plague," tuberculosis, killed and disabled indiscriminately. Like smallpox and typhoid fever, it took its biggest toll in the lower reaches of the Circle. In one year, for example, the mortality rate from tuberculosis in the lower West End was 525 per hundred thousand. It dropped to 443 in the Central Avenue and George

Street district just to the north. It was but 58 in Westwood, on Western Hills.[33] Dr. John M. Withrow, a leader in Cincinnati's public-health movement, summarized succinctly the plight of the Circle resident.

> If I were a cartoonist I would picture society as an anaemic man in the useful period of life, wearing a silk hat, a sack coat of quality, cheap, ill-fitting trousers and bursted shoes. The hat would represent the wealthy leisure class; the coat the active business man; the trousers, the low salaried and skilled working-man, and the shoes, the unskilled workers. Beneath the picture it would read: *Old man, the reason you have consumption is because your feet are on the ground!* [34]

Yet poverty alone did not explain the prevalence of disease. Much of it was due to ignorance of and indifference to rudimentary sanitary precautions. The situation was aggravated by fear and suspicion of hospitals and public health measures. A school medical inspector found Circle parents and guardians "a very unreliable, ignorant and sometimes an obstreperous quantity . . . who resent the interference of a medical officer, do not respond to his advice, and refuse to go to a clinic or district physician." [35] And there were "many," grumbled an Associated Charities visitor, "who utterly refuse to enter a hospital. . . . A horror takes possession of them at the mention of such a place, believing, as they do . . . that the 'young doctors will cut them up.'" [36]

To escape their cramped quarters, stifling poverty, and the ubiquitous shadow of death and disease, Circle dwellers spent much of their leisure time in the public and sometimes disorderly pursuit of pleasure. One observer thought their only recreation was talk. The neighborhood saloon offered opportunities for amusement, sociability, and comradeship, but coffee and tea houses were also popular gathering spots. After the turn of the century the younger people thronged to the concert or dance halls, where they learned the Turkey Trot, Grizzly, Humpback Rag, Gotham Gobble, Bunny Hug and Flatfoot Glide.[37]

Older and less strenuous pastimes were also common. One West Ender noted that "magic lantern shows, prestidigitators, lecturers

. . . phrenologists, religious fanatics, and tightrope walkers were on the menu every year."[38] Many attended the theater, but silent movies, which eliminated the language barrier, became even more popular.

Cheaper entertainment was available outdoors. On Saturday nights crowds promenaded along Central Avenue. Living close to downtown, the people of the Circle had ready access to the parades that marked neighborhood, city, national, and religious celebrations and political campaigns. For the children the streets, alleys, canal, and river made up for the shortage of parks and playgrounds. Older youths loitered about street corners, candy stores, and billiard and pool rooms, engaged in pranks, and brawled with those from near-by neighborhoods. Some drifted into "juvenile delinquency," creating a demand for "innocent amusement . . . to take the place of the saloon, the cigar store, the concert hall, the public dance, and that abomination, the cheap theater."[39]

Churches, too, played a large role in Circle life. Religion was as variegated as the population. Parishes of Irish and German Roman Catholics antedated the Civil War, and in 1874 Negro Catholics set up a separate church. As new immigrant groups arrived, additional buildings gradually appeared. By 1914 Polish, Italian, and Syrian churches had been established, and steps were being taken to organize one for Hungarians. In the same period a Greek Orthodox church and a Syrian Maronite as well as Polish, Roumanian, Austro-Hungarian, and Levantine Orthodox Jewish places of worship sprang up. Although many Protestant congregations fled the Circle, those which remained added to its religious diversity. Besides the older Negro Methodist and Baptist and several German sects, there was a Roumanian Baptist and an Italian Presbyterian church.[40]

The Circle, moreover, was the scene of most of the activities of the city's Protestant missionaries. They concentrated their efforts on the riverfront and even established an outpost among the houseboats on the Ohio. Although the proliferation of churches suggested otherwise, many observers felt that significant "leakage" and widespread backsliding if not outright immorality and atheism prevailed in the Circle. One Protestant investigator claimed that most

Roman Catholics there, "in the stress of earning money in this new land . . . simply neglect religion." He urged that Protestants continue to take advantage of the situation.[41] Jews were also regarded as vulnerable, and repeated attempts were made to win them over. In 1896, for example, the *American Israelite* condemned the "neophyte medicine man of Clinton Street" and called his mission "an outrage on common decency . . . [and] a breach of the peace, throwing a firebrand of dissension into our city and our peaceable society."[42]

Apart from church affiliations, it is difficult to identify organizational connections peculiar to Circle dwellers. A remarkable number of organizations flourished in the city, and many of them met in the Basin residential district. There is, however, little evidence to indicate that they were inspired or sustained by people living in the Circle.

The Orthodox Jews, for example, formed workers' circles, burial and mutual aid societies, a Talmud Torah society, cultural preservation groups, religious Zionist and socialist Zionist clubs, and, by 1914, had gathered some $8000 for a "Kosher Home for the Aged." But the leadership and financial support for these came largely from "outsiders" and "generous friends" who seldom lived in either of the two Circle "ghettos."[43]

Especially illustrative is the case of the Levantine Jews, separated from both the Orthodox and Reform communities by language and religious differences. They arrived in the Circle about 1908 and in five years had managed to set up but one organization, the Society La Hermandad. It was supposed to acquire a cemetery and synagogue, neither of which it accomplished, and supply members with a physician, a service which "atrophied." Because of these failures and rumors that its officers had mismanaged funds, the society was shot through with dissatifaction and, in 1913, seemed about to collapse.[44]

Boris D. Bogen, the director of the United Jewish Charities, deplored not only the inability of immigrants to organize themselves but also the fact that the groups they joined were "narrow" and disinclined to take an interest in political issues or social conditions.

The struggle for existence leaves little room for any other serious interest but his own narrow, personal sphere. He becomes indifferent to social conditions. . . . He joins lodges, clubs, and so on. The professional politician takes hold of him.[45]

It was for this reason that the Jewish settlement offered courses designed to "throw light into darkness, to shock inertia and foster a healthy and stimulating discontent." [46]

Similarly, most Italian societies were associated with the Santa Maria Institute, a Catholic settlement which drew its volunteer workers and finances from outside the Circle. The many Negro organizations, too, were dominated by politicians and economically successful businessmen and professional men, many of whom did not live in the Circle. There was, moreover, no Negro settlement house to stimulate the formation of clubs and societies and provide them with meeting places.

Whatever influence churches and clubs may have exerted upon the lives of Circle dwellers, it was not pervasive enough to prevent the section from becoming the center of illegal activity and disorderly behavior in the city. Police statistics reveal, for example, that disproportionately large numbers of the 13,297 people arrested in 1900 belonged to occupational, national, or racial groups concentrated in the blighted area. "Domestics" and "laborers" led the occupational categories with 1216 and 1602 arrests respectively, and 3708 were foreign-born and 2780 colored. More significantly, 11,884 of the arrests were made in police districts located in the Circle. These districts led in virtually every category of crimes reported, including cuttings, shootings, rapes, aggravated assaults, and suicides.[47] The *Catholic-Telegraph* claimed that the nature and frequency of criminal acts there "pollute the atmosphere" and warned that "like Sodom and Gommorah, God will chastise and humiliate those cities that daringly and openly offend him." [48]

Many believed that poor living conditions caused the chronic lawlessness. As a young county prosecutor put it, people

. . . reared in squalor, surrounded by prostitution and drunkenness are the meat of the machinery of the law. Weak in body and will, by reason of insufficient food and vitiated air, they can not in the nature of things, be proof against temptation. . . .[49]

Other factors also played a part. The close proximity in which the various racial, ethnic, and religious groups lived fostered outbreaks of group violence. Russian Jews were harassed by "grown ruffians who surround[ed] them on the streets, called them vile and obscene names, pulled their hair and beards, and often assaulted them with refuse, stones and clubs." [50] Clashes between Negroes and whites were even more common. In 1903 a fight between Negro and white youths in the lower West End erupted into a "race war" when white spectators at a near-by baseball game joined in. The Negroes "were knocked in the head with bricks, rocks and every kind of a missile that could be reached." [51] And in 1910 racial tensions ran so high that the mayor forbade the showing of a movie of the Reno heavyweight boxing match in which a Negro, Jack Johnson, defeated a white, Jess Willard, for fear it would set off a race riot.[52]

Most of the criminality, however, did not involve violence and grew out of conditions peculiar to the Circle. Prostitution, for example, was restricted by law to the confines of the section. And the frustrations of life in the Circle helped make petty gambling, especially policy- and book-making, a flourishing activity. The extreme competitiveness of the crowded business community of saloonkeepers and small retailers accounted for many arrests. Saloons opened as early and closed as late as possible and operated clandestinely on Sundays. Many featured "sitting rooms"—where women, some of dubious virtue, could be served drinks—and nearly all ran backroom crap or poker games. Gambling devices, too, were widely used to stimulate trade. Confectionaries, poolrooms, drug and cigar stores as well as saloons installed slot machines, many of which paid in kind rather than cash.

Other and more legitimate small businessmen, owing to ignorance or perversity, frequently ran afoul of laws regulating their undertakings. Hawkers ran the risk of being arrested for disturbing the peace. Central Avenue merchants with sidewalk displays and handcart vendors were repeatedly picked up for obstructing traffic. The butcher, greengrocer, and baker had to meet health department standards of sanitation and avoid selling by light weight. These and a host of other similar offenses kept the local courts jammed and added to the chaos characteristic of the Circle.

Variety, instability, and disorder characterized the Circle in the new and divided metropolis. Its business districts were a curious amalgam of new and old, containing virtually every kind of enterprise represented in the city. Its residential section, aged and decrepit, housed members of every national, racial, religious—and almost every occupational—group. Their horizons were circumscribed by poverty and ignorance, and their lives revolved about the institutions in their home neighborhood. They led a harrowing existence, threatened by destitution, disease, and violence and harassed by strange and unknown laws and ways of life.

2

The Zone

"The suburbanite," wrote Graham Romeyn Taylor in 1915, "who leaves business behind at nightfall for the cool green rim of the city would think the world had gone topsy-turvy if at five-thirty he rushed out of a factory set in a landscape of open fields and wooded hillsides, scrambled for a seat in a street car or grimy train and clattered back to the region of brick and pavement, of soot and noise and jostle." Yet this was "daily routine for many thousands of factory workers," a situation created, Taylor noted, by the "shifting of factories one by one to the edge of the city." [1]

The process had been under way for some time. As early as 1870 that portion of Mill Creek Valley between the Mohawk-Brighton district on the edge of the Basin and the village of Cumminsville already bore the mark of the exodus. By 1880 some 115 plants had located there, about three-quarters of an hour from the downtown financial center. After a lull during the depression of the 1890's the march resumed. By 1904 the miles of barren wasteland in the valley to the north and northeast of Cumminsville had been converted into the Mill Creek industrial belt.

Its northeastern terminus at the turn of the century was the "junior suburb" of Norwood, a hamlet within one-half mile of the city, known to its residents as the "Gem of the Highlands, the brightest jewel in Cincinnati's sylvan crown." By 1909 Norwood was "the Chicago of Hamilton County" and had forty-nine manufacturing establishments annually producing goods valued at $10,000,000.[2] The adjacent village, Oakley, was also transformed. In 1907, a group of industrialists purchased four dairy farms and established a factory colony, making the suburb the center of the city's machine-tool industry.

The flow of factories up the valley created new residential districts in its wake. By 1886 it was obvious that "the tide of population now rolling toward Eastern Hills" would be "turned to Millcreek [sic] Valley and the hills" on either side of it.[3] The migration persisted, engulfing old villages, creating new suburbs, and putting unheard of value on real estate. From 1880 to 1910 Cumminsville, Camp Washington, Westwood, and Winton Place tripled in size and Saint Bernard grew fivefold. Norwood registered an increase of about 150 per cent between 1900 and 1910 alone. Most of this territory, excepting Saint Bernard and Norwood, was annexed in this period. Yet Cincinnati's population increased by only 11.6 per cent and Hamilton County by 12.5 per cent. Clearly, the peripheral area of the old walking city grew most rapidly over these years.[4]

This development contributed to the physical bulk of the new city. A series of annexations between 1890 and 1910 more than doubled the size of Cincinnati. This, in turn, helped reduce the city's over-all population density. It also made people beyond the Circle increasingly mobile. In these years the city's rapid-transit system converted to electricity and extended its lines. Its clients, moreover, became addicted to streetcar travel. Cincinnati's "riding habit"—the number of rides per capita per annum—rose 45 per cent between 1890 and 1910.[5]

The movement of industry and people from the Basin covered the hills and valleys which surrounded the center of the city with a great industrial-residential district which lay between the fashionable suburbs* and the Circle. Conditions in the middle district

---

* Contemporaries consistently referred to the Hilltop districts, even when they lay within the city limits, as suburbs. That is the usage I have adopted. The

roughly paralleled those discovered in a similar section of Boston in 1915 by Robert A. Woods and Albert J. Kennedy, a section which

Table 3

MILL CREEK AND NEIGHBORING VILLAGE GROWTH, 1870–1920*

Neighborhood or Village	1870	1880	1890	1900	1910	1920
Camp Washington	—	3,000	—	11,520	10,890	10,450
Carthage	1,000	—	2,257	2,559	3,618	3,525
Clifton	—	1,000	—	3,555	5,540	6,740
College Hill	800	740	—	1,104	1,979	3,525
Cumminsville	4,108	5,622	9,974	14,036	17,275	19,650
Elmwood Place	—	—	—	2,532	3,423	3,991
Finneytown	—	—	—	125	125	275
Monfort Heights	—	—	—	—	—	250
Mount Airy	—	—	—	400	497	720
Mount Healthy	—	—	—	1,354	1,799	2,255
North Fairmount	—	—	—	4,975	5,715	6,055
Saint Bernard	—	1,022	1,779	3,384	5,002	6,312
Westwood	—	852	1,050	2,050	3,675	6,075
White Oak	—	—	—	300	300	300
Winton Place	—	—	—	1,219	2,750	3,475

* Robert C. Schmitt, "Cumminsville: A Study in Suburban Growth and Structure" (unpublished M.A. thesis, University of Cincinnati, 1944), p. 104.

they dubbed the Zone of Emergence.[6]

The outer and inner boundaries of the Zone were blurred and unstable, but, as in the Circle, the vague outlines can be traced in the census reports on home ownership and mortgages. Generally speaking, Zone wards contained relatively large numbers of houses in both categories, but both figures tended to rise progressively in the wards farther from the Basin.

Not surprisingly, while ownership and mortgages increased in the Zone, congestion tended to decrease. But housing conditions,

---

term "suburbs," unless clearly indicated otherwise, refers to a fashionable residential region on the fringe of the city and is synonymous with the term "Hilltop[s]."

while generally superior to those in the Circle, varied greatly. The
residents of the inner Zone lived in the aging brick tenements characteristic of the Circle. Those farther out, however, possessed neither hovels nor mansions. They occupied either a single home or
shared a two- or three-story brick or frame house with one or two
other families. Most enjoyed a degree of privacy, fresh air, and living space unequaled in the Circle. In the better Zone neighborhoods, as one resident put it, men could "rear their families out
where the sun shines, out where at least a fair portion of pure air
and sunlight will be theirs." [7]

Death, moreover, haunted the Zone less relentlessly than the Circle. In 1890, the city's mortality rate was nearly 22 per thousand.
Only Zone wards closest to the core of the city, or those containing
a specific health hazard such as bottom lands or territory bordering
the canal, had rates a few points above the city average.

The people of the Zone, like those of the Circle, were diverse.
Indeed, by 1910 every significant racial and ethnic minority in Cincinnnati had representives living in the Zone. The more recent arrivals tended to bunch in the wards that straddled the Circle-Zone
border. Others, however—by 1910 almost 61 per cent of the city's
foreign-born population had arrived prior to 1890—scattered
throughout the area. Of the total foreign-born white population in
1910, just over 50 per cent lived in wards lying wholly or partly in
the Zone. In the same year, moreover, 60 per cent of the native
whites with foreign or mixed parentage resided in the Zone. Negroes populated the area in lesser proportions. In 1910, slightly less
than 50 per cent of the city's 19,639 colored citizens lived there.[8]

Most of the groups in the Zone had lived on the periphery of the
walking city. As the new city emerged those who successfully ac-
commodated themselves to the novel conditions of life moved up
and out. Thus, after 1880, Mt. Adams and the territory immediately
beyond it became a haven for Germans and Irish and a heavily
Catholic area.[9] The Germans of the Over-the-Rhine district moved
north into Corryville. The Germans and Irish of the near West End
and Mohawk-Brighton district spread up and across Mill Creek
Valley. They also ascended the western hills from the lower West

End into Price Hill, and moved up Harrison and Queen City avenues in Lick Run Gap toward Westwood and Cheviot.

Many of the early residents of the Zone, then, were second- and third-generation immigrants mixed with older native Americans. The Germans, however, constituted a major exception to this rule. From 1830 they comprised the largest single immigrant group entering Cincinnati. But after 1880, unlike other foreign newcomers, most Germans avoided the Circle and settled immediately in the Zone.

The first two waves of nineteenth-century German immigrants had by 1890 achieved considerable economic success and social acceptance and were already well established in the Zone. Some also helped maintain a visible German community despite the dissensions eroding it from within and the attrition of Americanization operating from without. The German language, periodicals and newspapers, Protestant and Catholic churches, charitable institutions and voluntary organizations of all kinds, constituted the cement which held "Germandom" together. In addition, the Zone contained successful German-speaking saloonkeepers, retail merchants, landlords, tradesmen, firemen, lawyers, doctors, manufacturers, and financiers.

Newly arrived German immigrants, therefore, entered a not wholly unfamiliar or uncongenial world. Their predecessors offered them not only the comforts and security of the visible German community, but also jobs and a place to live, making them the most economically and socially mobile immigrant group in the city. Once settled, the newcomers repeated the experience of those who preceded them. Most assimilated rapidly, losing all contact with and interest in the formal German community, while others, with mounting desperation, entered the lists for the preservation of Germandom in Cincinnati. The newcomers did so well that the German Immigrant Aid Society, founded at mid-century to aid needy immigrants, disbanded in 1893 on the grounds that nothing remained to be done.[10]

Other immigrants did not have the advantage of a large, old, and well-established community to pave their way into the Zone. Hence they penetrated the region more slowly and in lesser numbers. Only a few Italians, for example, made the jump from the Circle to the Zone before 1900, and another decade passed before Russian Jews moved out of the Circle in significant numbers. The Negroes of the Zone were the only group that lived in distinct clusters. These enclaves, many of them composed of domestic servants who worked in the elite residential Hilltops, existed in virtually every section of the Zone. But the growth of the Zone black communities was impeded after the emergence of the new city by the peculiar situation facing the city's colored inhabitants.

In the 1880's and 1890's Negroes in Cincinnati were legally liberated by state legislation. The last remnants of the Black Laws were repealed, two public accommodations bills were passed, and legislation was enacted which granted Negro children the right to attend white schools. The new freedom, however, proved illusory. The *Commercial-Gazette*, in 1889, accurately assessed the situation when it declared that the "color-line is everywhere." [11] And in 1909, Frank U. Quillan, a doctoral student in history at the University of Michigan, investigated race relations in Cincinnati and concluded that the historic strong antipathy of whites for Negroes had been increasing steadily, especially since the 1880's.

Quillan found that the tightening noose of discrimination had virtually cut off all contacts between Zone Negroes and the city's white community. Negroes were refused jobs as health department investigators because they would enter white homes in which "wives would be subject to insult in having to accept the orders of a colored man." They were excluded from the fire department because white firemen objected to eating and sleeping "alongside them." There were only twelve black patrolmen on the 610-man police force, a figure amounting to one-half "their quota" on a population basis. Other areas of employment were just as tightly closed. Quillan found no Negro stenographers or bookkeepers, no clerks in stores or factories, no teachers in the public schools. Negro workers were excluded by all the trade unions except the hodcarriers' and building laborers'. Law, medicine, and the ministry were "open," but blacks could "scarcely make a living" in these professions. Whites avoided them, and Negroes were shy of the black professionals out of "jealousy" or "lack of confidence." According to Quillan, the "legacy of slavery" was: the "white man's word is law."

Segregation affected every facet of life. Virtually all hotels, restaurants, and other eating and drinking places were closed to Negroes. Theaters either rejected them or sent them to separate galleries, often at an advanced price. All three amusement parks were closed to Negroes except on the annual " 'nigger day.' " When the new Municipal Bath House "became practically a Negro institution," officials barred all blacks. Housing, too, by 1910, was segregated. Negroes, according to Quillan, could not "rent or buy a house in a decent section of the city without paying an exorbitant price." Few could afford it, and the man who could, found that whites would "threaten his life" or, more usually, "buy him out."

Quillan thought there were several reasons for the strong anti-Negro feeling in Cincinnati: sensational treatment of Negro criminality in the press, the city's dependence on Southern trade, and the "unusually large number" of Cincinnatians who had spent time in the South and been infected with its attitudes on race. In addition, there were the large numbers of "ignorant colored people coming in from the South . . . many of whom" mistook "liberty for license." The mixing of the lower classes of the two races in the Circle, moreover, created "jealousy and ill feeling in these classes and revulsion and . . . fear in the higher classes." And, Quillan observed, "the Negro is more and more entering politics as a Negro" and "demanding rewards for Negroes," a development which met "much strong opposition and secret resentment." [12]

The color line, in any case, prevented the black bourgeoisie from moving freely among the city's residential sections and limited their economic contacts to dealings with members of their own race, a relatively small and poor group. As a result, even the more successful Negroes seldom commanded the financial resources or social facility necessary for life in the Zone and many remained trapped in the Circle. Those who could, moved out. The black population of Walnut Hills grew from 1963 in 1890 to 3611 in 1910.[13]

School attendance figures reflect the relative economic well-being of most Zone residents. Young people in the Zone generally attended school, either public or parochial, in larger proportions than their Circle counterparts.[14] In 1912, moreover, a map plotting the residences of families of students at the University of Cincinnati showed that more than half lived in the Zone. The University of Cincinnati, commented one patron, was "an institution for the worthy poor rather than for the well-to-do." [15]

The university study suggests that Zone residents were largely skilled or semi-skilled workers with little formal education. They traveled all over the city to their jobs, usually by rail or streetcar. A survey of 4500 of the 10,000 workers employed in six plants in the Norwood-Oakley area revealed that all lived within the Zone, but less than one-third were within walking distance of their jobs.

The consequent dislocation of the normal routine of factory and home created several problems for the commuting worker. Among them were "the need for travel and its curtailment of leisure and income . . . lunches to be got by thousands of employees" away from home and "customary city facilities," and "less tangible effects on the permanency of the working force and their isolation from their fellows." [16]

The transportation problem, judging from the laments of labor spokesmen, was particularly annoying. "In the morning, and at night," complained one union man, "when the working people are going to their labor and returning to their home . . . the street cars are crowded, jammed, loaded down, and decorated like bequilled porcupines" with tools.[17] These lines proved "a traction bonanza," for the "same cars which carry factory workers out at 7:30 each morning are loaded on the way back with Cincinnati office workers going into the city. The reverse happens each afternoon." But the sixty cents per week amounted to almost 10 per cent of the weekly wages of many workers.[18]

There were, however, some compensations. The big, new plants of the Zone featured well-lighted, ventilated, clean, and roomy workshops. Few new factories were built without providing a dining room for workers; telephone operators in some had a kitchen, dining room, and lounge, and many of the large factories by 1909 had physicians on their payrolls. These, too, were the companies which offered bonuses and profit-sharing schemes.[19]

Yet it was "possible to find not a little discontent among workpeople in the various plants." One factory hired "negroes and 'hunkies'" and was accused of trying to cut under the wage standards demanded by " 'white men.'" None of the new plants shortened the standard fifty-five-hour, six-day week or raised wages to cover the inconvenience and cost of commuting. Isolated from workers in other factories doing the same kind of work, the employees had less chance to "compare work conditions and hours . . . less opportunity to learn of new jobs offering real or fancied betterment." [20]

The undertow of dissatisfaction among the Zone workers, however, was not produced solely by material deprivation. "It is useless," a labor editor noted in 1902, "to sigh over the vanishing conditions of long ago. . . . The resistless evolution of modern industry . . . has brought about . . . a massing of workingmen under one head" and made it "impossible for the employer to know . . . the employees. . . . They . . . see them as trees walking." [21] And the *Brauer-Zeitung* wanted to know "why workers . . . can't . . . have the best of science, art, and literature, and music, poetry and dance. Why shouldn't the factory girl be an educated lady?" [22] Labor, apparently, felt the pangs of status deprivation.

But the Zone was not exclusively a working- or lower-class district. It harbored a vast array of entrepreneurs and their employees, in part because before the urban explosion most of the Zone had been composed of autonomous villages. Their indigenous businessmen and professional men were joined, after 1880, by a host of newcomers, whose economic success depended to a large degree on their racial and ethnic connections. There were foreign-language, Negro, and religious newspapermen, Irish and Negro undertakers, and Irish and German contractors, bartenders, and saloonkeepers in every neighborhood.

Many of them ranked among the city's new rich. Behr Manischewitz emigrated to Cincinnati in 1885, set up a bakery on Fifth and Baymiller in the Circle, invented a machine which produced fifty thousand pounds of matzos per day, and died in 1914 in his

Walnut Hills home on the outer edge of the Zone. J. J. Castellini, one of the city's "most progressive and enterprising businessmen" and, in 1912, the president of the Commission Merchant's National Association, lived in Evanston. Even bankers resided in the Zone. In 1896 a meeting of fifty representatives of Brighton, Camp Washington, and Fairmount business interests subscribed $60,000 to the new Brighton German Bank. Henry Imwalle rose from undertaker to president of both the Saint Bernard Building Association and the Citizens' Bank of Saint Bernard. And Fred Tuke, a German-Catholic immigrant, parlayed his dealings in Zone and Circle real estate into a successful savings and loan business.[23]

In many respects the Zone population resembled what the *Post* referred to as the "so-called middle class." This was, according to the paper, "the class that makes any city or any country what it is," and in it "the soul of a city grows." For this was the class which built up "many organizations, societies, associations, fraternities and clubs that bring together people who are striving upward, trying to uplift themselves, and hence human society." [24] The penchant for organization both reflected and sustained the modest prosperity of the various elements of this "middle class." It helped them protect themselves from the economic disasters, legal pitfalls, and social injustices that made life insecure for the people of the Circle.

Perhaps building associations, "the people's banks," as Fred Tuke called them, were the most characteristic Zone organization.[25] They came into vogue just after the Civil War, and by 1909 there were over 217 of them in the city, in which an estimated 80,000 people were directly or indirectly interested. At least 75 per cent of the mortgages were furnished by the associations, and some 60,000 homes had been paid for through them. "But for them," claimed one observer, "it is doubtful that Cincinnati would have made the tremendous development of the past ten or fifteen years." [26]

They were also credited with making Cincinnati a city of homes second only to Philadelphia and the leader among the nation's twelve largest cities in homes owned free of encumbrance. According to the secretary of the Cincinnati Chamber of Commerce, a large percentage of the working element lived in homes "acquired through the medium of building associations." Since their homes "represent years of their personal savings . . . the workingmen of Cincinnati are interested in the welfare of their own city, and there is almost a total absence of that floating and uncertain foreign population which characterizes the cities further north, and of strikes which invariably follow in their wake." [27]

The Germans constituted the most thoroughly organized single element of the Zone's population. There were German unions among the brewery workers, bakers, and typographers, and a maze of singing societies, rifle clubs, mutual aid associations, charity organizations, and groups dedicated to cultural uplift. In 1915 there were 114 of these groups. They were valuable institutions, one spokesman thought, and he wanted "to set aside the opinion held by many that German societies exist only to promote social sessions" by emphasizing "the real work done . . . in bettering the conditions of members, not only socially, but financially as well." [28]

Yet some hoped that the German organizations would perform another service. Increasingly after 1880, the *Vereinsmeier* emphasized the notion of preserving a German culture, of shoring up the sinking but still visible German community. They faced a frustrating task. It was difficult to find a common denominator among the Forty-eighters (those who arived after the German Revolution of 1848), socialists, Lutherans, Catholics, and Methodists who comprised the German Zone population. There were, moreover, barriers of dialect, and throughout the period Germans scattered geographically throughout the Zone and suburbs beyond. [29]

The Irish of the Zone also built up an organizational structure, but compared with that of the Germans it was rickety and aimless. There were no "Irish" cemeteries, orphanages, old folks' homes, charity societies, or newspapers, and there was only a handful of mutual aid societies and building associations. This, in part, helps explain the relatively small contingent of Irish immigrants living in the Zone, for in contrast to the Germans their rate of social and economic mobility was sluggish. In addition, they lacked a distinctive language to emphasize a sense of separateness; their tight association with the church provided them a ready-made emotional and material guide, and the disproportionately large numbers of Irish among the leadership of the trade unions diverted many from spending much time developing a concern for cultural unity.

Some second- and third-generation residents of the Zone, however, did attempt to preserve a sense of Irishness. Numerically the largest and socially the most prominent were the Friendly Sons of St. Patrick—which in 1906 had a membership of "nearly three hundred of the most progressive Irishmen of the city . . . all Democrats" [30]—and the Ancient Order of Hibernians. These and the six others devoted most of their nonsocial activities to rallying support for Irish independence and celebrating St. Patrick's Day.

But their influence was dwindling. St. Patrick's Day became more of an all-Catholic religious than Irish national event. In 1889, the *Catholic-Telegraph* was pleased to announce "that the German Catholic Societies of Cincinnati will participate in the parade of the Irish Catholics on Sunday next. Catholic America," the paper observed, "is a wonderful institution. Three cheers for the three nations—red, white and blue!" The celebration was a success, "decorous . . . peaceful," and "religious" in nature. By 1913, there was no parade, only a banquet, to commemorate the occasion.[31] The city, in fact, virtually ignored Irishdom.

Although the Negroes of the Zone developed an organizational life which rivaled that of the Germans in its pervasiveness, there is little surviving evidence of any desire to build up a visible Negro communty based on some special virtue of the race or the uniqueness of its history. Many of the organizations were black counterparts of those found in the Zone's white population. Between 1880 and 1900, however, at least two civil rights groups appeared. The more powerful was the Cincinnati branch of the National Progressive League which, in 1897, claimed 1000 members and control of 3000 votes. Neither the National Association for the Advancement of Colored People nor the National Urban League, however, had appeared in Cincinnati before 1914.

Although Negro political-social clubs flourished, only two were self-perpetuating. The Douglass League was Negro-led; it was also the most prestigious, occasionally took an independent line in local elections, and possessed a clubhouse of its own. Most of the ephemeral variety had white Republican sponsors, usually a candidate or prominent party supporter whose name was attached to the club.[32]

With the exception of this kind of venture, the leadership and membership of the colored organizations came, as the white press expressed it, from among "the better class" or "the better element" of Negroes struggling to escape the Circle. They represented a variety of occupations, but newspaper editors, preachers, lawyers, physicians, teachers, undertakers, and real estate agents predominated. Like the Irish, however, the Negro organizations were virtually ignored outside of colored circles, except when politics, crime, or the social relations of the races were discussed.

Despite their absorption in secular voluntary organizations, Zone dwellers made religion a prominent part of their lives. Church edifices dotted the district. Most of the city's immigrant and Catholic congregations as well as a majority of the Negro sects had buildings within the boundaries of the Zone. Generally, the German Protestants, German Catholics, and Negroes attended services in facilities located on the inner rim of the Zone. Older and wealthier Protestants constructed new buildings farther out, but their membership was Germanicized steadily during this generation. Within the Catholic Church, the English-speaking congregations—assimilated Irish and Germans—also moved to the outer edge. By the end of the period, the Russian Jews, too, began to move their synagogues into Zone sections. All of these contributed a layer of clubs and societies to the pyramiding structure of voluntary organizations.[33]

Compared with the city's other two residential districts, the Zone was Catholic territory. The percentage of Catholics among the city's church members dropped from 62 per cent in 1890 to 61 per cent in 1900, but then rose to 70 per cent in 1910. German stock, the largest ethnic group within the Zone, predominated within Cincinnati Catholicism. In 1910 there were 72 Catholic parishes in the city, caring for 27,536 families. Of these, 65 per cent of the parishioners came from German backgrounds, a situation perpetuated by continued German immigration.[34]

Catholic spokesmen, nonetheless, did not feel secure in their Zone haven. The *Catholic-Telegraph* was concerned about the Protestant "axiom" that "where a Roman Catholic Church is built in a good neighborhood, the social quality of the population . . . is apt to deteriorate, liquor saloons are . . . likely to be opened, moral offenses and interruptions of good order occur more often, and the tendency is down hill decidedly." [35]

The paper also expressed concern that the church could not compete with other institutions and ways of life in the Zone. In 1889 the editor explained that "as Catholics . . . advance in wealth and social position and mingle on terms of equality with their Protestant fellow citizens . . . they [must] understand with clearness that it is not lawful for them to join in any other than Catholic worship." [36] In 1900 another editor in the same paper broadened the warning. "Outside of the Church," he complained, "there are many societies offering various inducements to allure our men." As a result, "not a few of our people have joined these associations . . . formed . . . intimate friendships with persons not of our faith . . . become liberal(?) lukewarm, and finally mere nominal Catholics, whose children grow up practical infidels, or join some sect 'just for the style of it.' " [37]

Regardless of the special temptations of Zone life, Catholic parents in the Zone responded to the call of the church to give their children a Catholic education. The percentage of youths between the ages of six and twenty-one that attended church schools in Zone wards in 1913 ranged from about 40 per cent in the Fifth on Mt. Adams, to 35 per cent in the Twentieth atop Price Hill, to around 26 per cent in the Twenty-third in Cumminsville. None of the Circle wards, except the Sixth, with a mark of nearly 30 per cent, or any of the wards beyond the Zone approached these figures.[38]

What remained of the Zone dwellers' leisure time after fulfilling his economic, fraternal, and religious obligations was devoted to recreation. Much of this was done on an organized basis through

the "co-operative neighborhood social clubs." But the trend after
1880 was toward participation in mass commercial recreation.[39]
Many Zone dwellers had the means and time to frequent the
middle-brow diversions downtown, and the large number of Germans arrested there for disorderly conduct and the complaints of
"rowdyism" on the Owl streetcars suggest that they took advantage
of them. At the four "hilltop resorts" located at the head of the
inclined planes a young man on a date in the 1890's could get a
bottle of wine, a soft drink, and chicken for two for $2.40. By 1900,
however, such places were falling out of favor, in part because of
their "rough house" reputations. They were replaced by amusement
parks, each of which possessed a gaudy and highly publicized
special attraction.

Zone inhabitants had, moreover, ready access to commercial
amusements in their own neighborhoods. The most common was
the saloon, but toward the end of the period there was an occasional dance hall. Zone Negroes seeking this kind of diversion,
however, had to go to "some out-of-the-way place or 'low dive.' " [40]
But they, like others with the price of admission, could attend the
democratic movie houses. Although there were only two in the entire city in 1906, by 1912 the *Post* counted 113 scattered throughout
the town, showing 369 films a day.[41]

Although the violence characteristic of criminality in the Circle
decreased in the Zone, the area was not wholly free of brutality.
Murders, rapes, and robberies were common in the "Murder Zone"
of Cumminsville and on the "Wicked Strip" along Spring Grove
Avenue. In addition, clashes of minority groups occurred sporadically. In 1905, according to the *Enquirer*, a "stabbing almost set off
a riot" between Irish and Hungarians who lived at the base of
Western Hills halfway up the Valley. The same year 500 citizens of
Saint Bernard tried to drive out of the village 50 Hungarian street
laborers temporarily housed in a two-room building. The Saint Bernard people, claiming that "the foreigners were filthy . . . attacked the house with a fire hose." A "lively fight followed in which
knives and guns were displayed by both sides," but no serious injuries were reported.[42] And in 1913 Cincinnati police had to "strug-

gle with a group of men who threatened to lynch" a Negro arrested near Norwood after an Oakley woman charged that he had "attacked" her.[43]

Disorder in the new city, then, was not confined to the Circle. Although the people of the Zone were generally more prosperous, healthier, better educated, and more secure than those of the Circle, they nonetheless found it difficult to strike new roots. The confusion of the novel routine of life in the Zone generated tensions which, at their strongest, could erupt into violence.

It also produced nostalgia for older ways. The *Catholic-Telegraph* mourned the passing of the "real home" of "a couple of generations ago" in which "the mother was competent to undertake all the duties that belong to that exalted title and to pass them on to her daughters that they, in turn, may be homekeepers and home builders." [44] And a retired leather factory porter who saved enough money to move to the outer edge of the Zone also had a complaint. "When I lived down on Richmond Street in a little house," he lamented, "we cooked the corn beef and cabbage in the house and ate it in there, and when we wanted to go to the toilet we went out into the yard, now I live in a fine house, I am made to eat . . . out in the yard, and when I want to go to the toilet I have to go into the house." [45]

Yet the discontented neither resigned themselves to apathy nor revolted in anarchy. Instead, through their social, economic, political, and religious organizations, they sought to realize their aspirations and control their communities.

3

The Hilltops

The top echelons of Cincinnati's social and economic register were not exempt from the dislocating forces which molded the Circle and Zone of Emergence. At the beginning of the period the two elite residential districts which had flanked the old walking city remained intact. The older, the East End, centered on Lytle Park and the Sinton-Taft mansion on Pike Street. Although the character of the district was teetering dangerously between the emerging East End industrial district and the Ohio River bottoms, a few residents, led by Charles P. Taft, managed to preserve their domain from the encroachment of factories and the expansion of the Circle.

The aristrocratic West End, however, changed almost entirely. In 1884 physicians and dentists with offices fronting on Garfield Park and residents along the other side complained that the park's benches "serve only for a loafing place for the most disreputable and worthless vagabonds of both sexes." And in 1892 wealthy residents of West Sixth Street objected that the growing cosmopolitanism of the neighborhood was destroying their privacy. That year a $25,000 home sold for $14,000. Thereafter the decline was precipitous. One former resident recalled that the West End "did not go down . . . imperceptibly. . . . It went to ruin almost as if a bombshell had sent it to destruction." [1]

Those who stuck it out lived in fear. Thomas Stanley Matthews, whose father was an Episcopal priest on Seventh Street, years later recalled that the door of their house was not only latched and bolted at night but had a chain, a precaution against sneak thieves. Every night the parlormaids had to draw the curtains of all the windows opening on the street and shut and latch the shutters. The "nightly battening-down of the house increased our sense of seige." After his West End childhood experiences, Matthews never understood why Cincinnati was called "The Queen City," for a city to him was "a place of horrors, an urban desert." [2]

The wealthy refugees from the Basin joined the flow of migrants pushing outward and settled beyond the Zone. There were by 1883, one traveler noted, "half a dozen beautiful suburbs" on "the amphitheatre of hills" where "the homes of Cincinnati's merchant princes and millionaires are found . . . elegant cottages, tasteful villas, and substantial mansions, surrounded by a paradise of grass, gardens, lawns, and tree-shaded roads." [3]

Before 1900 much of this silk-stocking belt lay beyond the city limits. Generally, it included part of Price Hill and the Western Hills as far north as College Hill, Clifton to the north of the Basin, Mt. Auburn and Avondale on the northeast, and parts of Mt. Adams and most of Walnut Hills to the east. As annexation and the flight to the hills continued, the atmosphere became less bucolic. After the turn of the century a residential hotel was built on Mt. Auburn to accommodate the elderly, and apartments sprang up in Avondale and Walnut Hills. The wave of emigrants continued to push north and east until they reached the isolation of Indian Hill, where lots could be bought for $200 per front foot.[4]

Nonetheless, the older Hilltop districts remained fashionable, and many retained their rural atmosphere. But within one generation Price Hill, the western part of Walnut Hills, and much of Mt. Auburn had been absorbed by the Zone and Mt. Adams pulled to the brink of the Circle. The growth of the city, according to one observer, seemed to be following a depressing cycle: "First, the

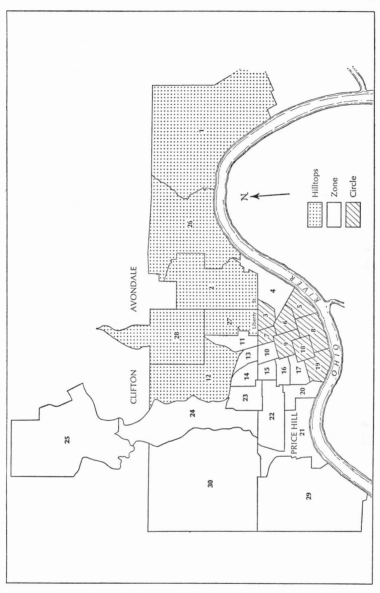

2. The New City, 1890

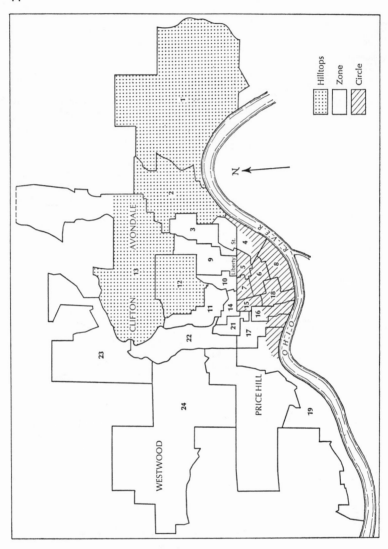

3. The New City, 1900

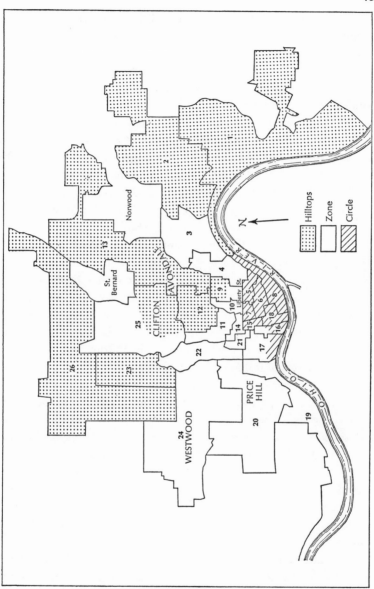

4. The New City, 1910

single-family house with its yard or lawn, the typical American home of which we are proud; then the crowded houses, the apartment house and tenement; then the slum." [5]

To the residents of the still uninvaded peripheral districts, however, "congestion" was a potential danger, not a present fact. Despite the continued construction of homes, hotels, and apartments, the Hilltops remained the least densely populated area of the city.

They were also the healthiest residential districts in the city. [6] Yet contagious diseases, despite their low statistical visibility, posed a serious threat. In 1891 David Taft, a student at Woodward High School and the son of Charles P. Taft, died of typhoid fever. It was "a ghastly satire on the poverty of riches," one member of the family wrote, that "money could not save the boy." [7]

While it was impossible to guarantee their children good health, Hilltop parents could, to a greater extent than others, provide them with an education. Public-school attendance in the outlying wards ranked among the highest in the city. While church-school enrollment in the Hilltops fell below that in the Zone, the number of students attending nonsectarian private schools in the Hilltop districts was exceeded only in those Circle or Zone wards that contained remnants of fashionable neighborhoods. [8]

The preference of many Hilltop parents for private schools was partly the result of a growing suspicion that the public schools were bad. After 1870 "there was a steady deterioration and starvation of our schools," protested one Hilltop lawyer, until in 1904-5, the "tax-rate . . . for the Cincinnati School District was the lowest in the State. . . . During this period . . . our schools declined and Cincinnati fell back step by step, compared with other cities." [9] Nonetheless, there was no rush to create new private schools for Hilltop students. Nor was there any marked increase in private-school enrollment.

The static condition of private education suggests that overt nativism was not widespread in the Hilltop districts, for they were not the private preserves of native-born whites. In 1910 native whites of native parentage constituted over 50 per cent of the population in only one of the four Hilltop wards, the First. Native whites of foreign parentage, most of them German or Irish, made up the largest single element in all four wards.

In fact, except for Indians, Chinese, Japanese, and Roumanians, every ethnic and racial minority in Cincinnati had at least a few representatives living on the Hilltops. The expansion of these settlements, however, was not welcome. In 1897 the owner of a vacant lot in the "aristocratic portion of May Street between Oak and Fern, Walnut Hills," vowed to "get even"—because a concrete sidewalk had been put down—by erecting a number of small cottages, each on a plot containing ten front feet, for Negroes. He was dissuaded by the inhabitants of the "adjoining palatial residences," who threatened to sue him for depreciation of property.[10] And in 1899 a Norwood politician complained that his neighbors were undemocratic because they claimed that the influx of working-class people was ruining their "village of homes."[11]

The Hilltops were also religiously diverse. In 1913, for example, 2515 pupils from Hilltop wards enrolled in church schools. Moreover, "the fact is historic," noted an excitable Gentile politician from Avondale, "that when West Sixth and Seventh and Eighth and Dayton Streets were encroached upon by Hebrew families the Christians fled to Walnut Hills as the haven of rest." But "when rapid transit came the Hebrews . . . flocked to 'the hill' until it was known by the name of New Jerusalem." Then "Avondale was . . . heralded as the suburb of deliverance, but again rapid transit brought the wealthy Hebrews to Avondale in numbers greater than the flock of crows that every morning and evening darken her skies." And now, he concluded, "it has been facetiously said that the congregation has assembled in force and that when Avondale is roofed over the synagogue will be complete."[12]

As that outburst implies, ethnic and religious selectivity was not uncommon in the peripheral high-income districts. Social registers, for example, listed only a few families in the relatively accessible yet prosperous Western Hills north of Price Hill. College Hill, however, at the remote northern end of the area, was well represented and almost totally Anglo-Saxon Protestant. So, too, was Glendale, although it contained some Catholics. It was a "preserve . . . inhabited and dominated by the Procters and Matthewses and their relations," some of them High Church Episcopalians who preferred services "smoky-sweet with incense and tinkly with sanctus bells." [13]

Other elite communities were more heterogeneous. Clifton, just north of heavily Teutonic Corryville in the Zone, was German enough to be known as "Dutch Clifton." But, in 1908, Lafayette Avenue—"the avenue of the barons"—housed not a single family with a German name. German Jews congregated in Avondale, the "Golden Ghetto," but so did others of German background, and there was a Presbyterian section of Avondale. German Jews, moreover, settled in every one of the northern and eastern Hilltop neighborhoods, though few moved into the Western Hills. Hyde Park tended to be Anglo-Saxon Protestant, but Walnut Hills housed Anglo-Saxons, Germans, German Jews, and Irish, in that order. The fashionable Hilltop residential districts, then, were less visibly divided into ethnic and religious agglomerations than either the Circle or the Zone.[14]

Occupational segregation, the only kind of selectivity operative on the Hilltops, excluded skilled and semi-skilled workers. Virtually every kind of business and profession, however, was represented. The city's oldest and most successful merchants, bankers, industrialists, lawyers, and doctors congregated there. Among their neighbors were businessmen whose fortunes grew with the emergence of the new city. This latter group included Bernard H. Kroger, who developed the chain-store grocery; Jacob G. Schmidlapp, an innovator in the savings-bank field; and George Puchta, the son of a Catholic immigrant who emerged from the Circle to become a manufacturers' supply distributor, bank director, and a founder of the Cincinnnati Frog and Switch Company.

Indeed, there were many routes to the fashionable districts. Heads of post-1880 big businesses like F. A. and P. O. Geier, Richard LeBlond, and Franklin Alter in the machine-tool industry, John Omwake of the American Playing Card Company, James A. Green, a Canadian-born executive in the iron and steel business, and public utilities magnates like Charles Kilgour in telephones and street railways and General Andrew Hickenlooper in gas and electricity all moved into the new section.

Like the businessmen, the professionals of the Hilltops stood at the top of their calling. The legal profession, however, provided little room at the top to accommodate the increasing numbers of young men attracted to the bar. Medicine, on the other hand, was more permeable. By the end of the period the sons of several German Jewish businessmen held positions of high respect within the field, as did other newcomers to the city. And in 1915, Dr. Otto P. Geier, who had opened his office as a general practitioner in 1900, took a leading part in organizing the American Association of Industrial Physicians and Surgeons.

Apparently convinced, as one Hilltop preacher put it, that "nature will tolerate no half-way successes," that the city must either increase or diminish, suburban businessmen and professional men founded a host of organizations to protect their stake.[15] They not only established improvement associations to uphold the interests of the downtown business section and their Hilltop neighborhoods, but also set up associations to promote the economy of the new metropolis.

Indeed, Hilltop residents, like the inhabitants of the Zone, were ardent joiners. This can be explained in part by the dispersal of population and the consequent reduction in semi-social contacts among businessmen and professional men. A plant manager in Norwood told Graham Romeyn Taylor that he thought the "advantages of the suburban location" were "all right," but, he added, "I find it hard to keep up the old interests and associations which means a lot to me. I don't have the same chance to run across old friends and join in the things at the club." Taylor concluded that "the quiet routine and distance from friends which the suburb enjoins" and the desire of the "better-to-do people" for "metropolitan advantages" accounted for the appearance of expensive apartments nearer the center of the city. Ready access to the theaters and opera, the life of the large hotels, and the pleasures of the "smart set," Taylor claimed, "have quite as strong a grip upon them as the

cheaper amusements and 'thrills' have upon the working people." [16]
The Queen City Optimists' Club was one product of this craving.
Founded in 1874 to serve the walking city, it became the nucleus
about which the club district developed. Before the period was
over there were five such downtown institutions—each housed in
large buildings and equipped with dining facilities, reading and
recreation rooms, a bar, and sleeping quarters—which provided a
central location where the suburbanites could gather for talk, conviviality, and business.

By 1900, however, the supremacy of these rich man's saloons was
already being challenged. Women, too, resented suburban isolation. In 1888 the city's first country club opened, a place to which
members and their families could get away from the dirt and heat
of the city. In 1904 there were three such havens.

The diffusion of wealthy families had other effects on the social
life of the elite. The practice of "calling" on New Year's Day disappeared owing to the difficulty and danger of travel among suburbs
divided by rough terrain. As early as 1884, William Howard Taft
noted that, except for "the cooks and servant girls . . . no one
called and no one received." [17] And because it was easier to get
from suburb to the Basin than from suburb to suburb, it became
increasingly common for residents of outlying districts to stay with
a friend closer to the heart of the city after an evening in town. It
was a fifty-minute carriage ride from Fountain Square to Grandin
Road, and more than an hour's ride when rain, snow, or sleet made
the hillsides slippery.[18]

Hilltop residents also proved resourceful in devising social activities for enjoyment in the home. Card games, especially poker, were
popular among the men. Mixed gatherings played whist and read
and discussed plays. Others, however, preferred amateur musicals.
When in town, Nicholas Longworth and his wife, the former Alice
Roosevelt, held such gatherings at least once and often two or three
times a week. "We would all have dinner first," Mrs. Longworth
recalled, "and afterwards waste no time getting started. In the
room next to the 'Picture Room' . . . there was a table with drinks,
a ham and a cheese, so that the performers could 'stoke up.' . . .

The music was not by any means serious. Nick had a perfectly amazing fund of games and stunts, and nearly every one else had some trick that was trotted out before the parties were over." [19]

Yet the suburbanites were sufficiently mobilized to take advantage of a broad range of commercial recreation. Between 1870 and 1900 Hilltop residents industrioulsy fostered the city's artistic development. In this "golden age" of cultural philanthropy the elite contributed funds to establish Music Hall, the art museum, the symphony orchestra, and Rookwood pottery and patronized the legitimate theater. They also kept alive older institutions, like the Literary Club, founded in 1849, which by 1910 numbered among its members, living and dead, many prominent persons—statesmen, ambassadors, jurists, and one President of the United States.

Tuesdays and Fridays were fashionable evenings at the Highland House, where, after dinner, young men and women drank wine, "sitting on a retired porch, with the lights and crowds of people below, and the gay music, and cool air." [20] And on one trip to Cincinnati Mrs. Longworth was taken to the races, to baseball games, to the Zoo, and some beer gardens.[21] Occasionally the pastimes were even less genteel. In January 1897 the *Post* reported that all the dancers and spectators at a Phi Delta Phi affair in College Hall which featured a "coochee coochee" dance would be arrested.[22]

Members of the fashionable set were also subject to fads. "Coaching" with a smart team of horses was followed by a "riding craze." The latter was institutionalized into the Cincinnati Riding Club, one of the most exclusive organizations in the city. On Saturday nights the members put on exhibitions, riding to music and demonstrating military drills. The highlight of one performance was a circus which featured "a Roman chariot race" between Nicholas Longworth and Julius Fleischmann. The evening climaxed when Max Fleischmann, in a blond wig and pink ballet shorts, and Carl Krippendorf, in white tulle and spangles, did dance steps on horseback." [23] At least one old social custom, however, flourished, for Hilltop residents in the early twentieth century continued the "summer migration" to other, cooler parts of the country.[24]

This level of society also built up and maintained a battery of secret and patriotic clubs and organizations. The membership lists of these organizations presented a group of names as diverse as that found in the social registers. It was, apparently, difficult to make them otherwise. In 1891, for example, there was an attempt to bring together natives of New England into the recently resur-rected New England Society. The respondents, though neither entirely Anglo-Saxon nor wholly Protestant, were at least largely British. But they soon made Theodore Roosevelt an honorary member. And guests at one of the club dinners in 1898 included Rabbi David Philipson, J. G. Schmidlapp, Herman Goepper, and the Reverend David S. Schaff. Finally, in 1899, the members amended the rules to open the society to any "lineal descendant" of a person born in New England, as well as natives and sons of natives.[25]

Social discrimination in suburban circles based on religious or ethnic differences remained at a low ebb throughout the period. German Jews of the fashionable districts belonged to all the elite social clubs and were excluded only from the Commercial Club among the businessmen's groups. Charles Fleischmann, because of his "warm hearted friendship, boundless liberality and fondness for sports of all kinds," became the leading spirit in an informal dinner and poker group which included Andrew Hickenlooper among its members. Fleischmann's sons, Julius and Max, along with the Forchheimer family, Dr. Christian A. Holmes, and Dr. John M. Withrow, who married Hickenlooper's daughter, made up a Jewish-Christian connection of relative newcomers to society that ranked just below the Taft circle. Beyond this clique, however, there was a general tendency to exclude German Jews from Gentile social gatherings attended by both sexes after six o'clock.[26]

Most of the few expressions of anti-Jewish sentiment among Hilltop residents occurred in the 1880's and 1890's, just after the first large migration to the Hilltops. None of them, however, were vicious or particularly effective. In 1893, for instance, Dr. Frederich Forchheimer resigned from the Univesity Club after a young Jewish attorney he and Charles P. Taft had sponsored was blackballed. But only three votes were required for rejection; a large majority had favored admitting the lawyer.[27] And in 1897 there was an at-

tempt to exclude Jews from the Avondale Athletic Club, but after
an editorial in the *American Israelite*, saying it was "strange" that
there was not one Jewish name among the one hundred original
members, "especially as the social and business intercourse between
Christian and Jew is as cordial in Avondale as anywhere else," the
club quickly dropped its constitutional proscription of Jews.[28]

There is little evidence that other elements of the elite received
discriminatory treatment. Hilltop Catholics, in part because they
were not numerously represented in the district, played an inconspicuous part in its social life. But their entrance was eased by the
conversion of members of prominent families such as Reuben
Springer, the originator and chief financier of the movement to
construct Music Hall, and Mrs. Bellamy Storer, whose social affiliations included members of Washington society, such as Henry
Cabot Lodge, Henry Adams, and Theodore Roosevelt.

The Anglo-Saxon Protestants of the fashionable districts, in fact,
possessed no generally accepted code by which to measure their
Catholic and German Jewish neighbors. Consequently, both groups
were accepted, but with reservations. Andrew Hickenlooper, for
example, in describing his association with Charles Fleischmann,
remarked that "he and all the members of his family looked like
Jews, but in Charlie there was not a single Jewish characteristic.
Our relations were quite intimate. I enjoyed his full confidence and
our friendship was only terminated by his death." [29]

This uneasy tolerance was abetted by the lack of any rigid ideas
about religion in the Hilltops. Specific theological beliefs and strict
religious observance were not, apparently, crucial matters. One
Presbyterian regarded his minister as "certainly up-to-date" because "Sunday a week ago he preached on the North Pole . . . and
yesterday . . . on the life of Harriman." [30] The members of the
Riding Club, moreover, took regular Sunday morning outings and
procured an "amateur chaplain" who went "to early mass" and "vi-
cariously prayed for the rest of us." They later were indignant when
the press branded them public enemies for taking religion so
lightly.[31]

Charles Dudley Warner concluded that Cincinnati was a city of art rather than theology due in part to the fact that in the suburbs it was difficult to get to church because congregations were so scattered "and society itself [had] more or less disintegrated." [32] A Catholic layman found that, since the father in a suburban household so often had to leave in the morning before the children arose and return at night after they were asleep, "it is not unusual to hear a suburbanite say that he stays at home on Sunday to get acquainted with his family." [33]

Yet Hilltop residents had not, by any means, abandoned religion. In many respects, they were the most conspicuously reverent portion of the city's population. By 1900 Catholics, Protestants, and Jews alike had sprinkled the suburbs with imposing houses of worship. Wealthy Catholics and Jews, moreover, attended services at St. Peter's Cathedral and Plum Street Temple, elegant edifices which faced each other across Plum Street next door to City Hall. Similarly, Episcopalians, Baptists, Methodists, and Presbyterians all kept up elaborate downtown buildings. The more liberal Protestant sects, however—the Unitarians, Universalists, Swedenborgians, and Christian Scientists—abandoned the Basin.

While welcoming churches, most suburbanites agreed that their neighborhoods should be kept free of taverns. One resident considered them a necessary evil but complained about the arrogant and defiant attitude of the saloon that "ignored and hampered the law" and demanded action be taken against them.[34] Throughout the period the saloon was a sore point with the Hilltop population. It offended the sense of public decorum of some, violated the moral code of others, and provided a source of drunkenness and crime which threatened the safety of the neighborhood.

Criminal disorder, in fact, was a major preoccupation of Hilltop residents. Although in 1900 police arrested 76 attorneys, 20 doctors, 22 manufacturers, and 19 merchants, most suburbanites believed that the serious threat to the security of life and property came from below. In 1891 Charles P. Taft complained that the two Hilltop parks had been "given over to the rascalities of the worst creatures to be found in a big city" and were so overrun by "scoundrels" that an unattended woman or child could not go there even in the daytime.[35] Suburban homes, moreover, offered rich pickings for burglars. "Bold hold-ups . . . continue with alarming frequency," protested the *Post* in 1905, "and the police seem powerless to find the crooks." Residents of Avondale and Walnut Hills were said to fear going on the streets at night.[36]

The elite residential districts, then, were havens for the economically successful. Inhabited by a mixture of old and new families, they were neither religiously, occupationally, nor ethnically uniform. Nor were they isolated from the rest of the city. Their residents were bound to the Circle and Zone by innumerable ties. Many had once lived there and others were connected by religious, ethnic, and family associations. Most had a business or professional interest in the fate of the interior, and all were threatened by disorders emanating from it. As commuters they were regularly exposed to the visible evidence of congestion and the spectacle of affluence and poverty.

Residents of the Circle, Zone, and Hilltops were all uprooted in the emerging modern city. It was physically larger, economically more variegated, and inhabited by a more diverse population than the walking city. Its incessant mobility was celebrated on May 1, "moving day," the date that leases expired. Businesses and residents alike got "even with the landlord" and sought out more favorable neighborhoods.[37] Everybody was a newcomer. Jostled by physical and social mobility, and confused by the search for accommodation with strange people and new modes of life, the residents devised new and modified old institutions in their search for stability. The new city provided a fertile breeding ground for discontent and turmoil, innovation and creative reconstruction.

II

DECADE OF DISORDER, 1884–1894

. . . the passion of American human nature for the gregarious
life of the city has its alarming as well as its agreeable aspect.
. . . The feverish hatred of solitude and calm contemplation,
the nervous eagerness to mingle in the multitude of men, the
anxiety of the struggle for success or for existence will make
men new creatures for statesmen to deal with, and the state-
manship of the past will have to give place to a statesmanship
of the future, the character of which no man at this present
time can predict.*

The waning decades of the nineteenth century were years of crisis
for Cincinnati. The constant moving of people from neighborhood
to neighborhood, the expansion of the city's boundaries, the increasing heterogeneity of its population, and the growing awareness of the lag in the race for regional urban supremacy placed a
severe strain on governmental and political agencies. Existing mu-
niciple institutions creaked under the burden. The new pressures
created discord among men and interests and triggered massive
disorders which taxed the limits of the city's political ingenuity.

The crisis would have been of greater magnitude had not annexation largely kept pace with the explosion of the population outward. Successive enlargements of the city's boundaries kept the
wealthy, highly educated, and politically experienced and active
residents of the Hilltop suburban fringe engaged in urban affairs.
They played an important part in determining the city's response to
the crisis in the years between 1884 and 1894.

* J. S. Tunison, *The Cincinnati Riot: Its Causes and Results* (Cincinnati,
1886), p. 19.

4

City in Crisis

During the decade of disorder law enforcement in Cincinnati virtually broke down. "Time was," complained the *Enquirer* in 1884, "when Cincinnati needed but twenty-five policemen to guard its moral safety." Yet "now, with . . . a police force of three hundred men . . . its streets reek with crime. Not a thoroughfare in its limits but has been stained with human blood." In the last year alone, the article claimed, police had made 12 arrests for malicious shooting, 29 for malicious cutting, 47 for cutting with intent to wound, 284 for shooting with intent to kill, 92 for murder and manslaughter, and 948 for carrying a concealed weapon. There was a total of 56,784 arrests.[1]

The *Enquirer*'s outburst was but one example of the growing public indignation over the failure of authorities to expedite the trial of criminals, and especially of some twenty-three indicted murderers who, in the spring of 1884, languished in jail. During March, then, public attention eagerly centered on the trial of two youths, Joseph Palmer, a mulatto, and William Berner, a German immigrant, accused of the robbery-murder of a white livery man.

On March 24, before a packed courtroom, the jury declared Berner guilty of manslaughter only. The decision touched off an explosive reaction. The judge called it "a damned outrage," and as the jury filed out, cries of "Hang them!" were heard.[2] The daily press blasted the decision. Even the *Volksfreund*, which had covered the trial in a comparatively judicious manner, joined the outcry and suggested that it was quite possible that "Judge Lynch would soon be honored in Cincinnati."[3]

Indeed, many felt the situation warranted some sort of action. Three days after the decision sixty-four prominent citizens called for a public meeting. In this fashion they hoped to start a legitimate reform movement which would eliminate the allegedly corrupt legal administration and stop the repeated miscarriages of justice.[4]

In response to their call, on the evening of Friday, March 28, a crowd of some ten thousand people packed Music Hall. The excited audience was composed mainly of "respectable" people, the wealthy, the middle class, and the working people. They were not, however, sure of the objective of the meeting. Many thought a vigilance committee was to be formed and brought ropes with them. At least one cry of "Hang 'em all" was heard, and the chairman had trouble keeping order. The crowd, nonetheless, sat through several speeches delivered by representatives of the prominent citizens who had called the meeting.

Afterward, as the crowd left Music Hall, a group of men and youths, including a few Negroes but dominated by whites, urged people to follow them to the jail to "hang Berner!" By the time the mob reached the county jail and courthouse in the center of the city its numbers had mounted to an estimated two thousand. Some of them stormed into the jail entrances. But police also rushed to the scene. They had succeeded in partially clearing the jail when a shot was fired and a young man fell dead. The mob then forced its way into the cell blocks. Before the cells could be broken into, however, the militia arrived, fired on the intruders, killed several, and cleared the jail. Thereafter the mob tried unsuccessfully to start a fire in an attempt to burn out both the militia and the prisoners. Mob and militia fought until 3 a.m.

The next day a larger contingent of troops arrived. But their appearance did not quiet the city. A handbill was circulated calling for the establishment of vigilance committees in each ward to "serve notice to criminals, criminal lawyers, gamblers and prostitutes to leave Hamilton county within three days . . . or suffer the penalty." Throughout the day men gathered in small groups to berate the militia and sheriff for obstructing the lynching. That night another mob gathered. This time some of its members entered the undefended courthouse adjoining the jail and set the torch to it. The militia opened fire. Another night of sporadic fighting had begun. The courthouse burned to the ground.

Sunday a special mayor's committee of public safety announced that the militia would be withdrawn as soon as possible since its presence seemed to incite the mob. Nonetheless at nightfall still another crowd gathered. Toward midnight a group of about sixty men and teenage boys opened fire. The militia responded with sweeping bursts from a Gatling gun. One final unsuccessful attack was made after that. Then the rioters dispersed and did not reappear. In the three nights of bloodshed fifty-four were killed and an estimated two hundred wounded.[5]

But the courthouse and jail were not the only scenes of disorder. Friday night a group of boys from sixteen to nineteen years old tried to steal a cannon from Music Hall and members of the mob broke into several gun shops for ammunition and weapons. Saturday night the "Sixth Street gang" joined with the "Deer Creek gang," a crowd of drunks, and "a rabble of boys" in looting the pawn shops on lower Central Avenue. The mass meeting, called by residents of the Hilltop suburbs in the name of law and order, had inadvertently led to a violent demonstration from the Zone and Circle.

For the rest of the decade the fear of a recurrence, fed by repeated outbreaks of violence, hung over the city. Just six months after the courthouse disaster, during the fall elections, violence erupted in the lower wards. A federal marshall killed a Negro. That night a policeman was shot and killed while trying to arrest a Negro during a brawl at Sixth Street and Freeman Avenue. The riot bell was rung and when additional police arrived "bullets poured from every window and every housetop." At day's end the casualty list recorded two policemen and one Negro dead and an indeterminate number of citizens wounded.[6]

Less than two years later law enforcement officials faced another crisis. This time it was brought on by the 1886 demonstrations for an eight-hour working day. They began with a parade. Oscar Ameringer, armed with a makeshift dagger, recalled that "Only red flags were carried in that first May Day parade, and the only song we sang was the 'Arbeiters Marsellaise'. . . . Even the May Day edition of the *Arbeiter Zeitung* was printed on red paper." [7] The marching was, however, quiet and orderly and culminated in a German party at the Bellevue House.

The following day the strike got under way. It spread rapidly like an epidemic. When news of the Haymarket incident hit town the tension heightened. What had started as a "jolly strike" for Ameringer and his associates now took on a grimmer aspect. City officials, with an estimated thirty thousand men on strike, took extraordinary police precautions. They placed some three hundred special police in charge of the suburban districts and assigned the heavily armed regulars to keep order in the Basin. The *Times-Star* urged them to be "swift, fearless and merciless" with the "rabid dogs" who threatened the peace and applauded when police investigated local socialists and discovered six hundred guns, including two hundred Winchester rifles.[8]

The crisis passed without bloodshed. By the fifteenth the workers had conceded defeat. As for Ameringer, he found his name "emblazened on the blacklists of Cincinnati's employers" and thereafter "experienced no trouble living up to the obligation . . . not to work . . . until our just demand, the eight-hour day plus a twenty-per-cent increase in wages, was granted." [9]

Although the general strike was not repeated, the workers of the Zone were not quieted. In 1887, for example, they organized the Union Labor party and came within an ace of winning the city election. That same year the brewery workers shattered the paternalism which had dominated the industry by organizing a union and launching boycotts against unorganized brewers. The "beer bosses" responded by setting up the Brewers Protective Association to break up the union.[10] The decade of labor unrest ended with the general railroad strike of 1894. Once again the city was gripped by the fear of riots. Circuit Court Judge William Howard Taft spent the hot summer days of late June and early July avoiding reporters and issuing injunctions. The emergency passed, however, after the strike leader was arrested and sentenced by Taft to six months in the Warren, Ohio, county jail.

Lynch mobs, election violence, and labor unrest were not the only sources of disorder. In 1889 the *Times-Star*'s editor, Charles P. Taft, claiming more than two thousand businesses were open on Sunday, launched a crusade against the "continental Sunday." If it "means fostering . . . and inciting debauchery," he asserted, "if it means opening the stores and pressing into service on that day the working people . . . then the modern Puritan intends to rise up and to oppose to the uttermost this kind of Sunday." [11] The *Catholic-Telegraph* also disapproved of people who made Sunday "exclusively" a "day for drinking, carousing and theatrical exhibits." [12] Even more disgusting, some argued, was the influence of the Sunday saloon. Because of it, a Methodist minister claimed, "Sunday in Cincinnati . . . [is] a high carnival of drunkenness, base sensuality, reeking debauchery and bloody, often fatal crimes." [13]

Indignation over these conditions spread rapidly and embraced prominent laymen. In February of 1889 a new organization, the Committee of Five Hundred, took the lead in the movement to enforce the Sunday laws. Backed by residents of the city's fashionable districts, the committee chose for its chairman a businessman who promptly announced that anarchy prevailed. The danger was increased, committee spokesmen thought, because of the connivance of politicians and the press. "It would be a serious matter," said one Presbyterian preacher, "if these mutterings of lawlessness . . . were heard only among the class of malcontents which is heard in every great city. [But when] this anarchy begins to display itself in high places (applause), when it is condoned . . . and encouraged by men who have assumed the attitude of mentors and moulders of public opinion through the press, then it is time that the moral and Christian element of the city assert itself (applause). . . ." [14]

The "liberals," of course, did not submit to this vituperation in silence. *Sam, the Scaramouch,* an avowedly independent local magazine, accused "the Puritans"—"mugwump organizations of played-out politicians . . . and religious fanatics"—of falsely describing Cincinnati as the most corrupt city in America.[15] And in 1886 a group of citizens, largely German, founded the *Bund für Freiheit und Recht* to protest against the agitation for a Sunday law.

The *Bund,* however, was concerned with more than just Sabbatarianism. Politicians failed to solve public questions, it felt, because of their tendency to leave the initiative in the care and management of public affairs to factions within parties, sects, corporations, and other groups. Thus the city seemed doomed to undergo a round of reforms that were shams and policies that were failures because they were introduced either from party or sect hate, or from inadequate knowledge of the needs of the whole city. What was needed, concluded the *Bund,* was "a sincere interchange of views and corresponding co-operation between the seemingly hopelessly discordant better elements of society." [16]

Instead, in 1889, the city got another near riot. After the spring municipal election the victorious Republicans announced their intention of enforcing the Sunday saloon law. Shortly thereafter a group of saloonkeepers, estimated to number between 500 to 1200, met at Central Turner Hall and decided to ignore the new policy. Some of the Puritans panicked. The Negro member of the Committee of Five Hundred warned Governor Joseph B. Foraker that hundreds of men stood ready to defy the law and show "their anarchial [sic] dispositions." [17] Alarmed by this message and the Turner Hall resolution, Foraker advised the mayor not to tolerate any defiance of the law.

The following Sunday the showdown came. The police, reinforced by the fire department, crossed the canal to close up Kissell's saloon. An unruly crowd gathered, epithets were hurled, but no violence occurred. Kissell's was closed.[18]

The dispute over Sabbath observance was but one of the cultural conflicts which divided the peoples of the Zone and suburbs. Residents of both sections expressed nativist sympathies, but the most articulate spokesmen of that movement came from fashionable residential districts. William Christie Herron, a member of an "old" and respected pre-Civil War family, described foreigners as "illiterates, full of superstition and semi-barbarism"—people who regarded the "inculcation of progressive civilization in the education and elevation of humanity, and in the dissemination of the Christian religion (unless Roman Catholic), as an encroachment upon their superior rights, independence, and personal liberties." [19]

Charles P. Taft, an advocate of immigration restriction, saw a complex of evils revolving about immigrants, especially Germans. He connected the Sunday saloon, runaway crime and violence, and the rise of radical labor to what he called "German Know-Nothingism"—that is, to the advocation, by some Germans, of the preservation of a separate German community.[20] Taft, however, did not engage in anti-Catholic agitation. Indeed, he praised Catholics who were co-operating with Protestants in securing legislation for a "proper, moderate" Sunday.[21]

Nonetheless, clashes between Catholics and Protestants provided still another source of social strife and civil disorder. In 1885, for example, the Salvation Army invaded the Sixth Ward, a "citadel of sin," according to *Sam, the Scaramouch,* and was attacked and driven out. The magazine was indignant: "The . . . toughs and cowardly ruffians who attacked the women belonging to the Salvation Army . . . are unworthy the name of men." Although they "call themselves Irishmen, no true Irishman ever knocked down women with rocks and foully insulted the gentle sex." [22]

A few years later, however, the Catholics were on the defensive. Throughout the late eighties and early nineties the *Catholic-Telegraph,* remembering the Know-Nothing riots of 1855, nervously chronicled the rise of the American Protective Association. It published scurrilous literature disseminated by the association, including a poem which invited good citizens to

> . . . come and join the A.P.A.
> We dine on Irish every day,
> We serve a German up for tay'
> Oh come and join the A.P.A.[23]

Although no violence grew out of this virulent verbal feud there was a pushing match among policemen in Cumminsville which pitted Catholics against Masons and members of the A.P.A. This incident suggests that the appearance of the A.P.A. may have caused most trouble among the religiously mixed peoples of the Zone. But the *Catholic-Telegraph* charged that the organization was also supported by prominent businessmen.[24]

While violence and verbal battles between the residents of the Zone and suburbs kept city officials in a chronic state of jittery tension, police were losing the fight against criminality in the Circle. Part of the department's ineffectiveness stemmed from the fact that the police force, like other municipal institutions, had been established to accommodate the needs of the walking city.[25] The police commissioners repeatedly complained that they needed more patrolmen and horses to meet the demands for protection made by the Zone and suburban residents. The board pointed out that the character of the various districts was constantly changing, that the population density in old districts was rising, and that the new parts of the city were being settled, all of which justified the allocation of more funds to the departments.

Other public services also suffered from pressures created by the emergence of the new city. In 1886 the fire marshall reported that in the past ten years there had been no significant increase in the fire department and predicted that if two large fires occurred at the same time the city would likely be engulfed in "a great conflagration." Even after the reorganization of old companies and the construction of six new fire houses in recently annexed territory, he claimed that Cumminsville, Price Hill, and the western hills near Cheviot still lacked adequate protection. The upper West End, moreover, was in danger because the small water mains made the water supply weak.[26]

Indeed, quenching the city's seemingly insatiable thirst for water was one of the critical issues of the decade. In 1888 the superintendent of the water works reported that despite the addition of 16 miles of main pipe—which brought the total mileage to 264—increased per capita consumption and new Hilltop demand required more extensions and increased pumping capacity.[27] In the summer of 1890, shortly after the legislature had refused to pass a bill for the construction of a new $6,000,000 plant, disaster struck. The city's water supply ran short and the city's health was endangered, its businesses disrupted, and grass and shrubs burned because of the resulting drought. For the rest of the decade the city had to put up with patchwork extensions, repaired machinery, impure water, and the annual summer threat of a "water famine."

Providing an adequate sewerage system for the suburbs presented yet another problem. In 1886 Walnut Hills, Corryville, Cumminsville, and Price Hill were still practically sewerless, a situation which, beside constituting a health hazard, forced the city's four-man building-inspection crew to spend a disproportionately large share of its time checking the crude facilities in these communities. As a result building-code violators in the Basin had to be neglected.

The health department found itself in a similar plight. It was, by the late eighties, short of manpower and without sufficient legislative and enforcement powers to meet the new conditions. Even mild epidemics, like those of smallpox in 1883 and typhoid in 1887, or merely the threat of cholera in 1892, occupied the full time and energies of its entire staff.[28] Frustrated health officials compiled a long list of nuisances which needed immediate attention. They deplored the pollution of the Miami Canal and Mill Creek caused by the extension of factory and residential districts beyond the Basin. They denounced the unsanitary streets, alleys, and public schools in the older sections of the city and warned of dangers created by the inadequate water supply and sewerage system. And they pleaded for the construction of city abattoirs, isolated buildings for the treatment of contagious diseases, municipal baths, and the establishment of public fumigation stations.

Other city institutions also ran into difficulties. The city hospital, completed in 1867, came in for increasing criticism in the eighties and nineties. Conditions at the city workhouse were, if anything, worse. It served as a temporary home for vagrants and drunks as well as a haven for the aged and lunatic for whom the police court could find no other institution. Originally built for 250 male prisoners, it housed as many as 600 of both sexes at one time, an arrangement which led to "moral pollution" as well as abominable sanitary conditions.[29]

The house of refuge for delinquent and dependent children apparently fared somewhat better. But adult refugees from the Basin created a serious situation in the infirmary. In 1884 the superintendent reported that the "Colored House" had been condemned by four or five grand juries. His successors elaborated on other prevalent evils. One was shocked to find an indiscriminate mixture of dirty, vermin-covered children, deranged adults and epileptics sharing overcrowded, filthy, and run-down quarters. And he also complained that the morgue, located below one of the dining halls, was required to keep corpses for at least twenty-four hours, with resulting discomfort to people in the dining rooms during the summer.[30]

Population growth, urban expansion and deterioration of old facilities also strained the resources of the school system. In the mid-1880's the president of the board of education suggested that the temporary intermediate school on Price Hill was inadequate. The population demanded not only more elementary schools but also high schools. There was especially strong pressure for a high school that would serve pupils in the territory embraced by Walnut Hills, Corryville, Mt. Auburn, and the East End.[31]

Indeed, there was scarcely a single municipal institution or service established to serve the walking city that had not been outmoded by the urban explosion. Officials felt they should expand the University of Cincinnati, improve riverfront wharf facilities, construct a new city hall, and consolidate and reorganize the city's public markets. And Cincinnati's average of 770 people for every acre of park, complained one mayor, was nearly twice that of any large city in the country.[32]

Beleaguered city officials were also bombarded with demands for new projects. Some of the most ambitious plans came from the business community, which in the 1880's developed an irritable sensitivity to Cincinnati's relative decline. Members of the Chamber of Commerce attributed the city's slow growth rate to the awkward and expensive system of intracity rail transportation. As a remedy, they proposed nothing less than an entire revamping of the railway system as a means of assuring a more rational and efficient urban development. After transportation into the Ohio River bottoms had been improved, the next step was to convert the canal into a belt railway. This, claimed the committee, would revivify the sagging businesses in the upper Basin and connect them directly to the wholesale commercial district and transportation center in the Ohio and Mill Creek bottoms. In addition, they recommended another belt railway to circle behind the northern hills and link the business houses and factories in the valleys of Mill Creek, Duck Creek, and the Miami and Ohio rivers.[33]

Some of the same men who pushed for the adoption of these ambitious transportation projects, however, also besieged city officials with demands for a reduction in municipal taxes. High tax levies, they argued, frightened off new industries and led those already located within the city to consider relocation.[34]

But the tugging and hauling to which public officials were subjected in these controversies never approached the intensity of the raucous debates which centered upon the technological innovations and expansion occurring in the public utilities. The streetcar question aroused the greatest excitement. In the mid-eighties the eastern hills were split into two camps by a proposal to introduce cable service. At the same time agitation developed for rapid transit connections to the northern and western sections of the city. In 1885 the *Times-Star* complained that Price Hill, Clifton, Cumminsville, and College Hill were still isolated. By 1887 the residents of Cumminsville were clamoring for an elevated railroad, and Westwood and Cheviot were demanding rapid transit.[35] Price Hill residents became especially frustrated by the poor service provided their community by the traction company. Some there even threatened to "secede" in a desperate effort to persuade city and traction company officials to provide more adequate service.[36]

Haggling between the public, city officials, and the traction companies, of course, did not end with the decision to extend service to a neglected neighborhood. Disgruntled Zone and suburban riders on established lines demanded the fastest, most efficient, cheapest, safest, and most comfortable service possible and expected the city government to get it for them.

City officials, moreover, had to decide whether, as the Cincinnati Consolidated Traction Company claimed, monopoly was preferable to free competition. And while it was generally agreed that the companies had to submit to some regulation, it was not yet decided what kind of regulations should be imposed, how much revenue they should return to the city, and which organ of local government should be held responsible for designing the regulations.

The haziness which prevailed in traction affairs was matched, if not exceeded, by the fog which surrounded the gas and electric-light question. Here, too, officials had to decide essential issues of public policy. What agencies of local government should regulate, how much, and on what terms? Their plight was aggravated by the existence of the Cincinnati Gas, Light and Coke Company, an energetically led and well-entrenched local corporation which supplied the city with manufactured illuminating gas under a franchise granted before the Civil War.

The late 1880's were especially trying years for the company's president, General Andrew Hickenlooper, his opponents, and city officials. He first had to down the "Natural-gas craze." At the same time the General was engaged in securing a renewal of his franchise. He was willing to accept a moderate reduction in rates in order to get a ten-year monopoly. His original and eventually successful strategy to get the new agreement was first to make contracts with large consumers at reduced rates and then have a "friendly member" of Council call attention to this discrimination, after which Hickenlooper announced that the company was willing to consider a general reduction under a new franchise.[37]

The General was also obliged to do battle with the advocates of electric light and power. As early as 1886 he had been called upon to meet and defeat the application of the Edison Light Company to secure a franchise. Nonetheless, Edison soon got a limited franchise, as did nine other companies. Hickenlooper retaliated by persuading city council to restrict electrical extensions, an undertaking which cost him $3000 in legal fees, and by gaining control of as many of the smaller companies as he could. By May of 1892 he worked out an arrangement with Edison. The General was immensely relieved. Yet at the end of the decade Hickenlooper still faced potential Edison competition. And by this time both firms were threatened by the forces of municipal ownership.

Surprisingly, the installation and expansion of the telephone and telegraph systems caused local government little grief. The Cincinnati & Suburban Telephone and Telegraph Company early established its hegemony in these fields. It was not wholly free from criticism, however. It was caught up, for example, in the debate on whether or not to require all electrical wires to be put underground. Yet the issue remained unresolved and by 1893 some sixteen thousand poles and over five thousand miles of wires graced the city's streets while only twenty-five miles of conduit had been laid. The *Post,* in exasperation, called for a "strong competent hand . . . to untangle the wires and make them safe."[38]

But, given the political situation, this seemed unlikely. At the outset of the decade many observers were convinced that partisanship, the use of money in local conventions, and the arrival of a new breed of politicians had produced a chaotic political system based upon unorganized bipartisan corruption which was incapable of orderly and efficient government. And in 1886, the Committee of One Hundred, a Hilltop organization,[39] made revelations which spread that conviction.

The committee began by investigating the fall 1885 elections and succeeded in convicting nine persons for fraud, one of whom had burned one hundred ballots. It also exposed a "voluntary organization" of Council members called the "Queen City Fishing Club" and discovered evidence of malfeasance in the board of equalization, board of public works, board of directors of the city infirmary, board of aldermen, board of education, and board of police commissioners. The committee concluded that all this was due to the fact that "greedy men" and "bosses" had captured the machinery of politics, most notably the primaries and conventions.[40]

The "slight boom [in] honesty and decency," as one observer described the committee's work, inspired a host of proposals for correcting the political system.[41] But Charles P. Taft was skeptical because of the influence of money and the "bummer," two new developments in local politics.

Taft claimed that money had first become a prime factor in local conventions in the early eighties. Its major impact had been to promote extreme factionalism, thus forcing politicians to make alliances across party lines. The most successful such bipartisan coalition had been that between John R. McClean and T. C. Campbell, a combination broken up by the courthouse riot and the revelations of the Committee of One Hundred. This created a vacuum in political leadership which had given the real power at conventions to the "bummer," the chief product of money applied to politics.

The bummer, Taft explained, was a "queer creature" of indefinite origin who came from the slums and may have started as a bootblack, a newsboy, or even a loafer. All he really needed was "a good standing with the saloon that has a fine lunch layout during the day. There he is solid and beguiles the unlucky candidate for office . . . introduces him to the proprietor, and then encourages a long drinking bout."

A "hustler at the polls and conventions," the bummer was in such demand that he could take money from two competing candidates, thus lengthening the convention and contributing to interfactional dealing. "The day of pure politics can never be in Cincinnati," Taft gloomily concluded, "until a riot, plague or flood kills off all the ward bummers." [42]

The required catastrophe did not occur. Factionalism continued, reformers pleaded for higher turnouts at primaries or the separation of national and municipal politics, and the city wallowed in disorder. The *Times-Star* commented wearily that the disclosure of official wrongdoing was an occurrence so common that there was almost no reaction when a new culprit was exposed.[43]

Clearly the residents of the Zone and suburbs felt the new city presented a challenge to order. Its old municipal institutions were overburdened, and the expansion of its boundaries and rising pre-eminence of industry, coupled with its relative decline, raised demands for new services. Simultaneously the fragile bonds of community were strained to the breaking point by the persistence of criminality, the militancy of organized labor, and the clash of cultures. The new circumstances, moreover, had created an undisciplined political system which served only to deepen the crisis. But it also encouraged men to grope uncertainly for a more effective means of meeting the challenge.[44]

5

George B. Cox and the Quest for Order

In 1885, on the eve of the repudiation of a Democratic administration, William Howard Taft predicted that "the clouds are beginning to break over this Sodom of ours. . . . It's the beginning of an era of reform." [1] He was, in a sense, correct. Yet for almost a decade no party could put together a decisive ruling majority. By 1894, however, a political order had emerged which, while imperfect by the standards of its critics, possessed flexibility and left the way open for further experimentation.

Taft's confident prediction was based in large part on what had happened at the 1885 Republican city convention. The platform committed the party to restore law and order to the city, rid its administration of corruption and extravagance, reduce taxes, and eliminate inefficiency. To carry out this program the convention selected Amor Smith, Jr., a candle and fertilizer manufacturer, as its candidate for mayor.

Smith won, and carried fourteen of the city's twenty-five wards, all but two of which lay beyond the Circle in the Zone and Hilltops. The Democratic candidate carried the entire Circle, except the Seventeenth and Eighteenth, and captured only one ward beyond, that on Price Hill. [2] If the citizens who voted the straight ticket "right or

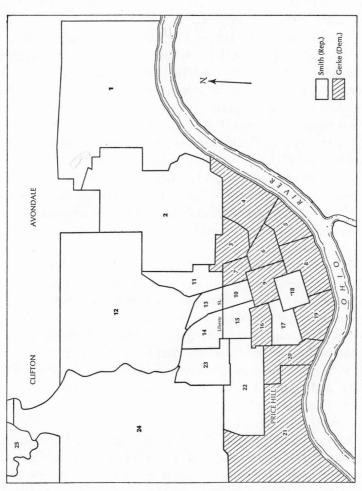

5. Election of 1885

wrong" were disregarded, asserted the *Times-Star*, "there never was an election here in which the friends of law, order and morality, were so unanimously on the one side, and the vicious and criminal element on the other."[3] The Republicans had united the Hilltops and Zone against the center of the city.

In the spring of 1887, however, at the next municipal election, a break in the solidarity of the periphery almost turned the Republicans out of City Hall. The serious challenge to the Republicans, moreover, came not from the Democrats, but from the recently established Union Labor party (ULP). The new party attracted the active support of a weird mixture. Knights of Laborites, trades unionists, socialists, Henry George men, temperance advocates, and Sabbatarians all rallied behind it. Its leaders were largely Zone residents, about half German and half Irish and Anglo-Saxon in origin. Reports also circulated that Democratic politicians in the lower wards were providing funds and workers for the new party.[4] Apparently the ULP leaders hoped to unite the diverse elements of the Zone and Circle.

The new party almost put together a successful coalition. Smith barely squeaked through with a plurality of some six hundred votes and carried only eleven of the city's twenty-five wards. W. H. Stevenson, the ULP candidate, ran second and took twelve wards. He won all the Democratic Circle wards except the Fifth and Eighth on the central eastern waterfront. And he cut deeply into Republican strength in the Zone. Stevenson took seven wards there which Smith had carried in 1885, losing only one German ward, the Tenth. Everything beyond this went to Smith, as did the fashionable wards in the West End.[5]

Despite the tightness of this election, harmony did not prevail within the GOP. Murat Halstead, a member of the "Smith crowd," was muttering about fellow Republicans who had "subterranean connections with the abodes of yellow doggery."[6] To Halstead, these abodes were located for the most part in the Eighteenth Ward.

The only Republican stronghold in the Circle, it was, in many respects, one of the most remarkable wards in the city. In the 1880's its eastern portion contained a few fashionable residences, most of which had been converted to tenements. Its population, although predominently white and native-born, included a growing number of Negroes. Houses of prostitution, saloons, gambling joints, and factories made the southern and western parts of the Eighteenth undesirable residential areas, and it had been the scene of violence during the tumultuous election of 1884.

Yet some of the city's most prominent citizens and successful politicians, including Amor Smith and William Howard Taft, had associations with the Eighteenth. And in the 1880's its chief professional politician was George Barnesdale Cox, a central figure in the intraparty strife of the late eighties.

Cox had grown up with the new city and received a liberal education in its ways. He was born in 1853, the son of British immigrants. His father died when he was eight, and young Cox worked successively as a bootblack, newsboy, lookout for a gambling joint, grocery deliveryman, bartender, and tobacco salesman. His school principal claimed that he caused no trouble in classes, exhibited an "undisguised love for his mother," and "never lied . . . bore malice, sulked, whined or moped." And somewhere along the way Cox was exposed to religion. Although not a churchgoer, as an adult he had, according to Gustave Karger, "dormant powerful sentiments, which rest on foundations of the firmest faith."

After acquiring his own saloon at the corner of Longworth and John—"Dead Man's Corner"—Cox's political influence grew steadily. Using the saloon as headquarters, he was elected to city council in 1879 and served two terms. At city conventions he was one of the few ward bosses who regularly delivered his delegation as promised, and by the early eighties he and Amor Smith were the party's recognized powers in the West End. In 1884, over the objections of some who were of the "better element" in the party, Cox was chosen to manage James G. Blaine's campaign in Hamilton County for the Presidency. William Howard Taft, as supervisor of the election, toured the polls with Cox in search of fraud. Blaine carried the county.

To help put Blaine over, Cox, Miller Outcault, a suburban lawyer, and William Copeland, a West End Negro leader, had organized the Young Men's Blaine Club. It quickly developed into a kind of political settlement house where Circle, Zone, and Hilltop Republicans met to eat, drink, play cards, and plan parades and campaigns. This and other similar groups were regarded as innovations, and their proliferation led the *Times-Star* to speculate that the day of the bummer was passing. Politicians, prospective candidates, and interested citizens could now meet at the club rather than at the saloon.[7]

In 1885, despite his previous achievements, Cox's position as a factional leader was challenged. That year the Eighteenth Ward sent two delegations to the city convention. Cox's group literally had to fight its way into the hall. The Credentials Committee listened to the Cox spokesmen plead that they were the victims of a conspiracy between Democrats and rebellious Republicans. Subsequently the committee chairman, William Howard Taft, ruled in favor of the Cox men. They then helped secure the nomination of Amor Smith.[8]

Cox received another and apparently unsolicited boost up the political ladder from Joseph Benson Foraker, who in 1883 had been the unsuccessful GOP candidate for governor. Supported by the Smith people in Cincinnati, Foraker was renominated in 1885 and won the gubernatorial race, although he failed to carry Hamilton County. In the fall of 1887 he ran for re-election with Cox as his campaign chairman in Hamilton County. On election night Cox telegraphed the governor that he left Cincinnati with a 5000 vote plurality. Foraker was re-elected, Hamilton County went Republican, and Cox was appointed state oil inspector, despite opposition from Marcus A. Hanna, the Cleveland businessman-politician.[9]

Foraker's alliance with Cox, however, nettled some respectable Republicans. And in the fall of 1888 Halstead protested to Foraker that Cox, now a candidate for county clerk, was being "crammed and rammed, and jammed upon the community" as a boss. The governor defended Cox, arguing that he was honest and that his leadership had not and would not, as Halstead charged, ruin the party.[10] Cox was, nevertheless, defeated, although the rest of the

ticket went through. According to the *Times-Star*, the returns were
"remarkable. . . . They show that every where . . . [Cox] was
scratched, though of course the heaviest lead pencil work was done
in the suburban wards, while in several of the lower wards Cox
really received a large Democratic vote." [11]

The circumstances surrounding his loss, plus Halstead's continued complaints to Foraker, led Cox to defend his conduct. In a
letter to the governor, Cox explained that he had been co-operating
on patronage matters with the Elm Street Club faction, led by
George Moerlein, a brewer. Cox also protested allegations that he
accepted money for endorsements or for the exercise of his influence in securing appointments. And Cox disputed the claim that he
represented disreputable elements in the party. He said he supported capable and honest officials known to be of the highest character.[12]

In the spring of 1889 this internal feud erupted into an open
fight. One of those who had refused to support Cox in the fall of
1888 was City Comptroller E. O. Eshelby, a businessman and a former president of the exclusively Hilltop Lincoln Club. As the city
convention approached, Cox declared that he would oppose the
renomination of Eshelby and, if that failed, vote against him in the
general election.[13]

Eshelby fought back. He got hold of the records of a club known
as the Loyal Republican League. Its membership, limited to 150,
was drawn from minor municipal, county, and state office-holders.
Representing every ward in the city, the members were oath-bound
to protect their political interests by working together in securing
nominations and elections and in the distribution of patronage.
Eshelby first showed these records to Hickenlooper, who in turn
revealed them to Halstead, and then to Charles P. Taft.[14]

On March 9 Taft published an editorial entitled "The Conspiracy" in which he described the organization in great detail and
charged that it was out to defeat Eshelby. This, said Taft, meant
that Cox, although not listed among the members, was actually the
power behind the league.[15] Cox, however, claimed that he had
never belonged, although he had been invited "over fifty times" **to**

become a member. The organization had originally been formed, he explained, to defeat Amor Smith for mayor, and Cox fought the order in his interest. The club, Cox said, then "reorganized against me for taking the stand I did . . . and for a long time no man recognized as my friend was admitted." [16]

As the city convention of 1889 approached, the *Post* reported that the Stranglers were determined to purge Eshelby for his party irregularity and replace his candidate for mayor with John Mosby. The *Times-Star*, ignoring Cox's disclaimer, insisted that a Cox-Strangler alliance existed. Now, asked the *Times-Star*, "will the Grand Old Party lie down before this band of conspirators?" [17]

It did. The convention rejected Eshelby, nominated four Stranglers to major city offices, and selected Mosby as its candidate for mayor. But Mosby, a wholesale grocery merchant, a resident of East Walnut Hills, an "ardent joiner," and a member of the Blaine Club, received such strong support from George Moerlein and his Elm Street Club that some observers regarded him as the candidate of Moerlein and the brewers. Even the *Times-Star* never decided just who dominated the convention, and it alternately denounced the Stranglers, the brewers, Moerlein, and Cox as the guiding influence.[18]

None of these factions, however, bossed the convention. Rather the ticket represented an alliance of these Zone forces and a compromise between them and the moderate suburban reformers. For the platform, while avoiding the law enforcement or Sunday closing issue, appealed to the reformers by promising a clean, economical, and business administration of all departments of the city government.[19] Mosby, moreover, had not previously been active in politics and was not suspected of having consciously entered into any arrangements with the professional politicians. Those credentials, apparently, were good enough for the *Commercial-Gazette, Volksblatt,* and *Freie Presse.* Pre-convention critics of Cox and the Stranglers, all three papers endorsed Mosby and the rest of the ticket.[20]

But the *Times-Star* refused to go along. On its call a mass meeting, organized by the Committee of Five Hundred, endorsed candidates from both the other parties—all but one of them Democrats or Prohibitionists—and nominated Daniel Stone, a coal merchant and head of the Committee of Five Hundred, for mayor on a Citizen's ticket.[21]

Stone's candidacy weakened, but did not destroy, the Republican reform coalition. Mosby won the mayoralty race with 21,998 total votes and a plurality of just 544 over the Democratic candidate. Stone received 7295 votes, but failed to carry a single ward. Generally, he ran strongest in the Hilltop wards, excepting those to the west. Otherwise the voting pattern was virtually identical to that of 1885.[22] The GOP's Zone-Hilltop coalition remained intact.

The Stranglers disappeared as an organized faction, but reform-minded Republicans still had to put up with Cox and Moerlein. In the fall of 1890, however, the two leaders began to drift apart. Moerlein had become disenchanted with Mosby because of his enforcement of the Sunday closing law. Cox, nevertheless, insisted on his renomination. Moerlein went along with this only after Cox agreed to support Valentine Heim, an employee at Moerlein's brewery, for sheriff on the fall 1890 slate. The reformers were placated by the promise to retain Mosby in 1891 and by the selection of Bellamy Storer, a member of the Lincoln Club, to run for Congress.[23]

The unexpected victory of Storer in the gerrymandered First Congressional District in 1890 plus Republican majorities of 9000 helped the Blaine Club members tighten their hold on the party. They now demanded that the "young blood" or the workers receive recognition from President Harrison, who had been favoring the silk-stocking faction. They requested that the President appoint John Zumstein, a native of Bavaria, a real estate man, and a member of the Blaine Club, as postmaster in Cincinnati. And Amor Smith, Foraker, the *Commercial-Gazette*, and Senator Sherman all recommended Zumstein. The *Times-Star* stood alone in opposition, and Zumstein got the job.[24]

The stage was now set for the eclipse of Moerlein and the emergence of George B. Cox as the leader of the Zone and Circle wing of the GOP. Cox held a strong hand as the spring 1891 city convention approached. As a result of the Zumstein appointment, it appeared that Cox had the inside track not only with Foraker, who planned to contest Senator John Sherman's renomination in the fall, but also with the local Sherman wing of the party.

George Moerlein, on the other hand, lacked powerful outside allies. He had, moreover, been harassing General Hickenlooper's gas company, for the Elm Street Club leader and brewer was involved in the Queen City Natural Gas Company, which, in 1890, narrowly missed securing a franchise to enter the city. During this raid City Solicitor Horstmann launched a vitriolic attack on Hickenlooper's gas company and suggested that a municipally owned plant might be the solution to these problems.[25] And the Queen City Gas scheme and Horstmann's attacks also coincided with the drive of the Edison Electric Light Company, for which former Governor Foraker was general counsel, to get a street lighting contract with the city. While there is no direct evidence that Moerlein, Foraker, and Horstmann planned and co-ordinated their assaults on Hickenlooper, it was these circumstances which led the General to seek a strong political alliance just as the intraparty maneuvering for the spring 1891 GOP convention began.

Instead of seeking relief by allying with Moerlein, however, he turned to Cox. The pact was sealed when the General agreed to support Frederick Hertenstein, Cox's choice for city solicitor, even though Hertenstein was the "last man," with the exception of Horstmann, that Hickenlooper would have chosen for the job.[26]

Cox had good reason to make a deal with Hickenlooper. After the fall 1890 county elections, Cox and Sheriff-elect Heim quarreled over the distribution of patronage. Heim appealed to Moerlein, who told the sheriff to "tell Cox to go to —— and make your own appointments." Heim did, claimed the *Post,* and Cox made no effort to conceal his resentment.[27]

The rupture was completed at the 1891 city convention. Moerlein's delegates were all pledged to Horstmann. Moerlein, moreover, directly challenged Cox's position by backing Amos Dye for the police court judgeship against the Blaine Club candidate, Ellis Gregg. This contest was regarded as a test of strength between the two factions and the Blaine Club battle cry became "If Dye lives, Cox dies." [28]

As the convention opened, Cox learned that he lacked the votes to get Gregg nominated on the first ballot. As a result "Cox threw out gas money right and left for Gregg forgetting in the excitement all about Hertenstein." Gregg and Horstman were nominated. Cox, reportedly, was not distressed about Horstmann's nomination because he thought the city solicitor would be a source of strength on the ticket. "In street language," the *Post* explained, "Gen. Hickenlooper got the 'double cross' all around." [29]

Despite this suggestion of scandal, spokesmen for the reform Republicans praised the convention and its work. The Lincoln Club agreed. And the *Volksblatt* called on its readers to vote for "Mosby Horstmann and Reform." [30]

The Democrats nominated Gustav Tafel, a German-born liberal who was expected to attract those who had grown suspicious of Mosby's temperance principles. He carried, moreover, the endorsement of the Municipal Congress, a Zone group composed of labor organizations, and the *Bund für Freiheit und Recht*, which advocated home rule, municipal ownership of public utilities, "personal liberty," and support for a party in which "citizens instead of the dollar should rule." [31]

Hilltop law and order enthusiasts were inflamed by Tafel's candidacy. The *Times-Star* charged that he represented "the socialistic faction of Germans who imagine that liberty means license to do anything they choose." And a spokesman for the Committee of Five Hundred claimed that Tafel, because of his membership in the Turners, supported principles on the separation of Church and State that could only lead to anarchy. But the Democratic and Catholic *Volksfreund* argued that, as a former member of the GOP and a Cleveland man, Tafel would be supported by all Democrats and "thousands of liberal Republicans." The paper was convinced that Republican rule in Cincinnati was about to end.[32]

It very nearly did. Mosby carried sixteen wards and was reelected with 25,582 votes to Tafel's 24,444, a plurality of only 138, some 400 less than his 1889 margin. The returns followed the familiar periphery-center division. With the exception of the heavily German Seventh and Thirteenth, Mosby held all the wards he carried in 1889, including the German Tenth and Eleventh. Horstmann, running stronger than the mayor in both the Zone and Hilltops, led the Republican ticket with a majority of 10,000, a vote which Hickenlooper regarded as a slap at the gas company.[33]

Hickenlooper, despite his treatment at the hands of Cox during the convention, also concluded, apparently, that the "Big Fellow" had something to offer. Just a month after the election the General confided to his diary that he had "concluded [an] arrangement with Geo. B. Cox for services at $3500 per year quarterly to last for 3 years."[34]

Cox now headed a formidable coalition. Both of the city's respectable English-language dailies, the *Times-Star* and *Commercial-Gazette,* had now reconciled themselves to his management of the party, as had the two German Republican newspapers. He could also depend on several wealthy and influential allies from the upper strata of Cincinnati society. These Hilltop backers, besides Hickenlooper, included Nicholas Longworth, a representative of one of Cincinnati's old families, and Bernhard Bettmann, a venerated figure in the German Jewish community.[35]

But perhaps the most important of Cox's Hilltop connections was Dr. Thomas W. Graydon, the liason man between Cox and Foraker. Graydon had emigrated from Ireland in 1866, and was educated in Iowa. He came to Cincinnati in 1876, enjoyed a lucrative practice, and promoted patent medicines on the side. An Episcopalian, a Scottish Rite Mason, and a member of the Elks, the Blaine Club, and the Elm Street Club, Graydon possessed ties in both Hilltop and Zone circles.[36]

After the overthrow of Moerlein, moreover, a host of ward and factional leaders who were rising from Zone to Hilltop status flocked to Cox. Like virtually all the top men in the organization they were newcomers to Cincinnati, largely German in background, and came out of the generation which grew up with the new city. Among them were Simon Krug, a photographer and county "subboss"; his son, Frank, a civil engineer, a member of the construction company of Police Commissioner Frank Kirchener, president of a cremation firm, and a bank director; Frederich Bader, elected in 1893 to the first of twenty consecutive terms as president of the Hamilton County League of Building Associations; and Herman F. Cellarius, an architect who was also active in building association circles.[37] These men all became close friends of Cox and members of a social-political office-holding group known variously as "the gang," "the sports," and the "bonifaces."

The core of this clique was made up of Zone politicians who joined Cox in the wake of Moerlein's downfall. These were the civil servants responsible for holding the politically volatile Zone for the GOP. It was a full-time job, and they mapped out plans nightly in the Over-the-Rhine district on upper Vine Street in "courts" held either at Schubert and Pels's saloon—where each of them had a special beer mug with his name gilded on it—or at their round table in Wielert's beer garden.[38]

August Herrmann was probably the most valuable of these recruits. He was born in 1859 in the Over-the-Rhine district and never broke his ties with that section of the city. Orphaned at eleven, young Herrmann worked as a delivery boy in a type foundry, learned the printing trade, and earned a card in the typographers' union. In the eighties he was elected to the board of education and then appointed to a clerkship on the police court. In 1891 he deserted Moerlein for Cox and was appointed by Mayor Mosby to the board of administration and reappointed two years later. At City Hall Herrmann became known as an uncanny shark for figures, in part because he carried the city's financial statistics in his head. Reporters, moreover, looked on him as a good public relations man, for during board meetings he made notes of what he felt the papers would like to know. And he thoughtfully epitomized complicated reports and explained them clearly for the benefit of the press.

Herrmann was also the most flamboyantly convivial of the Cox coterie. According to legend he often drank beer from four until midnight in the Over-the-Rhine saloons and then frequently joined a more exclusive set of drinkers at the Havlin Hotel. Yet he unfailingly appeared at his office at nine the next morning. Something of a dude, he wore a flower in his lapel and was reportedly fond of perfume. Herrmann also maintained an active interest in sports. He liked to bowl and eventually became head of the American Bowling Congress. He also joined Cox and Max and Julius Fleischmann to purchase the Cincinnati baseball club from its Indianapolis owner and became influential in professional baseball's official circles. An ardent joiner, Herrmann belonged to a long list of organizations.[39]

Second only to Herrmann was Rudolph K. "Rud" Hynicka, yet another defector from the Moerlein faction. Younger than Cox and Herrmann, he was described by one reformer as "a cleaner faced and clearer eyed" man who did not bear "the look of a professional politician who has been getting things by devious ways." He moved to the city in the 1880's, took a job as a reporter for the *Enquirer,* and held appointive posts in the county auditor's and treasurer's offices as a representative of the Moerlein interest. In the nineties he was elected police clerk and became captain of the Ninth Ward.[40]

Besides Herrmann and Hynicka there were a host of other Zone politicians who joined Cox as "higher lieutenants." This group, as the *Post* put it, were men "who sit under the drippings of the sanctuary" because they possessed "special ability, conviviality, friendship [or] positions useful to the gang." [41] They included, from the Negro community, William "Big Bill" Copeland, a chief in the West End, and Ford Stith, a real estate man known as the "Tuscaloosa Bull" and the "King of Walnut Hills." [42] William H. Leuders, a lawyer and a leading figure in German charitable associations, provided close ties to the successful Germans of the Zone. August H. Bode filled a similar function and gave the organization an intellectual light as well. Born in Germany, Bode was educated at the Polytechnical Academy in Hanover and the University of Berlin, emigrated to the United States in 1866, and came to Cincinnati the following year to take up a teaching post. He became the principal of an elementary school, and by 1883 had earned a law degree and started to practise. He also wrote a history of elementary reading, a book on elementary mathematics, and a series of seven readers, all of which were adopted by the city schools.[43]

Equally important to the Cox coalition were the ward leaders who frequented and ran the Over-the-Rhine and down-town saloons and gambling joints. Among then were Lewis Kraft, Cox's political heir in the Eighteenth Ward and the operator of a poker and crap game; Dan Bauer, proprietor of one of the fanciest saloons and dance halls in the Basin and the son of Morris Bauer, the city street sprinkler and a former barber; Joseph Schweniger, a saloonkeeper and city council member from the Fifteenth Ward; and James Keenan of the Twenty-third, a former catcher for the old Red Stockings.[44]

The occupations and attitudes of this Zone coterie are conveniently summarized in the 1901 *Police and Municipal Guide*. According to the guide, they were good fellows—friendly, well-known bonifaces who liked a good joke or story and belonged to several social and fraternal organizations. They were invariably charitable, especially kind to the sick and poor, and boosted the city enthusiastically.[45]

Cox is portrayed in the guide as an adherent to this code of the Zone who had risen to the top. He is depicted as a bon vivant who enjoyed good stories as well as good cigars; a man of wealth and refinement whose recently constructed Clifton mansion was adorned with tastefully selected works of art and decorated with impeccable taste; a philanthropist of impressive but quiet charities. Moreover, it was Cox and his colleagues, claimed the guide, who were responsible for the "many meritorious points of the peerless police department and the present administration of municipal affairs" through the application of what the anonymous author, without definition, called business methods.

Indeed, Cox and his top civil servants—surrounded by a motley crowd of former boxers and baseball players, newspaper reporters, vaudeville and burlesque performers, and other Vine Street characters—provided an attractive model for men awed by the glamor, wealth, and power so visible yet so elusive in the new city. Zone spokesmen seldom attacked this inside group directly.

In the spring of 1894, this singular coalition of Zone and suburban Republicans demonstrated its cohesiveness and loyalty to Cox. The seventy-five minute "convention of new faces," as the *Post* described it, met in Central Turner Hall. Cox, looking like a businessman in a grey suit, wearing a black tie with a small diamond in his shirt bosom, set the tone for the proceedings by refusing either to smoke or to drink. Cox's patron, General Andrew Hickenlooper, admiringly noted that the "candidates [were] all nominated just as Cox said 3 weeks ago. It's wonderful the ability of one man to handle such a mass." [46]

But the gas company president was not at all optimistic about the prospects for a Republican victory. Theodore Horstmann, running for mayor on a Citizens' ticket, seemed overwhelmingly popular among the workingmen. The socialist *Cincinnatier Zeitung* endorsed his candidacy, as did the Central Labor Council, now an affiliate of the American Federation of Labor, and one faction of the Populist party.[47] Yet a workers' uprising was not the source of either Horstmann's candidacy or the Citizens' party.

During the early months of 1894, Horstmann, backed by rebellious factions in the Elm Street and Lincoln clubs, had angled for the regular Republican nomination. They threatened to start an independent movement if Horstmann did not get the nomination. When it became obvious that Cox preferred Congressman John A. Caldwell, however, Horstmann pulled out of the GOP contest.[48] Then, on February 25, before either of the major parties had held their convention, a six-man bipartisan Citizens' committee of Hilltop Democrats and Republicans announced that it had chosen a ticket headed by Horstmann. The slate was composed, the committee said, "of gentlemen whose character for honesty, integrity, and independence is a guarantee of their giving a clean administration of municipal affairs" and who could be depended upon to consider "the welfare and prosperity of the city as a cardinal motive" while reducing expenses to the lowest level consistent with efficient and capable government.[49] They had determined to make the issue the people against the machine.

Before starting the venture, moreover, they asked for and received assurances from John R. McLean in Washington and Lewis Bernard, his local representative, that the Democratic party could be expected to endorse the entire Citizens' ticket, thus giving it vital Circle and Zone strength.[50]

McLean and Bernard had promised more than they could deliver. The Cincinnati Democrats were now split into four factions over local and national politics. Three of these united and put up a reform candidate, Isaac J. Miller. He had the support of Hilltop Cleveland men, the *Volksfreund*, and the Circle regulars. But Miller had been nominated at a convention which, according to Hickenlooper's information and to the *Tribune*, had been arranged by George B. Cox. The paper also claimed that Cox later had concluded that Miller could not pull enough votes to assure the defeat of Horstmann. Consequently, it charged, the Circle Democrats had agreed to work secretly for Caldwell. As a reward for their cooperation, the "Cox Democrats" were to be let in on the fifteen hundred jobs available to the two Democratic members of the board of administration.[51]

In the campaign the Republicans virtually ignored the straight Democratic ticket. But they reacted to the Citizens' slate as if civilization were at stake. Horstmann was accused of being a socialist for his alleged advocacy of publicly owned municipal utilities. A rumor circulated that he belonged to the A.P.A. and had, as a member of the board of education, voted to fire a teacher just because he was a Catholic.[52] And the *Commercial-Gazette* labored hard to tie Horstmann to McLean and Bernard and "the order of things . . . ten years ago." Claiming that McLean had inspired the Citizens' movement, the paper gave the charred shirt of the courthouse riot a thorough airing. "Fresh in the minds of all," it asserted, "are the stormy scenes of political demoralization in Cincinnati," the "reflections of the fires that consumed the Court-house" and "the rattle of the Gatling guns and rifles of the state militia that strewed the streets with dead and wounded citizens of the Queen city." [53]

Republican spokesmen also ridiculed the Citizens' pretensions to political respectability. One described it as a "Dolly Varden movement" composed of a strange combination of Avondale Democrats, Republican mugwumps, office-seekers, Lincoln Club traitors, dudes, "Society Leaders . . . too good to mingle with common mortals," a "Relative or dependent" or two, "and the hired help at the club." [54]

Despite the incongruous coalition put together by the Citizens—Bernard's men in the lower wards, socialists, trade unionists and old Moerlein followers in the Zone, the *Post*, the *Tribune*, and Hilltop independents[55]—Horstmann did not pull through. Caldwell won by 6755 votes, the largest plurality secured by any of the Republican mayors elected in the decade of disorder. It was, in fact, the first decisive city election in ten years.

Horstmann ran second with 19,912 votes. He carried but four wards, the German Seventh and Thirteenth and Price Hill in the Zone, and the Twenty-seventh on fashionable Mt. Auburn. He ran second in all the other Zone and suburban wards, and third everywhere in the Circle. Miller, the Democratic candidate, received 11,657 votes and took only three wards, the German Third, and the Eighth and Twenty-first, all of them in the Circle.

Caldwell held all the wards carried by Mosby in 1891 except the Twenty-seventh. More significantly, he added eight new ones to the Republican column. One of them, Thirty, lay in the Zone on the side of Western Hills north of Price Hill. The other seven were former Democratic wards located in the Circle. This was the first appearance of a political alliance between the suburbs and the Circle. The Cox organization had, temporarily at least, bridged the chasm between the center and the periphery of the city.[56]

The emergence of Cox in the late eighties and early nineties marked the arrival of a new order in Cincinnati politics. By the end of the decade of disorder he had the nucleus of an organization which, ten years later, was described as "more compact and closely

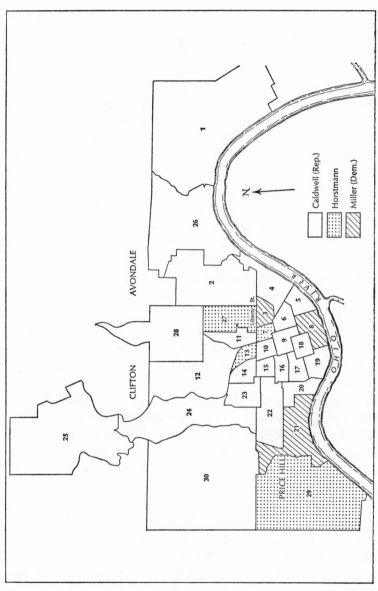

6. Election of 1894

knit than any of the political machines which have dominated New York, Philadelphia, Chicago, St. Louis or San Francisco," and which made him a ruler "more autocratic than Tweed or Croker ever dreamed of being." [57]

Indeed, some local observers were already convinced he had such a machine. To them, Cox seemed an evil genius, a master at the manipulation of men who possessed an almost magical power to inspire trust and secure obedience from his followers. And he utilized these powers, they believed, in a ruthless and carefully planned drive for power and wealth. [58]

Cox saw it differently. In an 1892 interview he attributed his success to careful adherence to two rules. "I never violated a pledge in my life," he claimed, and "I never supported a man . . . without being asked to do so." For this loyal backing Cox demanded only that "the men who made possible the nomination should be first considered when favors were passed around," a position which he made clear to Heim and Moerlein in their fight over the sheriff's patronage. Otherwise, Cox asked for nothing except strict party loyalty. He admitted that he had "probably made enemies, but unless I had done so I could not have made any friends."

Furthermore, Cox told the reporter, "I never aspired to be a boss, and never considered myself one." [59] Cox believed, apparently, that his simple code, combined with coincidence, explained his rise. This was not necessarily a naïve assessment, for the circumstances of his life and position were a major factor. He was born in a part of town where he could make a wide variety of acquaintances. As a bartender and a lookout for gambling houses he met many of the city's most prominent men. Politics in the heterogeneous Eighteenth Ward in the seventies and eighties cut across class and racial lines.

Once in the profession, Cox, like others, entered into a series of alliances. He first joined with the West End factional leaders, then the Smith, Foraker, and Moerlein groups and the Hilltop reformers, and finally, in 1894, the Circle Democrats. Instead, however, of trading one ally for another, or selling out, Cox pyramided them with the cement of personal favors and party loyalty. He had not created an organization, rather he pasted it together from pre-existing elements. As leader then, he managed a diverse coalition, serving each of its interests.

He saw himself, moreover, as an honest broker. With respect to his employment by Hickenlooper, Cox seemingly felt that he was, like Foraker, a political lawyer, lacking only a law degree. Cox consistently maintained that he never received an illegal payment. He attributed his affluence, like his political power, to coincidence and his adherence to a few simple and honorable articles of faith—hard work, frugality, and wise investment in real estate, business, and stocks and bonds. He saw nothing wrong with his quest for wealth. "You don't blame a man," he once asked a reporter, "for looking out for No. 1, do you?" Or, as his wife put it to a hostile critic, he "made his way up in the world. It was a hard fight. Other men are given credit for making their own way." [60]

Yet Cox's leadership produced more than a personal fortune for himself and a disciplined and successful Republican party. Looking back over the nineties he once boasted that he had taken the schools and the fire and police departments out of politics. But, he added, "my chief work as boss [was] in preventing graft and seeing that the city [had] the right men to serve." [61] He had also, by removing both cash payments and the bummer from conventions, made them brief and decorous affairs. All these accomplishments made his leadership more palatable to Halstead and the other Hilltop reformers who demanded order as well as efficient and business-like government.

Cox's readiness to go along with the Hilltop reformers proved one of his most valuable assets. He accepted the Australian ballot and voter registration laws and co-operated in securing a series of state laws designed to provide the city with a stable and centralized government. These statutes replaced the bicameral legislative body with a single board of legislation. The mayor's term was extended to three years and the office endowed with additional appointive powers. City departments were placed under bipartisan boards, the most important of which, from Cox's point of view, was the board of administration. Set up in 1891, its jurisdiction expanded until it enjoyed concurrent power with the board of legislation in granting franchises and contracts and possessed the sole authority to extend franchises. Gradually, more and more departments were placed under its control. By 1896 it ruled over every administrative field which commanded extensive patronage.

It was this emerging order in municipal politics and government which reconciled Charles P. Taft to the rise of Cox. The editor-reformer had apparently concluded that "a boss," as Cox put it, was "not necessarily a public enemy." [62]

6

Boss Cox and the "New Order" in Action

On the eve of the election of 1891 the *Times-Star* called on its readers to support the "new order" in Cincinnati by voting for Mayor John Mosby. The paper contended that the Democratic candidate, Gustav Tafel, was not "politically representative of the citizens who would make the city government something better than a weak apology for a municipal system and vastly better than [a] nerveless, bloodless, chaotic no-system." [1]

The key to the new order was the so-called new charter. Endorsed by the Commercial Club, the Chamber of Commerce, and a bipartisan committee composed of the city's most successful and prominent lawyers, its major feature was a board of administration of four members, appointed by the mayor, no more than two of whom were to be from the same political party. This bipartisan device, it was hoped, would abolish inefficiency in administration and purify politics by eliminating the necessity for wholesale hirings and firings in the aftermath of a turnover in elective offices. And it was expected to reduce the temptation of entrepreneurs and city legislators to raid the local utility companies. It was to open the way, in short, for the establishment of effective and positive city government.[2]

The Municipal Congress, an alliance of Zone organizations, saw this last objective clearly, but not favorably. Its Committee on Municipal Government charged that the real intent of the charter was to muzzle the press, "unite partisan boodling bosses" in a division of patronage and profit, and permit corporations and favored individuals to obtain franchises, privileges, and rights without fear of public criticism. The committee concluded its criticism by blasting the members of the Commercial Club as responsible for the anarchical condition of the city government.[3]

This denunciation calls attention to one of the persistent difficulties encountered by the Republican regime from 1885 to 1897 in its efforts to bring positive government to the city. Although the new functions and activities taken up by the city government, like the charter of 1891, were conceived to suit the party's Zone and Hilltop constituency, they had to be designed and carried out in such a way that they could not be used to inflame the politically volatile GOP supporters, particularly those in' the Zone.

This policy was most successfully applied in the reorganization of the police force after the riot and election violence of 1884 and 1885. To eliminate the political factor from police administration, the new force was administered by a nonpartisan board of police commissioners appointed by the governor. The mayor appointed the members of the force after they had passed a preliminary examination given under the direction of the board, but the board possessed sole authority to demote or remove a member from the force. The commissioners tried to provide the city with a professional police force. They wanted each patrolman to be "drilled into perfect subordination," and to understand that he had undertaken "real business,—that he is not merely a clubber, a thing in blue . . . decorated with a badge." [4]

To help develop this attitude the commissioners set up the city's first extensive training program for police. Newly recruited patrolmen had to serve six months as substitutes and attend school twice weekly to study the police manual, reading, writing, spelling, and "city locations." Regular patrolmen were required to work out in the gym twice a week, take a physical exam twice a year, and attend a "school of instruction" with the rookies once a month. The new and highly skilled police officers were also well trained in the science of "wielding the baton," the truly professional application of which would eliminate the appearance of prisoners in police court bearing "the regulation two inch cut on the forehead," the symbol of the crude methods of the old force.[5]

A heavy emphasis on military discipline transformed the police into a veritable urban army. City and state officials regularly reviewed the city's troops. The demonstrations featured mounted drill, "baton" exhibitions, an assembly on riot call, precision drill by signal flag, and, on one occasion, a staged battle between the department and a riotous mob.

All this, of course, was expensive, and the commissioners constantly requested larger appropriations. One board member admitted that economy in local government was a laudable objective, but he did not believe it should be pursued at the expense of the police department. Cincinnati, he warned, was a railroad and industrial city in which violence, bloodshed, and even insurrection were quite possible. And another contended that a city of 296,908 people needed and could afford more than a 482-man department. One riot, he noted, could well destroy in a single day more than an increase in the force would cost in twenty-five years.[6]

Demands for the total suppression of crime and vice and the regulation of disorderly saloons also presented the commissioners with a delicate policy problem. Too strict enforcement might antagonize those businessmen and Zone politicians who did not want the lid tightly closed. Yet at least a facade of respectability had to be maintained to placate the law and order element.

The department sought out a safe middle ground. The board boasted that it had eradicated all public games of keno, faro, and poker. But the commissioners contended that policy, dice, and pool could only be harassed, not eliminated. In addition, while claiming success in closing saloons on Sunday, they admitted that the side- and back-door trade flourished. Since this illegal commerce was said to be impossible to suppress, arrests were made only for disturbance of the peace or where "perceptible loitering" occurred.

Prostitution proved equally intractable. The commissioners tried, but failed, to eliminate the streetwalker, restrict houses of prostitution to the Circle, and regulate their operations. Brothels were placed under close surveillance, but orderly houses were not molested. The force co-operated with the police court and city hospital in an attempt to stamp out venereal disease by setting up a system of examination and treatment. Each prostitute, moreover, had to register with the department and have a conference with the chief, during which he lectured her on the appropriate standard of behavior. If she were new to the city or to the profession he questioned her about her circumstances, advised her of the grief and mortification she faced, and urged her to take up another line of work.[7]

Despite these compromises with vice and the continuing manpower shortage, the new force won the praise and respect of the Hilltop community. One Democratic reformer called it the most creditable branch of local government, and General Andrew Hickenlooper boasted that the new chief had organized and disciplined the best force in the United States.[8] Zone groups, though occasionally nettled by a specific policy, never agreed that the new force constituted a major irritant. Law and order, discriminately applied, had a strong appeal in both regions of the periphery.

In no other field did the new order reformers make such dramatic changes so successfully. In sharpest contrast stood the attempts to halt the deteriorating conditions at the workhouse, infirmary, refuge, and hospital. Repeatedly officials decried the deplorable conditions and requested increased appropriations. But all these institutions dealt primarily with Circle people or politically insignificant groups from the Zone. Consequently, so long as costs were kept down and outrageously scandalous conditions avoided, their operations remained hidden from the view of most Zone and Hilltop supporters of the new order. Their improvement was not a top priority project.

Those institutions and services which seemed more obviously related to the welfare and prestige of the city, however, received more attention. For example, the major improvement in the city's educational facilities involved the University of Cincinnati, which not only had many students from the Zone but also attracted the interests of the educated and wealthy men of the suburbs. The city donated some forty-three and a third acres of land and issued $100,000 in bonds to move the university from its old site in the Circle to Burnet Woods Park on the hill north of the Basin.

At the same time, the board of trustees worked persistently to bring other educational enterprises in the city into association with the school. Before the end of the century the Cincinnati law school and several of the city's old medical colleges had affiliated with the emerging university. By that time, too, a search had begun for a man to fill the presidency, vacant since 1890, and to build up and reorganize the faculty.

These improvements were based upon a filter-down concept of urban educational reform. The trustees hoped to create a civic institution whose influence would "be felt in elevating the course and thoroughness of study in the schools below it." They expected the new university, moreover, to aid the reform cause by "promoting higher practical knowledge in public works, public economy, and public virtue." Such a school, they believed, would not only assist all "those men and women who are promoting industrial, religious, and moral undertakings," but would also broadly educate the "industrial classes . . . for the most useful places in our industrial and political state." [9]

Fire protection, no less than higher education, was regarded as a service too vital and too visible to be neglected. The Republican reformers expanded and modernized the fire department, adding eight new companies in 1889 and four more in 1896. In addition, they increased the number of chemical engine companies, revamped and extended the fire-alarm telegraph system, and set up a telephone communications network. By 1896 the board of administration was satisfied that, as soon as the four newest companies were fully equipped, the city would be adequately protected from fire.

The GOP administrations also tried to carry out a variety of other reforms which appealed to both Zone and Hilltop residents. Beginning in 1887, they attempted to regulate private building. By the end of the period, however, the inspector felt the building code would need extensive revisions if private construction were to be effectively controlled. Serious efforts were also made, especially during Mosby's administration, to deal with the smoke nuisance, but little of significance was achieved. His smoke abatement campaign bogged down when the city inspector and a committee of businessmen failed to agree on how to eliminate excessive smoke.[10]

In addition, both Mosby and the board of administration talked enthusiastically about park improvement and expansion. The board was particularly proud of its park record. It congratulated itself for keeping the parks free of athletic activities, for refusing to make them into show grounds or zoological gardens, and for retaining the restful quality of scenery in the "rural" parks. This policy was based on the conviction that the "whole class of nervous diseases, resulting in prostration, insomnia, discomfort, ill health, and a high death rate among children and people of very modest means" arose from the "combination of circumstances which surround daily life in the harried and feverish activity of American cities." [11]

But the Republican regime worked most earnestly toward those objectives of the new order deemed essential to the economic well-being of the city or the comfort and convenience of the party's supporters in the suburban fringe. Virtually all these projects were opposed by Zone and other groups concerned about costs.

The Republican administrations persistently advocated the construction of a new city water works. In 1896, without a referendum, the state legislature authorized the city to issue $6,000,000 in bonds for a new plant and set up a five-man bipartisan board of waterworks commissioners appointed by the governor to oversee the project. The board elected August Herrmann as its president. The suburban districts promptly indicated their satisfaction. A committee representing the Commercial Club, Optimist Club, Board of Trade, Chamber of Commerce, Young Men's Business Club, and Manufacturers' Club assured Herrmann of its support and assistance.[12]

The GOP also tried to settle the controversy over the municipally owned Southern Railroad. The new policy emerged only after the locally owned Cincinnati, Hamilton & Dayton Railroad purchased a controlling interest from the original lessee, the Cincinnati, New Orleans and Texas Pacific, a company headed by men outside Cincinnati.[13] While this transaction was being worked out, the board of legislation passed an ordinance providing the Southern with land— a privilege pledged in the original lease—on which to build terminal facilities. Mayor Mosby, however, vetoed the ordinance on the grounds that the grant was not perpetual. The railroad took its case to court and Circuit Court Judge Howard Hollister ruled that the terminal project was valid and that the city had to provide the land in accordance with the board's ordinance.[14]

At this point, however, the board of sinking fund trustees decided to submit to a referendum a proposition to sell the road to the C.H.&D. for $19 million. A virulent opposition to this proposal soon developed, led by the *Post*, the Central Labor Council, and a citizen's protective association, which was fed information on the value of the road from the members of the sinking fund trustees who opposed the sale. The opponents of the arrangement charged that the Southern was actually worth $30,000,000, and claimed that the C.H.&D. had "bought" the "Cox machine" to secure an affirmative vote on the referendum. Despite the backing of Cox, Senator Foraker, and most of the daily papers, the proposition failed by the hairbreadth margin of 428 votes.[15]

The returns reflected the division of political power which had first appeared in the 1894 city election. Although characterized by contemporary observers as a German revolt, the vote represented a victory of the Zone over Cox's new Hilltop-Circle alliance. The proposition carried in fourteen wards, all of them Hilltop or Circle districts. It failed in all sixteen Zone wards and in one Circle ward, the Eighth, an unreconstructed Democratic stronghold.[16]

The fight over terminal facilities for the Southern and the sale of the road clearly demonstrated a major defect in Cox's alliance— that is, its inability to hold the Zone and Hilltops together on specific issues. This obstacle had been circumvented in the waterworks question by going to the state legislature. The GOP had adopted a similar strategy to carry out its public utilities program.

It became increasingly evident after 1890 that the new order pre-

ferred locally regulated monopolies to either municipal ownership
or wide-open competition. The policy was put into effect by limit-
ing the number of municipal agencies involved in granting franchises and extensions, and by working out the details in behind-the-
scenes negotiations between the lawyers of the dominant utilities
corporations and the representatives of the Cox-Foraker wing of
the Republican organization. The major cases involved the traction
and lighting interests. In both instances settlement came through
August Herrmann's board of administration, while Cox and Foraker, both of whom acted as paid advisors to the corporations, ma-
neuvered in the background.

The regulation of traction affairs began, paradoxically, with what
was called a raid on "the octopus," the Cincinnati Consolidated
Traction Company. Early in 1893, the board of legislation granted
a three-cent-fare franchise to a company which planned to build an
electric line to Price Hill. Route 25, as the new company was called,
was said to be dominated by Cleveland interests, but it was nonetheless strongly supported by the *Commercial-Gazette* and several
improvement associations in the Zone neighborhoods it was to
serve.

Mayor Mosby, noting that the franchise did not stipulate the
payment of 5 per cent of the company's gross earnings to the city,
decided to veto the measure. Under intense pressure from the
newspapers, politicians, businessmen, and building and improvement associations, however, he reluctantly changed his mind. The
mayor contended nonetheless that Route 25, "the push-button three-
cent strap combination," was nothing more than a raid on Consolidated and predicted that the new line would never be constructed.[17]

His prophecy proved only half correct. Instead of buying out
Route 25, Consolidated decided the time had come to extend
electric service to the isolated western sections of the city. But the
company was unwilling to make these changes at its prevailing
four-cent fare, much less at the three-cent level demanded by the
supporters of Route 25.

Before the year was out Consolidated and the city reached a

compromise solution. In September of 1893 the traction company secured an agreement from the board of administration under which it was to convert entirely to electricity, extend more lines into the western portions of the Zone, and raise its fare from four to five cents. For these privileges it was to provide free transfers throughout its system and pay 5 per cent of its gross earnings and a car license of $4.00 per lineal foot (inside measurements) to the city.

This arrangment, by renewing all the franchises held by the company, eliminated a round of competitive bidding which would have accompanied the termination of the old grants gradually accumulated by Consolidated. It also killed off Route 25. Under the new contract Consolidated promptly set about extending one of its old lines to Price Hill, thus cutting the ground out from under the Cleveland interests and its three-cents fare.

Herrmann, in defending the board's action, claimed that Cincinnati now had the best traction contract of any city in the country save Baltimore. He argued that it represented a new approach to the problem, for in the past the city's street-railroad legislation had looked only to local and individual interests, while this contract made a comprehensive system. Herrmann regretted, however, that the six remaining independent lines had not seen fit to accept the terms offered to Consolidated. He advised the board not to grant them franchise extensions unless they did so.[18]

The foundation for completing the comprehensive traction system for which Herrmann longed was laid three years later. The crucial decisions were made at the state capitol and in the board of administration. In 1896 the state legislation enacted the Rogers Law, authorizing the city to grant a fifty-year traction franchise. The fare was to be five cents, and was subject to revision twenty years after the original grant and every fifteen years thereafter. The law also permitted the consolidation of all local lines into one company. Shortly after its passage, Herrmann's board granted Consolidated a franchise on these terms.

Outraged reformers and Democrats later charged that the company, in violation of local sentiment, had initiated the law for the express purpose of obtaining a monopoly and an exorbitant five-cent fare. They also claimed that the company's lawyer, Senator Foraker, facilitated both the passage of the law and the board of administration franchise grant by the skillful distribution of $250,-000 of Consolidated money and federal patronage.

Yet it is not certain that the scheme originated with the company. According to the president of the Walnut Hills Improvement Association, the members of his organization first proposed the idea. They felt that "if Walnut Hills was to hold its place in the struggle for supremacy among suburban localities, something must be done to change the situation with reference to street railway transportation." [19] The Rogers Law was their solution, and other Hilltop commuting districts hastily lined up behind the plan. At the time of its passage it evoked strong opposition only from the *Post* and a few spokesmen for organized labor. In short, commuters who preferred speedy and efficient rapid transit got their way by joining with Consolidated and the Republican organization. Neither home rule, low fare, anti-monopoly, nor municipal ownership sentiment could stop this combination.

Resolving the question of who was to light the city's streets was more difficult. Arrangements were made less smoothly than in the traction matter, took longer, and were not entirely settled when the twelve years of Republican rule ended. The techniques used, however, were similar to those employed in the traction settlement. That is, the dominant company co-operated with the Cox-Foraker wing of the GOP to bring order to a chaotic situation and to mute the rising demands for cheap and effective lighting.

In the 1890's those demands grew increasingly insistent. In 1893 the board of legislation tried twice to lower General Hickenlooper's gas rates below the $1.15-per-thousand-cubic-feet level. By this time, however, Cox was on the gas company's payroll, just as Foraker was being paid to represent the Consolidated Traction Company. Neither proposition succeeded. Mosby, under pressure from the organization, vetoed a sixty-five-cent-per-thousand-cubic-feet ordinance and Cox and Norman G. Kenan, another Hickenlooper aide, "cornered" an eighty-five-cent proposal before it was introduced into the board of legislation. The company then accepted a compromise contract cutting its price to a dollar.[20]

During this fight pressure mounted for lighting at least some of the city electrically. In 1889 the board of legislation passed an ordinance which, Hickenlooper thought, posed yet another threat to the gas company. The law provided that companies or individuals could enter the electric-light field if they secured permission from city council by special ordinance, posted a $50,000 guarantee bond, paid one-half of 1 per cent of their gross receipts to the city, and refrained from selling their franchise until six months after the date they started supplying electricity.[21]

Hickenlooper first tried to secure legislation permitting the gas company to produce electricity. Failing in this, he organized the Cincinnati Electric Company and got a street-lighting franchise. But other companies, despite the stiff bond requirement, flocked into the business, convincing Hickenlooper that no one could profit under such rigorous competition.[22]

The General then launched a three-pronged offensive. He first persuaded city council to stop granting franchises to new companies. This provided only temporary relief, however, for two entrepreneurs promptly secured grants from the probate court. Meanwhile, Hickenlooper proceeded to buy up controlling interest in the locally owned independents. At the same time he began negotiations with Joseph B. Foraker, counsel for the Cincinnati Edison Company, for a consolidation of all electrical interests.[23]

In 1891, when Cox was emerging as the dominant force in the GOP and had signed up with Hickenlooper, the General's strategy began to pay off. By that time he controlled all the local independent companies. And late in 1891 or early in 1892 he entered into an agreement with the Edison people, the mayor, and the Cox-Foraker wing of the Republican organization to secure the passage of a general electric-street-lighting ordinance granting the lowest bidder the privilege of lighting all the city's streets. Although the details are not clear, the two companies apparently planned to rig the bidding and then consolidate under Hickenlooper's Cincinnati Electric after he had been granted the franchise.

On the appointed day, Hickenlooper, confident that he would not be underbid, offered to light the streets for $94.50 per lamp per year. He was dumbfounded when Edison submitted the low bid of $84.90. For the first time the General realized he had been deceived. Hickenlooper was dazed.[24]

The General decided to fight for the contract. He proposed a deal to city council. He sent it a guarantee bond of $100,000 and offered to light the streets for $75 or less if council would reject the other bid. The Edison people countered with an injunction from common pleas court restraining council from taking up this proposition. Hickenlooper then tried to get enough votes to prevent the granting of the franchise to Edison. Council was about evenly divided on the question when the General decided that, even if his Cincinnati Electric Company got the contract at $94.50, he would go broke. Greatly relieved, he retired from the fray.

But only temporarily, for a scheme now developed aimed at uniting all the gas and electric illuminating interests. In 1893 Cox got an ordinance through city council and the board of administration which permitted the gas company to enter the electric-light field. Mosby was disposed to veto it, but Cox, Foraker, Kenan, and Thomas Graydon persuaded him to sign. Thereafter the gas company consolidated with those electric companies under Hickenlooper's control, and negotiations were opened for the purchase of the Edison Company's local plant by the gas company. Cox, Foraker, Kenan, and Graydon urged Hickenlooper to make the deal. The talks broke down, however, when Hickenlooper insisted that Edison first abrogate its city franchise. His position seemed assured. Edison was operating at a loss and Herrmann, from his post on the board of administration, had already criticized it for overcharging and advised against permitting it to expand its service into the suburbs.[25]

By 1894, then, the GOP seemed well on the way to settling the question by granting Hickenlooper's company a regulated monopoly to provide the city with electric lights. In the course of the struggle the new order had rejected both municipal ownership and free competition. But this was not a uniformly popular solution, for Theodore Horstmann's 1894 independent mayoralty campaign derived much of its backing from elements in the Zone dissatisfied with the public utilities program of the new order.

At that same election, however, the voters overwhelmingly endorsed another top priority policy of the new order, namely its five-year-old pledge to annex the ring of wealthy suburbs which encircled the city.

In 1889 Mayor Mosby noted that the recent growth of the suburban population and the approach of a census year made the question of annexation one of unusual importance. A "large increase of population over that of the last census," he explained, "conveys the idea that there is great prosperity; that . . . business must be good [and that] opportunities for employment and the investment of capital [are] greater." It followed, then, that "persons seeking to better their condition in life naturally remove to these apparently prosperous centers." Yet the only expansion of the city boundaries since 1873 had been made in 1888, during Amor Smith's administration, when a wedge of territory in South Avondale around the Zoological Gardens was added.[26]

The expansionists now focused their attention on five villages—Avondale, Clifton, Linwood, Riverside, and Westwood—which, as one councilman put it, had been "built up at the expense of . . . the wealth and population of Cincinnati." [27] But the people to be absorbed objected. To eliminate the possibility that the villagers might upset the venture, the Republican organization in the spring of 1893 secured from the state legislature the Lillard Law, which provided that the votes of the city and the villages on the proposal would be counted together.[28]

Anti-annexationists in the villages exploded. They claimed that the Lillard Law was unconstitutional. Representatives of Riverside protested being made a part of a city they saw as already overwhelmed with debts which they had no part in creating. Spokesmen from Linwood claimed that Cincinnati's only object was to regain "the distinction, somewhat doubtful in its character, of continuing to be the metropolis of the State of Ohio." And a Clifton resident protested that the law would permit Cincinnati, where the tax rate was excessive, to assassinate his village in broad daylight. Although he admitted that Cliftonites loved the old city, he concluded that they were "not ready to allow her to destroy us." [29]

The outraged villagers never had a chance. In the city every precinct rolled up an overwhelming "yes" majority. The returns revealed neither a partisan split nor a division along Circle, Zone, or Hilltop lines. Among the villages, moreover, only Clifton, Linwood, and Westwood voted against the measure. The combined total read 49,467 for, and 4467 opposed.[30]

Part of the justification for annexation was the desire to secure more tax revenue, for a low tax rate was one of the cardinal principles of the new order. That was not easy to maintain, however. During the years of Republican ascendancy the city government took on some nineteen new functions apart from those discussed here. At the same time, it expanded and improved the city's streets, water mains, and sewers.[31]

Yet the tax rate did not soar. It stood at $26.86 per $1000 valuation in 1885. During the next ten years it never exceeded $28.14, and in 1896 it stood at $26.40. This stability was maintained in part by issuing bonds for major improvements and services, such as the $1,000,000 for a new city hall in 1887, the $100,000 spent to make work for the unemployed in the winter of 1893, and the $6,000,000 allotted for the construction of the new water works. But the Republicans claimed the low rates were possible because they administered municipal affairs in a business-like fashion and avoided extravagance.

Nonetheless, in 1894 a Democratic candidate for the state senate charged that the city government cost too much. "Cincinnati is pre-eminently a manufacturing city," he claimed, "and unless her taxes, expenses and assessments are reduced her factories can not compete with those of other cities where these burdens are less. . . . The power to tax," he warned, "is the power to destroy, and it should be used only for public purposes, not for the support of a

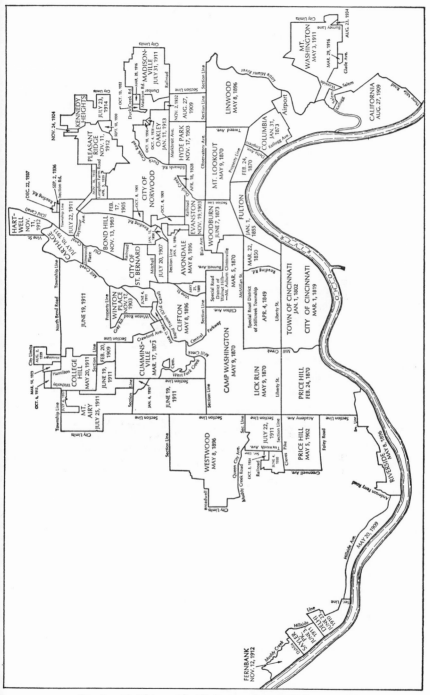

7. Cincinnati, Ohio, with All Annexations to February 5, 1940

body of political retainers or the enrichment of political bosses." [32] Another reformer, moreover, claimed that the new charter had proven an expensive failure. "Mr. Box or Mr. Cox or whoever happens to be the boss of the moment," he argued, controlled the $3,000,000 paid annually to the officers of the city government.

> So long as the present system prevails and the offices are distributed after every election [by a man] who has this fund to draw upon and who is hampered by no moral scruples and who devotes his whole time and energies to that business, he can defeat the unconcentrated action of honest citizens who are unable to provide themselves with the sinews of war [because] they are so heavily taxed to furnish the very money which their opponents use against them.[33]

Whatever the cost, the political and governmental reforms and programs supported by Cox and his allies represented an attempt to meet the demands of the new city in the decade of disorder. They provided Zone and Hilltop residential districts with most of the services they demanded and kept the price as low, or as invisible, as possible. To check crime and violence they created a deterrent, a professional police force which followed a compromise law enforcement policy symbolized by the backdoor saloon. They laid the foundations for a real university; they tried to unravel the knotty traction and lighting question; they expanded the boundaries (and tax base) of the city; and they tried to prepare for the next census report. And they made the processes of government, like their political system, more efficient. Only the Circle, which had few spokesmen and was not yet an integral part of the Cox coalition, was neglected.

III

PHILOPOLISM AND THE
NEW URBAN DISCIPLINE

> To attend a meeting of these delegates from associations rep-
> resenting every suburb and natural division of the city . . . is
> to be made profoundly certain that a civic consciousness of some
> kind is actually being born. . . . Today that comprehension is
> penetrating the minds of men, women, children and institutions
> in an amazing manner.*

The rise of George B. Cox and the Republican party helped suppress the immediate crises of the decade of disorder. But it did not
mark the end of municipal reform in Cincinnati. In many respects
it was only the beginning. For although the methods and policies of
the Republican organization held together a varied Zone-Hilltop
coalition, the machine represented but one response to the pervasive uprootedness which accompanied the urban explosion. A host
of other groups appeared, each in its own way engaged in a quest
for community based on a new urban discipline, and each seeking
to resolve the city's deep and persistent problems. Advocates of the
new civic spirit demanded that the ruling political coalition and its
perspective ought to be truly city-wide. They, like the GOP, tried to
transform the Circle, giving its residents powerful allies. As a result,
politics drifted unsteadily away from its preoccupation with order
and toward a concern with social justice and the preservation of an
open society.

* Charles Frederic Goss, *Cincinnati: The Queen City, 1788–1912, An Interpretation*, Vol. II (Chicago and Cincinnati, 1912), p. 283.

7

Boosterism and Reform

In 1909 the National Municipal League and the American Civic Association held their joint annual convention in Cincinnati. They had, according to Clinton Rogers Woodruff, hesitated about coming to Cincinnati because they had heard so much about its lack of civic spirit. But the stories, he said, were false. Elsewhere, the two groups had been the guests of one or, at the most, three or four civic organizations, but in Cincinnati they found more than forty active progressive organizations working for the city's betterment.[1]

Local observers felt that the outburst of civic spirit and organizational enthusiasm among businessmen was something new, and the Young Men's Business Club, founded in the 1890's, was widely regarded as characteristic of the movement. Charles B. Wilby, a lawyer and veteran of the civil-service-reform movement, praised the club because its members were drawn from no single business or profession and thus would not identify the welfare of Cincinnati with that of their own field. And Judge William Howard Taft thought that the great good of the organization was that it educated members on practical politics and the issues of local government.[2]

It had begun modestly enough. In 1892 a group of young businessmen, finding existing groups beyond their financial and social reach, decided to form an organization of their own devoted to civic and social as well as business purposes. The membership quickly grew. Leading businessmen and professional men from every field—German Protestants, German Jews, and German and Irish Catholics, as well as Anglo-Saxon Protestants—joined the organization, and Hilltop people predominated. In 1896 they incorporated to promote the best interests of Cincinnati.[3]

Boasting a membership of some one thousand men by 1900, the club was led by a hard core of seventy-five members known as the Knockers or the Gridiron Club of the West, so called for its satirical plays and burlesques. Yet its members had joined for more than just horseplay. Every Knocker, one member claimed, worked hard for the good of the city and had to be willing to give time and money to boost Cincinnati.[4]

But the Knockers were not the only civic zealots in the Business Men's Club. The booster spirit dominated the entire organization. In 1904 its president announced that the club stood for whatever was progressive and that it was composed of energetic businessmen, to whom the club motto, "The Honor and Glory of Cincinnati," was no empty phrase. The following year he exhorted the members to keep the faith and asked that they all realize that Cincinnati was undergoing a great transformation and recognize that they "must keep our municipality abreast the times [sic] by cultivating civic patriotism and concentrating our energies for the upbuilding and uplifting of our beloved city." [5]

The club created a battery of standing committees which kept a close watch over city government. Through this kind of pressure, and by means of endorsements of particular measures voted by the membership, it urged a wide variety of reforms. It wanted the sewerage system extended and improved. It agitated for cleaner streets, additional paved thoroughfares, and the construction of boulevards. It demanded the opening of the tightly sealed city to more interurban railroads. It supported a movement to increase terminal facilities and construct a belt railroad. It worked for more playgrounds, urged the development of a park system, and backed the anti-smoke campaign. It advocated manual training in the public schools. And it endorsed a series of political reforms, such as the adoption of a small city council elected at large, a separate nonpartisan judicial ballot, the federal system of municipal government with a strong mayor, and the extension of civil service.

But the club never limited itself merely to economic development and administrative and political reform. Toward the end of the period its concern with poverty and social issues intensified. It launched an investigation of what was being done in other cities for Negroes. It also looked into the plight of Cincinnati's immigrants, especially those of southeastern Europe who lived under unhygienic conditions and were taken advantage of because of their ignorance of the language and customs. It displayed an interest in better housing, a concern related to its insistent campaign to persuade the traction company to extend the street railway system and improve its service as a means of alleviating congestion and social disorder in the center of the city.[6]

Older organizations, too, like the Chamber of Commerce, joined the growing ranks of Hilltop advocates of reform boosterism. Between 1910 and 1913 the Chamber of Commerce experienced a renaissance.[7] The old-time business organization, explained the new superintendent, operating through voluntary committees of merchants and manufacturers who devoted "a few moments of their leisure time to the passage of sonorous [business] regulations" had been transformed into a new and effective organization "equipped with efficient departments and trained experts." [8] Its membership, moreover, was more than doubled, and the new Chamber of Commerce, like the Business Men's Club, created a shadow administration of standing committees to help municipal officials run the city.

The reorganized Chamber of Commerce delved into a wide variety of public questions. It concerned itself with "problems of a sociological . . . importance," such as better housing, city planning, prevention of disease, and the growth of educational facilities commensurate with the city's development.[9] The scope of its interests was reflected in the proliferation of committees. By 1913, they numbered thirty-three, twenty of which were created after 1910.[10] And in each of the areas covered by these committees the Chamber of Commerce took some positive action.

But not all the civic groups dominated by Hilltop members were business organizations. The Federated Improvement Association, for example, originated in the neighborhood improvement associations which dated from the eighties and nineties. They were set up by residents of new Zone and suburban districts to secure improvements for their locality. Later, however, several of the associations decided that many of their problems transcended neighborhood lines. In 1907 seven of them joined forces to form the federation, whose objective was the promotion of the general welfare of the cities, villages, and other communities in Hamilton County, and particularly that of the suburban and residential districts of the city.[11]

The federation flourished. By 1913, it claimed some thirty-six constituent societies which represented eight thousand men. They came from both Zone and Hilltop districts, but Hilltoppers held most of the offices. With a membership including men from a vast array of businessess, professions, religions, and ethnic groups, the new organization had a city-wide interest.[12]

The public meeting was perhaps its favorite means of proselytizing. "Public opinion," claimed one federationist, "moves the world, [and] one of the best ways to mold a wise and enlightened opinion is by public meetings where men of all classes meet and discuss the needs of the people without political, religious or personal bias." Yet the city itself, as a kind of gigantic town meeting, was the best teacher. "Cities are playing a more and more important part in the life of the nation," he noted, and "in cities men have many interests in common to all, such as the use of streets, police, fire and health protection." There men "learn best how to work together, learn best the great truth that each must give up something for the good of all." In short, he concluded, "it is in cities that men, if given the chance of home rule, will learn most quickly the true foundation principles on which rest real freedom in a representative democracy."[13]

The federation backed virtually every project for city improvement which arose. It took part in the smoke abatement campaign and the movement for fire prevention. It supported dairy inspection and urged the construction of better housing in the slums. It thought the abolition of gambling among children especially important lest there "raise up among us a race of gamblers and produce a condition worse than those which have been suppressed." [14] Plans for the creation of more and better parks and playgrounds, the construction of a convention hall and an enlarged budget for the University of Cincinnati also received its endorsement.

Like the other Hilltop organizations, the federation felt it held a special relationship to local government. As the secretary of one of the affiliates put it, a link was needed to connect the citizen with City Hall, and the Federated Improvement Association provided it, allowing businessmen who wanted to do more than just vote to participate in city affairs.[15]

Although the city had many civic organizations, and although thirty of them had a combined membership of over six thousand businessmen and banded together in 1905 to form the Cincinnati Associated Organization, few pursued broad-gauged programs. More commonly, they concentrated on a single field of reform. Some dated to the 1890's and focused on political or governmental reforms. They continued to proliferate, but were probably the weakest of the new single issue groups. Here, too, as with those organizations of more diverse interests, the emphasis fell increasingly on special questions.

The Social Center Federation, for example, urged the city to join the social-center movement and to construct a building equipped with a stage, stereopticon, gymnasium, and reading, game, and dancing rooms and halls. In 1914 a drive began to promote a professional men's and businessmen's immigrant welfare league. Circuit Court Judge Howard C. Hollister, one of its leaders, believed that immigrants had been too long neglected, misled, and exploited, and consequently many of them had grown "distrustful and anarchistic." [16] The Juvenile Protective Association, founded in 1912, concentrated all its attention on "particularly unfortunate children" as a champion of the new idea—preventing trouble by removing the causes, protecting society, and reforming the guilty, instead of only punishing the criminal.[17]

After the 1880's, in short, it became increasingly difficult for the businessmen and professional men of the Hilltop to ignore the new civic spirit. And they found no respite in their homes. In 1911 Mary C. Gallagher, of the Cincinnati Woman's Club, announced that "the steel engraving type of womanhood [was] long out of style. The ringleted damsel of wasp-like waist, simpering voice, and satin slippered feet, is, thank God, dead" and has been replaced by a "noble army of broad-minded women [who realized] that they, too, are responsible for gang rule, graft, greed, child labor, pauperism and prostitution."

Also gone, claimed Miss Gallagher, were the days when a women's club meant a society which raised "funds to clothe the naked little negroes in Africa by selling antimacassers [sic] and worsted dogs." Women's clubs now aimed at definite and specific evils relating to "Educational Problems, Local Option, Joint Property, Education Reforms, Direct Legislation, Pure Food, Domestic Science, City Politics, County and State Institutions, Sociology, Political and Industrial Reforms." [18]

The largest and most prestigious group in the maze of women's organizations was the Cincinnati Woman's Club, founded in the winter of 1893–94. Although the Kindergarten Association, established in 1879, was perhaps the earliest women's organization to engage in civic work on a continuing basis, the Woman's Club was the first to match the new businessmen's groups in spirit, technique, and strategy. Its founders wanted to create a representative body of women, drawn from all sections of the city, all religious denominations, and all interests and pursuits. This diversity, they felt, would inevitably broaden and widen their mental horizons.[19]

Although the club by 1914 had more than one thousand members, it had not wholly fulfilled its democratic aspirations, perhaps because of the $15 initiation fee. The board of directors "elected" women without regard to age or marital status from every section of the Hilltops and outer Zone with occupational, religious, and ethnic background characteristic of those regions. German Jews, however, appeared in less than proportionate numbers. And while Catholics were not excluded, the overwhelming majority of members came from the predominantly Protestant Hilltop communities of Clifton, Mt. Auburn, East Walnut Hills, and Avondale. With but twenty-one Germans represented, the club was largely British in ethnic background. Negroes were entirely excluded.

The club proceeded gradually but more surely toward becoming "a literary and political training school, a maker of citizens with a broader outlook in the world of affairs, a powerful engine of moral force." By 1895 it had eight sections—education, social science and philanthropy, household economics, civics, literature, art, music, and current topics—but had not, "even at the risk of seeming too conservative," taken any steps toward active reform work.[20] Instead, it gave the women time to get acquainted with each other and the workings of the organization. Before the turn of the century, however, the club had begun to act.

By that time other women's groups were moving in the same direction. They came in a bewildering variety. There was the Julia Ward Howe Club, a group that made a transition from culture to civic spirit between 1890 and 1903. The city's three suffrage organizations became more aggressive and ambitious than the reconstructed culture associations. Beside these, there was the Cincinnati Section of the National Council of Jewish Women, a German Jewish Hilltop clique. Indeed, by the end of the period, women's clubs, mothers' clubs, and neighborhood organizations could be found throughout the Zone and Hilltops, including the Civic League, the Federation of Colored Women's Clubs, several Junior Leagues, the DAR-sponsored Children of the Republic, the New Citizen's Educational League, and the Consumers' League. Scarcely a single occupational, geographic, or ethnic interest was not represented. Although records of their activities and make-up are scant, it is clear that the impetus came from the Hilltops and the thrust was toward the new civic spirit.

In 1914 Emilie Watts McVea, dean of women at the University of Cincinnati, surveyed the development of club life among women since 1875. The growing wealth and removal of industries from the home, she wrote, gave many women much leisure time. At first they interested themselves in art and literature, but they soon realized that their clubs must contribute to the community, must leave their isolation and "go down into the tenements. . . ." The clubs then enlarged their scope, concerning themselves with questions of civic importance, and began to exert an influence on public opinion by espousing municipal experiments. In case after case, she noted, the pattern was the same—"imitation, experimentation, success." Then the project was relinquished to the city so that the proved plan might be made more useful to the community.

The women's club, Dean McVea concluded, had produced a new ideal of education and culture which found no field of study foreign to the life of its own time.[21] The women of leisure, like the men of the Hilltops, had found a new usefulness.

Despite the great number and diversity of the Hilltop booster organizations which carried the banners of the new civic spirit, they had much in common. They drew their membership from among the women and businessmen and professional men who lived in the expanding peripheral territory beyond the Circle and Zone. Their members were divided among the Catholic, Reform Jewish, and Protestant religions roughly in proportion to the representation of these groups in the Hilltop population. Negroes and southern and eastern European immigrants were almost universally excluded. The movement was largely a native-born and second-generation British-, Irish-, or German-American affair. It was neither overwhelmingly white Anglo-Saxon Protestant, nor exclusively old family.

The Hilltop sponsors of reform boosterism, moreover, had ethnic, religious, and economic ties to all sections of the city. Far enough from the slums physically and socially to feel safe, they were still close enough, by virtue of their backgrounds and their commuting habits, to be appalled by Circle conditions. And they had the finances, time, and education to act.

Walter A. Draper of the renovated Chamber of Commerce interpreted the sudden interest in reform among Hilltop businessmen to mean that "the problems that confront us will not be settled by the radical nor by the stand-patter, but by the progressive conservative." These men realize, he claimed, that a "new order of things must prevail . . . [and] have determined that the knife that will perform the operation must not cut deeply enough to kill." [22] Yet the Hilltop boosters' groups were not as embattled as Draper saw them to be. They frequently found allies in the Zone who were also pushing the new civic spirit, and their attitudes and programs meshed nicely with those emanating from the Hilltop boosters.

The Taxpayers' Association, for example, was composed of some two thousand members, most of them Zone residents of German background who owned property on the Circle-Zone border. Founded in 1886, it did not begin its career in reform until 1896 when it was revitalized and reorganized by its secretary, Fred Tuke, a German immigrant. By the time he took over the organization Tuke had come to believe that crime and dishonesty in public and private life were increasing. A pious Catholic, he thought that revolution against authority, anarchism, and nearly all crimes were founded on disbelief in any supreme authority.

In recruiting members for the association, however, Tuke took a more earthly approach. He pointed out that the bankers, brewers, businessmen, and workingmen were well organized and thought that the same should hold true for the "taxpayers who are, in fact, the stockholders of the city." The association promised to work for a businesslike and economical administration of public affairs and an equal division of the burden of taxation. And it favored, as a general rule, "necessary and beneficial improvements," but opposed "extravagance." [23]

Of all the booster organizations, the Taxpayers' Association fought perhaps the longest, most consistently, and most outspokenly against bossism and expensive spoils politics. It struck with a variety of weapons. Beginning in 1897 it backed a series of reform mayoral candidates. There were few proposed alterations in the structure of local government which it did not support. It went down the line for the initiative and referendum, a small council and small school board elected at large, civil service, the strong-mayor federal system, and a nonpartisan judiciary.

With respect to public improvements, the association's program differed little from those of the Hilltop organizations. It wanted clean, well-paved, and promptly repaired streets, public comfort stations, cheap and efficiently run monopolistic public utilities (but not municipal ownership), a centrally located Union Terminal and more interurban railroads, and additional parks and playgrounds, especially in the congested districts of the city.

Favoring "efficient" public education to teach civic duties and other modern courses, the association nonetheless disliked extraordinary increases in education taxes just to provide for fads. It preferred a sufficient levy for a progressive system of education, especially "more mechanical training." [24] And Tuke fought the expansion of the University of Cincinnati on the grounds that it was a haven for the wealthy who laughed at poor and ambitious young men.[25]

But Tuke's organization was not wholly representative of the new boosterism in the Zone. Compared with the Cincinnati Anti-Tuberculosis League, the Taxpayers' Association was more conservative than progressive.

The league was founded in 1907 to create public awareness of the great annual loss owing to the prevalence of tuberculosis in Cincinnati. Its fifty-four delegates from forty-eight organizations, thirty-three of which were labor unions, established a program of "educational propaganda" on the prevention of the disease. To the ill-informed, ill-educated, and poor it issued warnings on the dangers of bad health habits and pointed out the benefits of good ones. If the campaign were successful, the league predicted, it would produce strong, healthy, efficient workmen who would seldom be absent from their jobs.[26]

By 1911, however, the league had expanded its mission. It now described itself as an educational and vigilance organization acting between the people and their employees, the public officials. It was educating the people to support better government and demanding efficient service from public employees. In addition, the emphasis in its propaganda had shifted and broadened markedly. Cne official complained of the money expended to "lift social wrecks, when a smaller expenditure and a little concerted courage and energy would remove the cause of these wrecks." Dr. John M. Withrow, the league's president, made that doctrine official policy in 1912. The battle, he contended, involved the sweatshop, child labor, low wages, impure milk, impure food, intemperance, and other social evils. "Consumption is a social malady," he explained, "and its entire uprooting will require wonderful social regeneration, [a] reweaving of the social fabric." [27]

The league hoped that the minimum result of its propaganda would be an enlarged health department budget to help cover the expense of educational work and increased efforts "for better civic health." And it insisted that this work could be properly done only by local and state government, not by private agencies.[28]

Somewhere between the Anti-Tuberculosis League and the Taxpayers' Association among the Zone proponents of the new boosterism stood the Central Labor Council. The organization had grown rapidly. In 1893, four years after its establishment, the council counted but eighteen affiliates and its monthly publication, *The Chronicle,* distributed only 10,000 copies. Thereafter, however, the Central Labor Council joined the American Federation of Labor and by 1897 its thirty-nine affiliated organizations claimed to represent 17,000 unionists. At the turn of the century it spoke for fifty locals. In two years this figure had jumped to eighty-one locals with a total membership of 35,000.

The Central Labor Council rejected both the political and the ideological approaches of the past. To be sure, it claimed that in the city's "wrong and immoral" society "wealth-producers live in poverty and idlers roll in luxury" while the "toiling masses" labor under the delusion that they enjoy political freedom. Yet it held the old trade and labor organizations partially responsible for this because they had protected workers as producers but not as consumers and citizens. With this in mind, the council drew up a declaration of principles, in the form of the Declaration of Independence, which defined the council's purpose as "organizing and concentrating the working classes for their own mutual protection, education and social advancement." [29]

Its spokesmen, moreover, relied on labor boosterism, a worker's version of the new civic spirit, to rally the workers and win the respect of the community. On May Day, 1896, for instance, "The Rajah," a columnist for *The Chronicle*, boasted that Cincinnati working men were superior, that they had built a great city and were proud of it. And, in the spring of 1912, *The Chronicle* glowed with civic pride. Cincinnati, declared one editorial, has had fewer labor troubles than any other American city of its size and has pointed the way toward progress and a spirit which has become the ideal of thousands of other municipalities. The editor brimmed with "love of home, of city and fellowmen." He could not restrain his enthusiasm. "My Queen City, my home! A place to live and a place in which to rear your progeny. A liveable condition; tolerant and progressive minds." [30]

But the Central Labor Council did not abandon more traditional means of educating the community. *The Chronicle*, for example, regularly printed a list of boycotted firms. And in 1904, after an eight-month plumbers' walkout, the editor of *The Chronicle* remarked that the lesson to be learned from this strike was that employers had to reckon with trade unionism as a vital factor, and that any attempt to denigrate labor would surely end in disaster. [31]

Despite its use of militant language, however, the Central Labor Council viewed voluntary arbitration as a reasonable means of resolving labor-management disputes. In 1900 it lavishly praised August Herrmann for successfully arbitrating a settlement in the seven years' war between Max Burgheim of the *Freie Presse* and Typographia No. 2. It also reacted favorably to a similar intervention by Republican Mayor Julius Fleischmann in the 1904 teamsters' strike. And in 1913 it supported the efforts of Democratic Mayor Henry T. Hunt and Walter Knight, president of the Federated Improvement Association, to secure arbitrated settlements of the teamsters' and ice drivers' disputes.

During this period of experimentation in employer and community education, the Central Labor Council leveled a steady and diverse barrage of instruction at the organized workers. They were beseeched to heed the slogan "Organize! Agitate! Educate!" *The Chronicle* also offered tips on the practice of thrift, individualism, and the pursuit of upward mobility. It printed a sample budget which explained how to divide expenditures to promote family savings. The paper also told its readers that every organized wageearner should be ambitious to own his own home, because home owners commanded respect and standing in a community. And the paper urged all workers to send their children to school so that "in place of being reared in ignorance, they may grow up like the children of business men, worthy and respected members of society instead of . . . crouching creatures . . . hunted by the law." [32]

The council also offered political advice. Officially it was not interested in partisan politics. Yet in 1893 *The Chronicle* declared that the Populists were the only party with a platform approximating that of the Central Labor Council. And the following spring the council, along with the Populists, endorsed Theodore Horstmann and the Citizens' ticket. The council claimed that the Citizens' candidates would not only add to the honesty, ability, and efficiency of reform, but also reduce taxes, cut rents, eliminate special privileges, and induce manufacturers to come to the city.[33]

Thereafter, however, the Central Labor Council's enthusiasm for party endorsements waned. Instead, it adopted a policy of endorsing "labor men" or individual candidates favorable to labor, regardless of their party label.

But the organization backed a broad range of specific political reforms. From 1911 to 1913 it conducted an intensive campaign for home rule, the initiative, referendum, and recall of local officials—including judges, a nonpartisan ballot, and the establishment of a local civil service commission so long as it included a labor representative among its members. In 1911, moreover, the Central Labor Council joined twenty-seven other civic organizations to form the United Constitutional Committee of Hamilton County. Its objectives were to draw up a list of constitutional reforms, nominate delegates to the convention, arouse public interest, secure ratification of the new document, and create sentiment against political-party activity in matters relating to the constitutional convention.[34]

The Central Labor Council, in addition, proposed a motley list of municipal improvements which it felt reflected a progressive spirit, most of them closely linked to the welfare of workingmen. It asserted that building parks and playgrounds in thickly populated areas for the families of workingmen was vastly more important than acquiring additional park area in the suburbs. It claimed, too, that public baths and swimming pools fulfilled one of the needs and comforts of a healthful civic life. It supported the establishment of a juvenile court and praised its enforcement of the child labor laws, and joined the drive for the construction of a new city hospital.[35]

Toward the end of the period, the organization took up the cry against criminality in the Circle. It protested that the city's name was besmirched by almost daily reports of violent crimes by "man, woman or child" in that part of the city. A strong hand at the helm, it claimed, "would be a tremendous power for a change in this undesirable and entirely unwarranted notoriety." It also believed that prostitution was too flagrant. The only way to clean up the city, suggested *The Chronicle*, was to post conspicuously the names of the owners of houses of prostitution.[36]

The Central Labor Council also displayed a persistent concern with poor housing and sanitary standards. *The Chronicle*, although proud that hundreds of the city's beautiful homes were owned by workers, nevertheless recognized that "there are thousands and thousands of them housed in the tenements of the congested districts, whom organized workers hope to emancipate." The council urged philanthropists to help out by building model tenements, including some of the "dumb bell" variety, insisted that the city should compel the abolition of unsanitary tenements, and warned businessmen that tenement sweatshops encouraged low wages. That meant poor business, "idleness, crime, misery and slavish conditions, and what must follow, revolt." [37]

As part of its program to protect the health of labor, the council also favored Sunday closing for workers, especially retail clerks. It suggested that the Business Men's Club, in its efforts to enlarge legitimate business interests, would surely not have "'fair' merchants robbed [so that] 'kike' produce venders may prosper [by] driving men to work seven days in the week hawking disease breeding, sweatshop rags." The council did not, however, look with favor on the Puritanical Sabbath. It argued that the overwhelming majority of Cincinnatians wanted to be able to go to baseball games, the theater, the zoo, and "saloons properly and decently conducted," and to enjoy excursions on Sundays. It opposed prohibition, moreover, as a conspiracy of fanatics and the trusts which, predicted *The Chronicle,* would destroy the livelihood of thousands, kill personal liberty, and "reduce workers to the position of the Negro before the Civil War." [38]

After the mid-nineties the Central Labor Council also showed an increasing interest in immigration restriction. It disliked the idea of Europe's "pauper classes" coming into contact with "legitimate American labor." In 1901 it noted that 70 per cent of all immigrants came from Italy, Austria-Hungary, and Russia, and labeled 53 per cent of them undesirable because they lacked a trade or regular vocation. Yet the editor of *The Chronicle* in 1903 disclaimed any nativist motivation. He noted that the American Federation of Labor had been founded by a Jew who was now its president. And, he added, "union labor has no better or more liberal friends in Cincinnati than among the Jews." [39]

That remark reveals a great deal about the new civic spirit in the Zone. Highly practical, it could be narrow, self-regarding, and defensive. But when, as in the Anti-Tuberculosis League and to a lesser degree the Central Labor Council, it was guided by men or groups operating from a secure base, it followed the drift of the Hilltop groups toward a comprehensive and positive urban discipline for the whole city. Reform boosterism, then, served as a link which helped hold the very different peoples of the Zone and suburban fringe together and united them in an effort to keep the city politically and socially open.

Although the organizations were avowedly nonpartisan, they

were regularly criticized for interfering in politics. The *Post* claimed that this charge was very pleasing to politicians, who, the paper argued, "prefer that civic organizations do not mix in politics either directly or indirectly," because then "politics ceased to be profitable to the politicians." [40]

The *Post* did not elaborate on this statement, but the implication was clear. The civic organizations' concern with social and economic problems undercut prerogatives formerly reserved for the politicians. The boosters' desire, moreover, to educate the people of the Circle, Zone and Hilltops to an awareness of city-wide problems and the measures required to meet them also led to "mixing in politics." Virtually all the organizations recommended an expansion and reorganization not only of private institutions but also of local government to cope with the new city. The reform boosters, in a variety of ways, threatened to usurp the role of the politician.

They also shared a set of attitudes indicated by the frequent use of "efficiency," "progressive," and "businesslike" as terms of praise. The civic organizations believed in the efficacy of organization and education. Addicted to the formula of boosterism and reform, they felt that they labored patriotically for the welfare of the whole city. None hated urban life.

8

The New Urban Gospel

In 1904 Boris D. Bogen, a Russian Jewish[1] immigrant who had failed to find a satisfactory place for himself in the cities of the Atlantic seaboard, crossed the Alleghenies to interview for the position of superintendent of the United Jewish Charities of Cincinnati. In that city he found "a seasoned and well-rooted Jewry" whose "leaders spoke English with a decided German accent." In a moment of pique, however, David Philipson, a young Cincinnati rabbi, thought them "loud, overbearing, conceited. . . . These people, having amassed a great deal of money, imagine they own the universe." [2]

Whether the German Jews were "seasoned and well-rooted" or "loud, overbearing, conceited," it is not an exaggeration to say that they had done well in Cincinnati.[3] Affluence earned them a place in the fashionable residential districts, and once there, they tried to conform to Hilltop customs. By 1900 their immigrant cohesiveness had all but disappeared. The two German Jewish downtown businessmen's clubs, the Wednesday Night Literary Club, the mutual aid societies, the secret orders, and the Young Men's Hebrew Association all floundered and lost members. Philipson, by 1890, felt that if such groups supplemented the work of the Jewish religion, they could do a great deal of good, but merely as exclusive Jewish organizations they had no raison d'être.[4]

The difficulty of establishing and upholding a visible Jewish community was due in part to the ease with which German Jews moved into Hilltop circles. With a reputation for intelligence, public spirit, and liberality, they had before 1900 been fully accepted in the Chamber of Commerce and other commercial and civic organizations, fraternal orders like the Masons, Knights of Pythias, and Odd Fellows, and the elite social clubs. They supported the theater and major musical events consistently and in numbers. They also took an active part in local politics—more so, perhaps, than the German Jews of any other American city[5]—but not as a self-conscious ethnic bloc.

By the turn of the century, the question of the existence of a German Jewish community seemed irrelevant to Max B. May, a prominent local lawyer of German Jewish background. He was surprised when asked to write a chapter on the Jews for a centennial history of the city. May agreed, but he contended that the Jews were no more entitled to a separate chapter than the Catholics, Episcopalians, Methodists, or other sects.[6]

This notion had long been preached by Rabbi Isaac M. Wise, the leading spokesman and chief organizer of American Reform Judaism in the nineteenth century. He had "the highest respect for Judaism, Christianity, the Islam and every other religion in harmony with the postulate of reason and the standard of conscience." And he also asserted that believers in one God—as proclaimed and defined by Abraham, Moses, and the Prophets—and in the ethical principles contained in and following from the belief in one God, believed in Judaism. "They are of Israel *de jure*," he contended, and if "this controls their conduct and directs their performance of duty toward God and man they are of Israel *de facto,* whether they know it or not . . . confess it, or confess it not, whoever or whatever their ancestors were. Judaism denationalized is universal religion."[7]

From this broad base, Wise and his Cincinnati colleagues led their opulent and respectable congregations toward the style of American Protestant religious practices.[8] They introduced the sermon, the use of English, choirs, and organs, the sale of pews, and the integration of men and women in the temple while de-emphasizing the dietary laws, the rigid schedule of prayers, and the elaborate ritual aspects of the Orthodox service of eastern Europe. The thrust of Cincinnati-style Reform Judaism, in short, aimed at making the German Jews as much like their Hilltop Gentile neighbors as possible without entirely abandoning their religious distinctiveness.

Yet by 1915 Wise's religious strategy, which had done so much to pave their way to Hilltop status, had been altered. The transformation began in the 1880's just as the German Jews were demonstrating their remarkable adjustment to life in the new city.

The coming of the Russian immigration forced the German Jews to look down from the Hilltops and introduced them to the seamy side of life in the Basin. The spectacle aroused their disgust, sympathy, and horror. Philipson had to repeatedly denounce from the pulpit the eruption of "inexcusable prejudices" against the newcomers, particularly the use of the epithet, " 'kike,' which German-descended Jews were fond of hurling at their Russian-descended coreligionists." Yet something more positive had to be done. Wise candidly remarked that unless the Russians adopted American culture quickly, they would disturb "our social status and do considerable damage to the good reputation which our coreligionists have established for themselves." [9]

The first positive response to the crisis was an outburst of charitability. Individuals and groups set up more than a dozen organizations to clean, feed, and educate the immigrants, to care for their orphaned, aged, and ill, and to secure jobs and provide capital to give the unemployed a start in small business. Some concentrated solely on the Jews of the West End, but others rendered service to all the downcast of the Circle.[10]

These early efforts were apparently based on the assumption that the Russian Jews, given a small boost, would repeat the experience of their German predecessors and rise to Hilltop status. By the mid–1890's, however, the conviction grew that the "indiscriminate alms-giving produced selfishness, laziness and abhorrence of honest work," along with "loss of self respect, lying, cheating, simulation and hypocrisy and crimes of grosser sorts." In 1895 Philipson and a few others began to push for a federation of the charitable agencies and a change of method. They finally persuaded the conservative elements that charity should be reduced to a science and practised in a systematic way and by concerted action.[11] As a result the German Jews established, in 1896, the United Jewish Charities of Cincinnati. By 1914 it was co-ordinating the efforts of a broad range of philanthropic agencies, all of which quickly adopted the most recent innovations in social-work programs and techniques.

Out of the experience garnered in the work of the United Jewish Charities, a group of wealthy, educated, and influential German Jews developed a new urban gospel. It sought to change the mode of life of the West End immigrant, alter the attitudes of Hilltop Jews, transform the physical appearance of the city, broaden the activities of the municipal and state governments, and rescue politics from the sordid abyss into which it had purportedly fallen in the waning decades of the nineteenth century. By 1914, as Boris D. Bogen remarked, "social service was par excellence the medium of religion in the Reform Jewry of Cincinnati; it was religion." [12]

Yet an insistence on philanthropy, social work, and political action was not the only message carried to the Hilltops by the charity workers. They asked the German Jews to accept a remodeled and more aggressive Reform Judaism. It was around the Jewish settlement, an affiliate of the United Jewish Charities, that all the components of the new religion were first put together.

The settlement traced its origins to 1899. By 1905, one member of the board of directors remarked, it had grown steadily "toward the ideal of an institution which will be the social and intellectual center of Jewish life in Cincinnati." He was not entirely happy about having to insert the word "Jewish," however. During the early years, he noted, Gentiles comprised a considerable proportion of the membership of the clubs that met there. But as the Jewish influence in the clubs and in the administration of the institution became predominant, the settlement seemed inevitably to grow more and more exclusively Jewish.[13]

From the beginning, workers at the settlement felt compelled to emphasize its peculiarly Jewish nature. In 1903 S. C. Lowenstein pointed out that it provided a central meeting place for Jews who might not ordinarily come into contact where they could discuss politics, literature, business, sports, or questions of Jewish affairs. Another put it only slightly differently. The settlements, he argued, must strive to become Jewish communal centers, neither Reform nor Orthodox, neither Zionistic nor socialistic, furthering what was good in the principles and aspirations of the whole community.[14]

There were other practical reasons for the adoption of Jewishness by the settlement. It helped prevent the continued defection of second-generation Jews from all forms of religion, for as Philipson put it, "the Americanization of the Russian Jew is in one sense the atheization of the Russian Jew." This goal, in turn, was closely related to the preservation of the home. Too often, Bogen explained, social workers had "forgotten that, besides the advisability of making the parents more modern and putting them, so to say, in a shape lovable to the children," it was "also important that the children should be able to realize the strong and positive sides of their parents." This oversight, he felt, produced a serious weakening of the moral structure of the Jewish people.[15]

The cultivation of a sense of Jewishness was climaxed in 1913 with a week-long "Jews of Many Lands" exposition, deliberately timed to coincide with the convention of the Union of American Hebrew Congregations, the central body of Reform Judaism. The event was organized and sponsored by German Jews but was put on with the co-operation of the Jews of the West End, including the city's "Oriental" or "Turkish" Jews. It was a spectacular show. For a week the participants presented music, readings, speeches, art exhibits, and tableaux and displayed 512 objects representing historical aspects of Jewish life in various lands. The object was to demonstrate that people might be different in things external but alike in sensibilities, and that "difference does not mean inferiority." [16]

This organized expression of the social workers' "Jewishness" provided a striking example of the way in which the attempt to discipline the ghetto had imposed new attitudes and behavior on the Hilltop philanthropists. The discovery of the Circle Russians had revitalized the dormant ideal or historic myth of the holy community among the German Jews. Paradoxically, this represented a sharp deviation from the uphill path of ultimate assimilation into the Hilltop community of sectarian equality which they had traveled throughout the nineteenth century.[17]

Yet it did not precipitate a religious crisis among Reform Jews. The leaders of the faith had, in fact, been keeping pace with the emergence of the new Jewish urban gospel. Philipson, who had wanted to go even further with reform in the 1880's and 1890's than Wise, confided to his journal in 1905 that although Reform Judaism stressed religious teaching against national, judicial, and legal elements, it recognized that Judaism is religion, historical development, and tradition "in the sense of historic consciousness of Israel." [18]

But Philipson had not retreated into sectarian, communal seclusion. Reform Judaism, he asserted, was "selected by Providence to be 'the light of the nations;' it is the genius of religion." And one of the obligations of that genius, he felt, was to create a solid, citywide phalanx of civic righteousness for lofty purposes and principles.[19]

Philipson, in his drive to make Reform Judaism the light of Cincinnati, had an ally in Kaufman Kohler, the president of Hebrew Union College. In 1911 Kohler delivered a succinct expression of his expansive version of the Jewish urban gospel. Hebrew Union College, he asserted, was creating a new type of rabbi whose vocation was to promote the personal, moral, and spiritual welfare of old and young, of members of his flock and strangers. He should manifest a deep concern in all community interests and "bring out in clear, ringing notes the message of Judaism to our age, the message of *social justice* . . . Judaism's teaching for high and low, for rich and for poor, for Jew and Gentile." [20]

Between 1880 and 1914 the German Jews of Cincinnati had found their way to the Hilltops without abandoning the Circle. By virtue of the effort to discipline the ghetto in the requirements of life in the new city, they arrived at a new concept of community. With it they broadened and deepened their philanthropy and enlisted in the drive for political democracy and expanded city and state governments. In the process they brought a sense of Jewishness to their religion while avoiding narrow sectarianism and a segregating sense of Jewish nationalism.

The city's Catholics, for similar reasons, arrived at a similar destination. In the late nineteenth century, under Archbishop William Henry Elder, Cincinnati Catholicism was in a deep crisis. Throughout Elder's tenure there were at least two churches in Cincinnati. One, attended by Germans and centered on the Zone-Circle border, not only held services in German but also supported societies, charities, and cemeteries exclusively for Germans. Although the number of German congregations declined with the passage of time, as late as 1897 two parishes listed themselves in the Cincinnati directory as German Catholic rather than Roman Catholic.[21]

For the most ardent Germans, neighborhood and religious separatism represented the safest strategy for Catholicism in the new city. Their chief spokesman, the Reverend Anton Walburg, a native American of German descent, strongly opposed overt attempts to urbanize and Americanize German Catholics by helping them adjust to life in the highly mobile new city. Indeed, in 1889 he declared that English-speaking Catholicism could not survive in an American culture which he described as a "hotbed of fanaticism, intolerance, and radical ultra-views on matters of politics and religion. All the vagaries of spiritualism, mormonism, free-lovism, prohibition, infidelity, and materialism generally breed in the American nationality," he argued.[22] To escape contamination Catholics would have to remain aloof and cling to the security of the presumably homogeneous neighborhood parish.

Owen Smith, the editor of the *Catholic-Telegraph* until 1890, spoke for the "other" church. A Hilltop resident, he exhibited a breezy confidence about the future of his religion in Cincinnati and felt that it stood on the threshold of acceptance as just another sect in a city of sects which shared common aspirations, political ideals, and modes of life. Public schools, he argued, posed no serious threat to the perpetuation of the faith, and the nationality problem within the church would fade under the benign influences af assimilation. He hoped that eventually all "strayed sects" would return to the church, but he urged that, for the time being, all true believers put up an increasingly united front against the "indifferentists and skeptics, blasphemous and pronounced infidels." [23]

Elder tried to bridge the chasm between Walburg's German isolationism and the Americanist assimilationism of Smith. He wanted to create a distinctive and united Catholic culture which would resemble the predominant Protestant society enough to foster peaceful coexistence without, however, acquiring the evil traits which Walburg attributed to the American environment. The result was a stress on loyalty to the church hierarchy and the vision of an enduring and united Catholic social structure, moderate reform in politics, and a "puritanic" sense of public morality.

One of Elder's first steps was to institute administrative reforms to bring all parishes and charities more directly under his supervision, which would weaken the autonomy of the parish priests. The two diocesan synods and two provincial councils held during his tenure, moreover, sketched out a code of satisfactory behavior for clergy and laymen. Among other things, they banned choirs from religious services, inveighed strongly against blasphemy and intemperance, and established rules for the conduct and encouragement of Catholic societies. In addition, Elder warned against raising funds for charities by holding picnics, excursions, and other entertainments at which "late hours, round dances, and other excesses have prevailed." [24]

In 1895, however, he vigorously supported the Papal ban on Catholic membership in certain secret societies such as the Knights of Pythias, Odd Fellows, and Sons of Temperance, which attracted young men seeking economic security and social respectability. But this was not a reversion to Walburgian isolation. According to the *Catholic-Telegraph*, these groups were neither inherently evil nor overtly anti-Catholic. They advocated, however, "a sort of religion of their own" through which weak Catholics might be led from the church. The rule did not apply to other fraternal or civic associations. Indeed, the church worked so closely with the Knights of Labor that it was frequently charged that the two institutions were in league to take over the country. And the archdiocesan council of 1882 issued a proclamation recognizing the right of workers to form voluntary unions.[25] Elder clearly did not want Catholics completely cut off from the city's mushrooming nonsectarian organizational life.

Yet all this was only part of Elder's vision of the new urban gospel for Catholics. He revealed more of it in an 1898 proclamation on Cincinnati's moral and spiritual needs. The press, he claimed, was corrupt because it reported dishonorable and immoral acts and it badly needed "reformation." Elder also urged the reformation of saloons through the enforcement of laws regulating the hours and days of operation. He condemned the promiscuous sale of alcoholic beverages to children and to the man whose drinking hurt his family. Legislation was needed, moreover, to forbid "accessory attractions" in saloons and to limit their size to one room fully visible from the street. He emphasized, too, the suppression of "immodest theatres," particularly the cheap ones, to which children had easy access, and of "sensational posters" which depicted crimes and scenes of drunkenness and vulgarity. And if a fear of God, he claimed, had more influence on legislators and voters, it would purify the city. At least, he added, "as far as human enactments are capable of doing." [26]

Elder was succeeded in 1904 by Henry Moeller. The first German archbishop in Cincinnati, he nonetheless followed the policies laid down by Elder.[27] Moeller made his chief contribution to the goal of creating a united Catholic culture which would be neither isolationist nor assimilationist by stressing the importance of parochial education. As a result, Cincinnati, although not among the country's twenty largest archdioceses, ranked among the highest in the number of children enrolled in parochial schools.

Some observers expressed surprise, then, when a 1911 pastoral letter announced that First Holy Communion would be permitted at age seven rather than at twelve or thirteen, thus abrogating a rule which had led parents to send children to church schools in order to complete their religious education. Although Moeller followed this announcement with a warning to parents that it was "a matter for confession" if they sent their children to a non-Catholic school,[28] the new rule represented a concession to the Catholics of the Zone and Circle tempted by the economies of the public school.

The cautious program of Elder and Moeller indicated the difficulties facing a hierarchy working within an institution which cut across Circle, Zone, and Hilltop boundaries. The *Catholic-Telegraph*, a lay paper approved but not controlled by the hierarchy, was not caught in this web. Although the paper was generally a strong supporter of the archbishop, its policy shifted with each change of editor. In 1897 Thomas P. Hart, a physician and, in his words, "a Catholic, an Irishman and a Democrat," replaced a German as editor of the paper. He became one of the most capable and progressive Catholic editors in the country.[29]

Hart accepted and elaborated the urban strategy outlined by the archbishops, particularly their emphasis on building up Catholic societies and improving and solidifying Catholic family life to prevent "leakage." But more bluntly than they, he addressed himself to the shortcomings of Hilltop Catholics, the would-be gentle folk who moved in the tolerant society of the suburban fringe. They were generally found among social climbers, Hart explained, and they imagined themselves so cultured that they looked down upon the Catholic newspapers, and they refused to subscribe, because they feared their circle would look down upon them.[30]

In the final analysis, it was the Circle which united Cincinnati Catholicism and prevented it from becoming isolated from the city. Hart told his readers to face the fact that there was a tremendous need for social work in the congested districts of the city and to realize that when the people needing it were Italians, Hungarians, Poles, Syrians, and Roumanians, they were almost certain to be Catholics. And Ernest F. DuBrul, one of the city's leading manufacturers, pointed out that his generation possessed a unique opportunity, for "among our fellow Catholics we find the poorest, most degraded, most ignorant citizens that this country is blessed with." Little was being done, he asserted, because fortunate, educated lay Catholics had "shirked their work" and shifted their responsibility to the clergy.[31]

Others, apparently, agreed. After the mid-1890's charitable projects and philanthropic social-work agencies multiplied rapidly, and older institutions began to bring themselves up to date. The Society of St. Vincent DePaul revived and expanded its operations; a Catholic settlement house, the Santa Maria Institute, was established and put on a sound footing; boys' clubs—including one patterned after the YMCA—boomed; federations of Catholic men and women developed and entered the burgeoning reform movement; Big Sisters' and Big Brothers' groups took up the fight against juvenile delinquency; an institutional church which provided a variety of social services was established for the city's Negro Catholics. All of these ventures were originated, financed, manned, and supported by Catholics from the periphery, primarily Hilltop residents.

In an analysis of Cincinnati's Catholic Charities in 1926, the Reverend John O'Grady noted that little emphasis had been placed on preserving home life before the appearance of the new Catholic philanthropy. But that was not all. The same development, O'Grady noted, also began to break down parish provincialism and, for the first time, gave the laity a chance to participate on a community-wide basis in Catholic charitable work.[32]

These changes culminated in 1913 with the organization of the Bureau of Catholic Charities. The bureau assumed that the parish was no longer a self-sufficient unit to care for the poor in their homes and recognized that in modern life the volunteer needed the aid of full-time trained workers to deal effectively with the problems of the poor and needy.[33]

The bureau became, by 1916, a well-established organization.

The Community Chest helped it overcome its financial problem, one of the first fruits of the church's movement away from denominational isolationism, and it planned to pool all money collected for charity so that "the burden would be equally proportioned and greater and more beneficent relief given." It was helping the Vincentians extend their work into new territory and acting as a clearing house for them through its Central Wardrobe and Waste Collection Bureau. It had established an employment bureau, taken over the juvenile court work from the Federation of Catholic Societies, and organized a children's department to place youths in Catholic homes and regulate the intake and discharge of children from the various Catholic orphanages. In 1916, moreover, the bureau distributed relief to 254 individuals, 31 of them American, 15 Hungarian, 71 German, 14 Italian, and 123 Irish. And in November of the same year it sponsored a course of lectures on social work because it considered the awakening of interest in social work among Catholics necessary.[34]

The emergence of a new approach to Catholic charity, by attempting to re-educate both the giver and the receiver, coincided with and constituted a part of a broader strategy. It was designed to build up a Catholic social structure based upon a commonly held Catholicism which would encompass all the nationality, racial, and occupational groups of the Circle, Zone, and Hilltops, and at the same time conform to the social and political standards of behavior being worked out by non-Catholic reformers. The new Catholicity preserved a reverence for the truths of the church. But it also placed a heavy emphasis on the service it performed for its adherents and on what it could do for the individual, society, and the new city. Stressing coexistence and co-operation with the "American" reformer, whether Protestant or German Jew, and imitating and adapting his methods, the new Catholic urban gospel became increasingly responsive to its environment and moved a step toward, without wholeheartedly embracing, the emerging urban "nondenominationalism" which sought to cut across all theological lines.[35]

Protestants had formulated this new ideal, which had begun to take shape in the mid-nineties. During the depression winter of 1893 and 1894, an interdenominational committee of Protestant ministers supervised the distribution of private relief. Warmed by the fellowship which the work inspired, they decided to form an organization to perpetuate this fraternalism. In March of 1894 they invited a number of ministers, varying in theology from rock-ribbed fundamentalists to "extreme liberals," to join the Catholic Club.

The group, later rechristened the Clergy Club, took for its motto "out of many one." According to one member, the club was the product of a new unity of spirit based upon a new faith which expressed itself in deeds rather than creeds. These deeds took many forms, including the founding of Christian philanthropic associations and institutional churches, and participation in civic charities, municipal reforms, and educational movements, and it also contributed to the promotion of fellowship. The Clergy Club was, he concluded, an "expression of the Christian spirit of our time." [36]

Yet as the new Protestant urban gospel emerged, it became clear that its leading advocates were seeking a religion broad enough to encompass all the groups in the city. Like their Catholic and German Jewish counterparts, most of the leaders of the new Protestant urban gospel came from the Hilltops and were preoccupied with and stimulated to act by conditions in the Circle. And they, too, responded with a burst of philanthropic and social work. Scarcely a religious institution in the city remained unscathed by the new interest. The Protestant urban gospellers, too, characteristically defined their objectives primarily in the language of reform boosterism, not in that of religion.

The development of the Cincinnati Union Bethel illustrates how broadly the Protestants cast their nets. Until 1900 it had been a missionary center for boatmen on the Ohio River, and emphasis was placed upon evangelical endeavors.[37] At the turn of the century, however, the institution set off on a new course, welcoming modern methods and seeking co-operation of people without regard to religious or party affiliation.[38] By 1910 it had been converted into a full-fledged settlement house, recruiting clients without regard to their religious background and providing services devoid of sectarian or denominational content.

Mr. and Mrs. Charles P. Taft, steadfastly refusing to move out of what remained of the fashionable East End, provided much of the money. But they did not bear the burden alone. Most of the contributors to the new Bethel were old family Protestant Anglo-Saxons, many of whom had lived in the neighborhood during its grander days. Some half-dozen German Jews also made substantial regular donations. The number of German Gentile contributors was relatively low compared with their representation in the city's total population, but this figure swelled disproportionately as the years passed.[39]

Spokesmen for the new Bethel described its goal precisely. One complained that the worst evil of modern city life in a democracy was the people's separation into classes, but he felt that the settlement was "a mediator of this separateness." Bethel had, in short, accepted the theory and practice of the most scientific and progressive philanthropy. And, like other settlements, it would "beneficially react upon all ranks and orders of people," "counteract mutual antagonism," "do away with class hatred," and "economize the intellectual and moral force of every community." He assured contributors, residents and volunteers alike, that they were enriching the city by creating good citizens, while insuring their own lives and safety and increasing the worth of their estates. The ultimate aim, he concluded, was not merely to relieve immediate wants, or even to better the outward conditions of life, but "to better the quality and increase the quantity of life, which shall be utilized for the happiness of each and all." [40]

Other familiar Protestant institutions went through a similar experience. In the mid-eighties Josiah Strong reorganized the Evangelical Alliance, a city-wide federation of Protestant clergymen. It dropped out of public view in the 1890's but, under the prodding of the Reverend John Howard Melish, it re-emerged in an aggressive mood after the turn of the century. Melish, a young Episcopalian minister, asserted that "civic patriotism" had been crushed by the Cox machine and that this constituted a serious moral problem.

Because of this, young men of ability and leadership lost their faith in democratic government and devoted themselves to a system of boss rule "which in their souls they hate." It was time, he argued, for clergymen to throw off the notion that preachers should keep silent about city government lest they offend parishioners.

In the spring of 1903, the Evangelical Alliance heeded Melish and endorsed the Citizens' ticket. A Citizens' victory, it announced, would be a rebuke to the alliance of the present administration with the corrupt elements of our city—an administration which had protected unsavory elements and encouraged the forces of lawlessness. The reform mayoralty candidate, if elected, would encourage virtue, diminish temptations, and guard the virtue and innocence of children. And he would administer affairs in a wise, efficient, and economic way.[41]

The city's four Protestant institutional churches also sought to influence a wide and diverse audience. Open to all who might come in, they, too, stressed a vaguely religious gospel of citizenship. As Frank Nelson, pastor at the East End's elaborately equipped Christ Church Parish House, put it, the "church is not here for its own sake. It is here to bear witness, and to spread a spirit. It should be the center from which radiates the forces of righteousness and the spirit of brotherhood . . . and interest in the community." [42]

Nor was this message reserved for Circle audiences or saved for appropriate political occasions. Several Hilltop ministers actively proselytized for the cause. The pastor of the Avondale Presbyterian Church warned that Cincinnati, like other cities, might soon share the reputation, if not the fate, of Sodom and Gomorrah, a crisis brought on by a serious shortage of "philopolism," or municipal love, the spirit which creates the beautiful city. Living in the suburbs did not excuse one from obligation. "Kneel down upon your knees," he commanded the businessmen of the suburban fringe, "and let the city Knight you!" [43]

The fullest expression of the new Protestant urban gospel, however, was the People's Church movement. Cincinnati had two, but clearly the most influential was that which grew out of the fashionable Congregational Church on Vine Street. As early as 1889, when there was a tendency among the churches to move toward the hills, much of its membership had already moved to the suburbs.[44] The church, however, remained on Vine Street.

In 1896 a new minister, Herbert Seely Bigelow, was elected to the pulpit. An Indiana farm boy who had been educated in Ohio, Bigelow was no stranger to the Circle. As a student at Lane Theological Seminary, he and his wife, a physician, had worked in a settlement house in the lower East End, and Bigelow had been an assistant to his predecessor at the Vine Street church.

Bigelow immediately ran into trouble with part of the congregation. Some accused him of preaching "unitarian principles." A disciple of William Jennings Bryan and a convert to Henry George's single-tax idea, Bigelow also offended those who regarded the institution as a "Republican Church" by insisting on his right to preach on social and economic questions. He aroused more dissatisfaction in 1897 when he tried to admit to membership a Negro who had been converted by Dwight Moody. In 1899 those whom Bigelow had offended seceded.[45]

The new governing board, elected under a proportional representation system, revamped the Vine Street church. They substituted discussions of economic and social problems for Sunday and Wednesday prayer meetings. Communion was dropped. They also redecorated the interior, inscribing on the walls quotations from Jefferson, Lowell, Lincoln, Henry George, Tolstoi, and Ruskin. Included among these was a lonely biblical maxim. "Ye shall know the truth and the truth shall make ye free."

The new church attracted a diverse group of followers. Unskilled white laborers and a few Negroes from the riverfront lodging houses came to the programs and discussions. So, too, did a good many union people, clerks from stores and small businesses, and tradesmen. A few Catholics as well as some Jews, none of whom were prominent, also participated.[46]

The leaders of the church also came from disparate backgrounds. One board member was a saddler, and two were white-collar workers. A member of the ironworkers' union and a staff writer for the *Times-Star* also participated. Fenton Lawson, president of the

Lawson Company, a Swedenborgian single-taxer and the only Democrat in his family, lent his aid.[47] And Bigelow's right-hand man in religious and public affairs was Daniel Kiefer, a retired German Jewish clothing retailer, a member of the United States Proportional Representation League, and chairman of the board of commissioners of the Fels Foundation, a single-tax organization.[48]

The church asked its members to hold but one article of faith, the belief that the great work of mankind and of organized religion was to aid in the establishment of the brotherhood of man in a world of social justice. It left theology and philosophy to the individual. According to the People's Church, one's religious duty was to strive for a just social order.[49]

Bigelow, moreover, taught this doctrine in language calculated to make the broadest possible appeal. The devil, he explained, was a pessimist and a hopeless reactionary, but God was a progressive who had implanted in men the desire for perfection and wanted his children to march ever forward. Bigelow exhorted Cincinnatians to make the city a sanctuary for the service of men and the worship of God. The standing order for all mankind, he believed, was "On to the City of God." [50]

To help make this vision a reality the church presented a series of free lectures beginning in the fall of 1907. The most optimistic supporters of this project wanted to make it a downtown people's college for training people to extend democracy and abolish "all forms of social privilege." Since unity, system, and continuity were considered the characteristics of the machine, Bigelow's band of reformers hoped that the college would gradually develop these three essentials for municipal reform. Convinced, too, that the city could not be regenerated by the efforts of businessmen or the men of the cultured classes alone, the founders of the college hoped to produce leaders personally acquainted with the Circle and Zone, who would assist in the broad movement for "civic righteousness." Participation in this work, Bigelow hoped, would "fire the hearts of the masses with a passionate love for their own city." [51]

The new Protestant urban gospel, a mixture of boosterism, enlightened philanthropy, and political sociology masked by a vague religiosity was designed to uplift the Circle, arouse the Zone, and inspire the Hilltops—to re-educate and unite the new city. In this respect it differed little from the Catholic and German Jewish strategies.

Yet it was, at bottom, more aggressive. Regarding divisive sectarian, denominational, and theological questions as irrelevant, it sought to cut across the class, ethnic, and racial lines which divided Cincinnati and to create a monolithic urban Utopia based on the religion of reform. By 1914, however, Jewishness had been rediscovered and the Elder-Walburg compromise was intact, and neither the Catholics nor German Jews were prepared to espouse completely the Protestant urban gospel. They preferred, instead, co-operation in "philopolism" and maintenance of a triple melting pot.

9

The New Philanthropy:
The Gospel of Efficiency

Although much of the reform impulse evoked by the urban expansion and disorder of the late nineteenth and early twentieth century received expression through religious activities, many preferred to operate entirely unfettered by religious boundaries. Most of the philanthropists cut across racial and ethnic divisions as well. They had to be free of all unnecessary, outmoded, or artificial restraints, they felt, if they were to control their new expansive and fluid urban environment. The expert was their hero, efficiency with justice and democracy their passion. And they proved adept at winning broad support for their causes.

Of all the nondenominational philanthropic innovations between 1880 and 1914, the Associated Charities of Cincinnati best reflects the interplay of these factors. Organized in 1879, the new charity had its beginnings in meetings of the Young Women's Christian Association. After comparing the good done and the permanent relief afforded to the outlay of money, time, and sympathy, several YWCA members concluded that a co-operative plan was needed. Only then could the work be done efficiently and thoroughly with little waste and demoralization.[1]

After studying the systems in Philadelphia, Buffalo, New York, and London, the YWCA group and others they had interested in the project set up an organization which included clergy and laymen, Protestants, and Reform Jews, and officials of private and city institutions on its board of directors. The public officials were predominantly Zone residents and frequently Catholic.[2] From the outset, then, the Associated Charities was nondenominational. Had it not excluded Circle inhabitants from its directing officials it would have constituted a community-wide organization concerned with broad governmental reform and social control.

Paradoxically, most of the families to which it tendered aid were Roman Catholic and lived in the Circle. In 1900, for example, it helped 806 Catholic, 733 Protestant, and 12 "Hebrew" families, 162 that indicated no religious affiliation, and 215 others which were listed under "church not known." In 1910, 4 per cent of the families aided were Negroes, a proportion which remained constant to 1914, and the breakdown by nationality revealed that most of the families aided were "native white Americans."[3]

From the beginning the Associated Charities emphasized the efficiency of its new system. It directed those who criticized the cost of its paid staff and bureaucratic procedures to note that the same principles were being applied in the business world, and explained that one of the Associated Charities' chief aims was to serve as an intermediary between existing charity and the poor. It offered relief applicants centrally located bureaus where they could explain their needs, undergo the "thorough investigation every honest applicant wants," and receive advice about the existing sources of relief and assistance to obtain it. They were to be referred to employment whenever practical and made self-supporting as soon as possible.[4]

Indeed, the Associated Charities was an educational agency in the broadest sense, a self-conscious instrument of social control. In 1892 it asserted that its work was that of progressive education and development of the city, leading to "higher thoughts, stronger sympathies, and better methods." And thirteen years later, an enthusiastic veteran volunteer claimed that one of its major achievements had been the education alike of those active in the society and of the public.[5]

Professional and institutional advocates of the gospel of efficiency were moving in the same direction. Their task, however, was to broaden the scope of their professions and institutions.

In 1911, Dr. Paul G. Woolley, dean of the University of Cincinnati Medical College, told the City Club that doctors and social workers ought to co-operate for the ideals of health and the extermination of diseases. The physician, he claimed, looking for the cause of illness, found vice, ignorance, overcrowding, sweatshops, and poverty. At the same time, the social worker, investigating the reasons for the troubles of a family or its children discovered poor nutrition, bad air, alcoholism, tuberculosis, and industrial injuries. It seemed obvious to Dr. Woolley that co-operation of doctors and social workers was necessary.

Such teamwork, he announced, now existed on an organized basis in the newly founded Hospital Social Service Association. Underlying the service was the concept of the connection of the mental and physical, a concept which had grown along with modern psychology. Behind physical suffering, the theory ran, lay the anxiety created by the stress of life. To combat this, the service helped resolve the most pressing personal problems of the client, instructing the family in hygienic measures and helping him to find a job after he recovered.

Hospital Social Service, Woolley explained, paid dividends to the community. It reduced the expenses of the city hospital by cutting the readmission rate and protected the city against chronic invalidism and the spread of contagion. And by reuniting families upon a basis of economic independence, it prevented many additions to the relief rolls. Most important, it restored to society efficient individuals with a keener sense of social responsibility who would bear their share of civic and social burdens.[6]

Indeed, physicians felt they had good advice for politicians as well as for social workers and businessmen. The Cincinnati medical profession had been actively participating in the democratic process as an organized faction for some time. Beginning in the 1880's and 1890's most of the city's medical associations—some geographically based and others organized by specialties—gradually merged into the community-wide Cincinnati Academy of Medicine. From the outset, the academy agitated for legislation to raise professional standards. But it also entered crusades to protect the health of the city. In the 1890's, for example, the academy had conducted an investigation of the water supply, found it polluted, and joined the civic associations in securing the passage of the Cincinnati Water Works Act of 1896. The academy also supported state legislation to prohibit the "slop feeding" of milk cows. And, in 1909, it demanded, and obtained, an autonomous board of health separate from the board of public service.

By 1911 the organization was conducting a public education campaign on a broad range of civic topics. The academy arranged for its members to give public talks all over the city on tuberculosis, parks and playgrounds, school medical inspection, sewage disposal, social service, quacks and nostrums, medical charities, smoke and dust, public health, "social evils," milk and food inspection, and blindness.[7]

Leading members of the profession were instrumental in the fight for the construction of a new, centralized city hospital in Avondale. The chief advocate of the project, and the man largely responsible for winning over both the academy members and other influential individuals in the repeated bond-issue battles, was Dr. Christian R. Holmes, a Danish immigrant who had received his medical education in Cincinnati.

Opposition to the proposal was composed of a strong network of allies centered in the Zone. Backers of the old charity hospital and doctor's hospital ideas joined with the proponents of economical local government against Holmes. Others, including some labor leaders and Fred Tuke of the Taxpayers' Association, rallied to Dr. John M. Withrow, who wanted a new medical center but preferred a Basin or West End site close to the current business, commercial, and industrial districts, and close to the homes of the workers and the poor. And George B. Cox, apparently persuaded by one or several of these objections, at first refused to support the project. "If Doctor Holmes wishes to build a monument to himself," Cox reportedly asked, "why does he not choose Spring Grove [Cemetery]?"

Nonetheless, the new hospital was built, and very much the way Holmes had planned it. His victory was due, in large part, to his success in putting together a broadly based coalition. Holmes was fortunate in having extensive personal connections with socially prominent and politically influential individuals. To this diverse crowd he added the support of the Central Labor Council, most of the women's and businessmen's civic organizations, and the *Freie Presse*. Time and again this coalition organized down to the precinct level to carry bond issues.[8]

By 1913 the medical profession had gained a reputation as a potent force for reform. The *Post* pointed out that the medical schools were turning out doctors with a passion for social service who were "so keen on preventing disease that they are actually working themselves out of fees." Other professions, too, claimed the *Post,* systematically produced reformers. The paper noted that the theological seminaries were producing young ministers who were more concerned with human rights than with their own comforts.

It could not, however, say the same of the legal profession. Why, one editorial asked, did not law schools send their students into factories, workshops, and prisons to study the workings of economic and social legislation at first hand? Clearly, the *Post* thought, something was wrong with the profession, for the bar, as a group, had been far more subservient to Cox than had the general public.[9]

Indeed, the profession had not compiled a noteworthy reform record. It contributed only the Legal Aid Society to the burgeoning list of new organizations working in the Circle. And although the Hamilton County Bar Association sporadically endorsed candidates for the bench, its recommendations usually ignited bitter partisan feuds, even after the adoption, in 1911, of a nonpartisan judicial ballot.[10]

Reformers in the legal profession were not sure what had brought about this sad state of affairs. Many thought that the profession's close ties to politics made it too easy an avenue of social mobility. One lawyer stated that many of his colleagues "were intended by God to be hod-carriers, [but] the weakness and vanity of indulgent parents directed them from an employment where they could have been useful to a profession in which they are worthless." The excess spilled over into public life, he complained, creating a polluting flow of poorly qualified politicians and civil servants.[11]

Some observers also felt that Cincinnati's educators, like its lawyers, had neglected their obligation as experts to meet the challenge of the urban explosion. But a new movement was emerging. The Teachers' Club, for instance, had been organized in 1893 for social purposes as well as for the provision of a forum for distinguished educators. At its meetings the club discussed teaching methods and the need for courses in mental and physical hygiene and civics. Similarly, the Mathesis, an association of women teachers founded in 1894, held a monthly session on methods. And the Cincinnati Schoolmasters' Club, founded in 1910, sought to enlighten both the public and teachers on new trends in education.[12]

These reform-minded educators were reinforced by a host of allies. Mothers' clubs, the Central Labor Council, and business- and professional men and women from the Zone and Hilltops all blasted the shortcomings of the schools. One citizen, appalled by the Cincinnati Board of Education exhibit at the St. Louis Exposition of 1904, wrote that after he had seen the magnificent exhibits of several other cities, he was pained and humiliated to think of what they were doing that Cincinnati left undone.[13]

Superintendent of Schools F. B. Dyer gave the crisis an even more ominous meaning. He argued that the public schools had too long overlooked the home and environment and had mistakenly tried to contain education within the walls of a school building. Teachers, he claimed, ought to become social workers who provide education for Circle parents as well as for children. And if more citizens had visited some of the so-called homes in the Circle, he observed, they would have recognized that slum conditions had to be eradicated before any kind of education could be effective. He hoped to convince Zone and Hilltop dwellers that "race homicide is the trouble in the basin."

Dyer thought, moreover, that the drop-out problem endangered the whole community. Because an estimated one-half of all students failed to finish the fifth grade, "the majority of our people remain practically illiterate [and] form a vast proletariat whose rule is king mob, the legitimate prey of the snolly gaster in politics and the bunco steerer in business." Anarchy, rather than revolution, was the likely result. The illiterate proletarians took menial jobs, soon outgrew their positions, but were fitted for nothing better. For them, "the next step is to loafing and vice, and the next to crime." [14]

The campaign to improve the city's school system produced what was called an educational renaissance. It began in 1904, and by 1913 the new education, a system which sought to enable adults as well as children to cope with the new urban situation, was already established in Cincinnati. The transformation of the public schools, moreover, was achieved under the large board system, a perennial target of the educational reformers, during the superintendency of F. B. Dyer. His success was due in large part to the leadership provided by a handful of board members, four from the Hilltops and one from the outer Zone.

These school reformers undertook a huge building program. Within four years, the board had provided twenty-five new heating plants, installed electric lights and new plumbing in thirty-seven buildings, and added eighteen gymnasiums, eighteen auditoriums, and twenty-one fire escapes. By 1915, moreover, at a cost of some $5,750,000, thirty new buildings had been constructed.[15]

The curriculum was revised to furnish an education to "all the children of all the people, in order to prepare them for service in the community." In 1905 kindergartens were introduced as one means of socializing the work of the school, "making every teacher a social worker." In 1907 summer-vacation schools, actually recreation centers, were opened to those children from homes in closely congested districts. The following year the board offered summer classes in academic subjects for students who wanted to make up work or skip a grade. And in 1909, the Continuation School, a supplement to the manual training and domestic-science classes introduced on a regular basis in 1905, began operation. This project permitted working boys who had dropped out of school to continue, at their employer's expense and with his approval, their secondary education.[16]

A program of special treatment for special cases was rigorously followed. A system of medical and dental inspection was inaugurated, and in 1912 eight school nurses began work at twenty-eight schools in the center of the city. Courses were set up for the deaf, blind, and "mentally defective." Immigrants were given English instruction and then integrated into a grade level commensurate with their previous educational achievement. Two fresh-air schools, one for consumptives and one for anemics, were opened. And penny lunches, first introduced by volunteer women, were taken over by the school board. Available only in Circle schools, the menu included Kosher meat and "Catholic soup" on Friday.[17]

To complete the process of developing a new discipline in the youth of the city, special courses in civics were introduced. These classes devoted much attention to the family and its benefits for the individual and the community and stressed the advantages of home ownership. Other topics emphasized were health protection, civic beauty, the delinquency problem, local government, taxation, and the public. All the while, civics teachers worked to "help the child realize that he is a responsible and helpful member of several groups, [and to] awaken and stimulate motives that will lead to the establishment of habits of order, cleanliness, cheerful co-operation, sympathetic service, and obedience to law." Children were also taught the history of Cincinnati and reminded of the dubious but grim idea that until the last century no city had perpetuated itself.[18]

The new educators also reached out for adults. The free courses given at night in high schools, begun in 1893 on an academic basis, were reorganized in 1904 to include commercial and vocational instruction. In addition, under the new arrangement the schools in the center of the city offered the English language "to fifteen nations."[19]

Little else was done, however, until 1909 when the school social center was introduced. Randall J. Condon, who became superintendent after Dyer resigned in 1913, thought the school center was necessary because the great danger in a democracy was in preventing people from expressing their ideas. The best place to bring people together for these discussions, he thought, was in their children's schools.[20]

Cincinnati's educational renaissance climaxed with the creation of "the university of the city," the phrase of Charles W. Dabney. A Virginian and former president of the University of Tennessee, Dabney came to the city in 1904 to revive the University of Cincinnati. Before accepting the presidency, however, Dabney paid a visit to George B. Cox. The boss pledged not to reduce the tax support for the institution and assured Dabney that there would be no political interference in university affairs.[21]

Cox, apparently, extracted no pledges from Dabney. College graduates, Dabney declared, should uphold civic righteousness against the hosts of corruption. "We hear a great deal these days," he told the City Club, "about efficiency—the getting of the greatest efficiency in transportation, selling, marketing and living," but what was really needed was "political efficiency—social efficiency." Cincinnati needed, he argued, a social conscience and a unity of spirit. And with Cincinnati's public schools and its university, why should it not have that spirit? He offered a motto: "Progressive Cincinnati; Why not?" [22]

Dabney believed the university had a natural role to play in making the new city. Historically, he claimed, the democracy had educated itself first through the common school and then through the high school and the state university. Now, with the development of the great cities, must come municipal universities. According to Dabney, this new university was to search for truth and teach the truth to all men and would recognize no boundaries to its field and no classes among its students. It stood for the democracy of knowledge. The "university of the city, as distinguished from the university in the city, should be not a mere co-ordinate organ among the many in the social body, but the brain, directing all the other organs" through "a broad, liberal policy of co-operation with all the educational, social, and industrial interests of Cincinnati." [23]

The university, supported by taxes, gifts, and endowments, neither a public nor a private institution, was to educate and uplift the whole city, to become a settlement house for all of Cincinnati. The new administration introduced evening classes in liberal arts and commerce and established a college of commerce. The Ohio and Miami medical colleges merged, affiliated with the university and co-ordinated instruction with the city hospital. A graduate school, too, was officially established and dedicated. A separate college of teachers was established in 1905, controlled jointly by the university and the Cincinnati Board of Education, to replace the haphazard system of pedagogical courses begun in 1900. The new school offered programs of professional study using the kindergarten training school, the art academy, and the public schools as training grounds, providing on-the-job experience for teaching candidates.[24]

Similarly, in 1906, the engineering school instituted Dean Herman Schneider's co-operative program. Under this scheme co-op students spent part of their time working in factories or on construction projects. Others studied "municipal engineering." They surveyed the streets for the city and charted the kinds of pavement used. Aspiring chemists and engineers ran qualitative tests for the board of public service through the new Bureau of City Tests, established in the engineering department in 1913 by city council.[25]

Other departments began to co-operate with the various branches of city government. Medical students spent part of their junior year in active service with the board of health, "following," as a critic put it, "fruit, meat and garbage inspectors in lieu of professors." And, in 1913, the political science department organized the Municipal Reference Bureau. The service, quartered in City Hall, was designed as a central library to assist councilmen, administrators, and the general public as well as students. Dabney hoped eventually to establish a chair of municipal affairs to supply urban specialists to meet all the increasingly complex problems of city government.[26]

In 1912 the university rounded out its program to make Cincinnati progressive by opening its first course in "philanthropy and sociology." In keeping with Dabney's preference for practical instruction, the teachers were recruited from city institutions and private social-work agencies.[27]

Dabney, too, wanted the university settlement to become part of his university of the city. Although consistent and total financial and administrative affiliations between the two institutions never developed, the close relation existing since the founding of the settlement in 1899 continued. It became a partial if unofficial branch of the university[28] and played its part in Dabney's drive to make the university a producer of men and women with expertise in helping others to meet the demands of life in the new city.

The concern for finding truly qualified experts in urban affairs was not confined to the university. In 1909 members of the Commercial Club, Optimist Club, Business Men's Club, and Chamber of Commerce subscribed funds to set up a bureau of municipal research. Its board brought in R. E. Miles, formerly of the New York bureau, as director, and recruited a staff of "experts" from among political-science majors at the University of Cincinnati.

The bureau was spawned by the civic organizations' passion for facts, their confidence in the ability of experts to accumulate and interpret correctly those facts, and their faith in the competence of a properly informed and educated public to act on this information in the interest of efficient public service. The bureau, mirroring this view, saw itself as a kind of professional muckraking association. According to its first report, its work resembled that of "expert accountants who are summoned by business men to examine their accounts and point out where savings can be made or better results secured." Unfortunately, however, "many business men" deemed it advisable to spend "thousands of dollars to discover improved ways of conducting their business" but forgot that "efficient government" was one of the "best assets" a city could have.[29]

The bureau did not confine itself, however, to applying the new standards of political science and business efficiency to local government. Between 1912 and 1914 it also investigated the operation of the city's private charities. With the exception of the United Jewish Charities, the bureau found all of them, in many respects, "unbusiness-like, wasteful and inefficient." While the average cost of raising funds was 15 per cent, some agencies spent two-thirds of all money raised in solicitation campaigns. Only a negligible degree of co-operation took place between church-related and nonsectarian charitable agencies. Catholic relief was administered through separate parishes and not under a centralized bureau. Negro welfare work, "a pressing necessity," was wholly unorganized. Cincinnati charities had, "in brief, no provisions for sound financing or for constructive social effort reaching far into the future." [30]

Yet the experts in charities and philanthropies had long been concerned with these problems and were, at the time of the bureau's report, on the verge of establishing an organization which would meet these criticisms. The problem of finances, plus the desire for co-operation and a co-ordinated program of social service, directed toward constructive rather than remedial ends, finally led, in the spring of 1911, to a conference on the co-ordination of charities. Out of this meeting came yet another organization, the Central Conference of Charities and Philanthropies of Cincinnati and Hamilton County.

The conference, however, made little headway until the great flood of 1913. During that crisis it worked with the Citizens' Flood Relief Committee. At one of the joint meetings several members moved that some of the flood relief funds be provided to an association composed of representatives of all philanthropic and charitable organizations in Cincinnati, to be known as the Council of Social Agencies. The motion stipulated, moreover, that upon the dissolution of the Citizens' Flood Relief Committee all remaining funds should be turned over to the council so that it could continue the work of "social reconstruction." The new organization was formally incorporated on May 28, 1913. In June delegates from sixty institutions and associations approved a constitution which embodied, according to the council's director, "the most progressive thought available." [31]

The council, however, was more than an enlarged version of the Conference of Charities and Philanthropies. It described itself as a federation of the charitable, civic, philanthropic, and public agencies of the city. Its executive committee was composed of business- and professional men and women from the leading civic organizations—with the notable exceptions of the Taxpayers' Association and the Central Labor Council—representatives of the Catholic, Protestant, and Jewish charities, prominent philanthropists and social workers, and the mayor and city health commissioner. The Council of Social Agencies represented a confluence of the institutions and personnel developed by the new civic spirit, the urban gospel, and the new philanthropy. And the inclusion of high officials from city government suggested that the politicians had decided to recognize and co-operate with these groups in what they had called the social reconstruction of the city. [32]

The immense variety of institutions and programs launched by the civic organizations, urban gospellers, philanthropists, and experts produced clusters of men and women of diverse backgrounds who shared common interests and experiences in social and political reform, if not in techniques and specific goals. Confident of their ability to gain their ends through what they thought of as the democratic process, they defined their mission as one of organization, agitation, and education. Hilltop groups far outweighed those of the Zone in numbers, scope of activities, and influence. Speaking a new jargon which pivoted on such terms as "progressive" and "businesslike" and enamored with the word "new," they aimed to make their chaotic society "efficient," a flexible concept which they applied broadly to virtually every facet of life from family conduct to local government.

Gradually, too, the welter of groups coalesced in order to improve their effectiveness in enlisting the uprooted inhabitants of the Circle, Zone, and Hilltops in the crusade for social control. And increasingly they called for an expansion of the activities of local government to help in their quest for community, for a new urban discipline in their mobile and divided new city. At least one of the new reformers felt they had succeeded:

> No longer does one portion of the city feel itself an independent factor, for a new and more righteous vision of a city has been implanted in the public conscience. We know now of a certainty that one part of a city can not be evil, ridden by disease, unsanitary, full of dissatisfied revengeful people, underfed, underpaid, isolated and the remainder be free, happy, prosperous and healthful.[33]

IV

PERIPHERY AND CENTER: THE POLITICS OF REFORM

Coxism may again feebly rise upon its feet, but it can only totter along upon groggy legs; its fangs have been torn out by the roots.*

In their quest for community and social control in the new city, Hilltop and Zone residents had created a complex network of voluntary organizations. It became evident, however, that these groups, singly or collectively, could not bridge the city's economic, social, educational, and geographical divisions. The spokesmen for the new urban discipline, rejecting the program of the GOP new order administrations of the 1880's and 1890's as insufficient, infiltrated both major parties and created new ones, taking with them ideas, methods, and programs which had developed from their experiments in boosterism, the urban gospel, and the new philanthropy. In the process, the Cox coalition was transformed and the anti-machine men discovered a formula for destroying the foundation on which "Coxism" in Cincinnati rested.

* Theodore Horstmann in *Cincinnati Post*, May 5, 1897, p. 4.

10

The New Order Attacked, 1897–1900

In January 1897 the *Cincinnati Post* published a series of articles dispassionately explaining the city's "superior and unrecorded government." Indisputable control of this behind-the-scenes apparatus rested with "the boss, whose power is absolute," George B. Cox. Then forty-three, he stood nearly six feet tall, weighed more than two hundred pounds, and resembled a retired businessman, taciturn but convivial.

Since 1894 Cox had been scientifically adjusting his voluntary organization. Although the Blaine Club, composed chiefly of "gangworkers," presented no problem, the Lincoln Club remained unfriendly to the new leader, despite the fact that Cox had succeeded in getting one of his men on its board of directors. The Stamina League, a Republican club which had only recently become prominent, had received no special attention, but two men were to be delegated there.

The *Post* reported, too, that Cox was concerned with the social status of his organization. Within the past few years, it noted, businessmen and prominent figures had run for office on all the tickets, while the old-line politicians, to whom the term "gangster" clung, had lost a little ground. Since judgeships, though conferring distinction, carried little patronage, Cox set them aside as indirect levers to move those of the wealthier and older families, who "do not train with the boss." Some doctors, and even more lawyers, were represented. Recently some younger Jewish men, "good mixers in certain wards, notably the Seventeenth, Twenty-Sixth, Second and Thirty-First," had received special attention. In addition, merchants, manufacturers, brewers, and saloonkeepers all formed distinct groups to be watched.

The paper also dissected the patronage system which had been built up around the nonpartisan boards. In the 1890's these boards had become completely bipartisan, with appointments divided in favor of the Republicans on a 3:2 ratio, thus assuring the loyalty of the Cox Democrats, virtually all of whom came from Circle wards.

Party finances had also been systematized. Lesser office-holders were assessed, in some cases through payroll deductions, at a rate varying from 2 to 2 ½ per cent of the salary of almost every Republican employee. Clerks and heads of departments and other high-ranking officials made voluntary donations, and candidates had to pay part of their campaign expenses. City and county contractors, as well as merchants and saloonkeepers who sold to public institutions, obligingly made liberal contributions. Betting on elections, moreover, was a favorite source of revenue for ward officials who needed more than the $20 allotted by the campaign committee to meet election expenses.

Party workers, asserted the *Post,* were kept in line by a spy system. Any mention of the workings of the machine or of Cox would be transmitted to the leader. The careless talker was usually reproved, for talkativeness was recognized as dangerous. Indeed, alleged the *Post,* office-holders, businessmen, and all others having dealings with the city or county were subject to this system of espionage.[1]

Nonetheless, as the spring 1897 city elections approached, a revolt erupted in the Hilltops. Its leaders, according to one spokesman, were not typical insurgents, but businessmen, who for years had voted for a ticket they had had no part in making. It was time, they felt, to put the welfare of the city above party and politics. Most members of the Citizens' Committee were Republicans, but they had agreed that the most promising strategy would be to co-operate with the regular Democratic party and name a fusion ticket.[2]

The Democratic organization, in an unusual display of unity, concurred in this plan. On March 3 some three hundred of the most widely known Democratic businessmen and professional men decided that, in order to prevent "the Cox ring . . . the police force and the City Hall crowd" from bringing influence to bear, no primaries would be held except to elect ward officials. Those at the meeting instead picked a committee to name a ticket on the following day.[3]

That night, however, the committee met with representatives of the Citizens' Committee and the two groups agreed to divide the major offices. The men selected were officially nominated by the Democratic convention the next day—with two exceptions. The "free silver" or regular Democrats from the Circle insisted that Thomas J. Noctor, a liquor broker, be put up for police court clerk —a post which paid $15,000 to $20,000 per year in "legitimate per-quisites"—and that Gustav Tafel once again head the ticket.[4]

Tafel, using Cox as a whipping boy, tried to arouse the Hilltops and Zone. He vowed, if elected, to conduct a strictly business administration, denounced the "gangs" which "threaten our prosperity," and promised to follow the example of Mayor Josiah Quincy of Boston in appointing an unofficial cabinet to help him make the city one of the most beautiful and prosperous in the United States.[5]

The *Enquirer* also joined the movement. It accused the Cox men of conducting a reign of terror against businessmen in the fusion movement by threatening boycotts or reprisals through Cox's brother, the city purchasing agent. The paper also tried to spread the impression that a massive revolt was brewing in the Hilltop districts. It pointedly remarked, for instance, that the new Thirty-first Ward, composed of the recently annexed villages of Clifton and Avondale and normally regarded as Republican, should be watched carefully because the inhabitants, businessmen and professional men, could be counted on to consider qualifications of candidates rather than party in local elections.[6]

The German-language *Volksfreund* tried to rouse its readers in the Zone to support fusion. But it treated Cox much more gently than the *Enquirer*. It called him an amiable man who had to be admired for his success in "becoming absolute King of Cincinnati." Yet the paper disliked his "one man rule," his bossing of "the gang," and the "dictatorial methods" he had imposed upon the GOP.[7]

The *Post* was the only other fusionist paper in the city. It concentrated on the alleged extravagance and immorality of Cox and his associates. It wondered how August Herrmann could afford expensive furniture for his home, and it gave front-page coverage to an Anti-Saloon League allegation that Cox owned disorderly houses in which beer and liquor were sold illegally.[8]

A tangled morass of alliances developed around Tafel. He had, for instance, the endorsement of spokesmen for the Anti-Saloon League. At the same time, rumors persisted that the Germans would bolt Cox because they were dissatisfied with the increase in the saloon tax and because Tafel was president of the Liberal League, a federation of German societies, labor unions, and the Central Labor Council which had been fighting a local option proposal on the sale of beer and native wine.[9]

Fusionist stock also rose when the Populists decided against running a third ticket for fear that it would help only Cox and the Republicans. Some Populists saw the election as a time for deciding who would rule—property owners, taxpayers, and those with the city's interest at heart or "boodlers, corruptionists and thieves." [10] The Central Labor Council, however, maintained a neutral stance.

A handful of new leaders in the Negro community, concerned with their low status in the city, were less complacent. In March an organization known as the Colored Citizens' Labor League was set up. It demanded of both mayoralty candidates a pledge to spend from $100,000 to $500,000 on public works for the unemployed and wanted "a remedy" for the police department's refusal to accept Negro applicants.[11]

One week before the election the Douglass League affirmed its allegiance to the tenets of the Republican party, the interests of true Republicanism, and municipal reform and endorsed Tafel and the fusion slate. The statement claimed that under the present administration prejudice had grown and that all interests of Negroes had been disregarded. It attacked the superintendent of schools, charging that he refused to hire Negro teachers and opposed "mixed schools." Moreover, the league noted, the Republican mayoralty candidate had "distinguished himself by being a party to the isolation of colored from Coney Island," an amusement park on the Ohio River. And the elite of the Negro community, protested one league speaker, were tired of hearing it said that Cox could vote them like sheep.[12]

Cox appeared undismayed by the growing fusion coalition. He and his allies drew up a slate which was ratified by a city convention of six hundred delegates in just forty minutes. The platform was brief, built around a pledge to continue Republican rule on "business principles." The ticket was headed by a businessman, Levi C. Goodale, the manager of the local branch of Bradstreet's Commercial Agency and a former member of the General Assembly. After surveying the situation, at about noon on election day, Hickenlooper recorded that everything indicated complete Republican success. "Geo. B. Cox [is] betting 5 to 7" and estimating the majority as "between 5,000 and 7,000." [13]

The final returns, however, caused dismay among Republicans and astounded the General. The fusionists swept every major city office and missed gaining control of the board of legislation by only one seat. Tafel led the ticket, garnering 35,868 votes to Goodale's 28,433. The Socialist Labor party candidate received but 250 votes.[14]

Cox's recently established Hilltop-Circle alliance had been smashed. Goodale carried but three wards in the Circle: the Fifth, Mike Mullen's; the Ninth, Hynicka's; and the Eighteenth, Cox's old home grounds now managed by Lew Kraft. In the Over-the-Rhine Zone wards only the Eleventh, Herrmann's responsibility, went for Goodale. Elsewhere in the Zone he won the Fifteenth, adjacent to

the Mohawk-Brighton district, and the Twenty-fourth, Cumminsville, and in both his margin barely exceeded 70 votes. On the Hilltops, only the Twenty-seventh, Mt. Auburn, went for Goodale, and
that by only 59 votes out of a total of over 1600 cast.

Tafel carried every other Hilltop ward, all of which had gone
Republican in 1891 and 1894 and, in 1896, for McKinley. Tafel also
held all the Circle and Zone wards which had been safely Democratic in the past, except the Fifth. The revival of the Democratic
party in the Circle was due in part to an enlarged campaign fund
which provided each ward captain with $100. But the Zone and
Hilltops entered the strongest protest and proved to be the crucial
factors. The returns meant, said one Republican, that political tyranny had become galling to the "better element" of Republicans
and that bossism had to go.[15]

Cox's fortunes, indeed, began to ebb. After the defeat came a
series of scandals involving lame duck Republican officials. The
grand jury indicted the county clerk, an ally of Cox since 1891 and
a former chairman of the GOP City Campaign Committee, for the
embezzlement of some $23,464 during his tenure as county re-
corder, and the health officer was charged with blackmailing a New
York drug firm. Then the board of administration discovered that a
secretary in the water works department was short an estimated
$10,000 to $20,000 in collections. The case was given additional
spice when it was revealed that Cox was the man's bondsman.[16]

Revelations of corruption on the part of new-order officials continued throughout the spring and summer. The *Post* announced
that the board of administration purchased bricks from a syndicate
of six firms which had appointed one man to make sales for all their
street-paving brick or block products. The *Enquirer* topped that by
announcing that Hynicka, as police court clerk, made $150 to $200
per week by arresting actors performing on Sunday, collecting bail,
and then freeing them without a trial because it was impossible to
secure convictions. The same scheme, added the paper, was used
on Sunday baseball games. And in both cases Hynicka had attempted to "systematize" the operation by collecting from the man-

agement before scheduled events in order to eliminate interference with theater performances and games.[17]

The spring defeat, the scandals, and the press's lumping of Cox and the bossism issue into the word "Hannaism" had made Cox such a liability that many Hilltop regulars concluded he might jeopardize the fall election and thus prevent the legislature from naming Marcus A. Hanna to the Senate. They decided to push Cox into the background. Jacob G. Schmidlapp was chosen to form a committee of twelve favorably inclined to the organization which would name the fall GOP county ticket. As Cox later explained, Schmidlapp's crowd "said they'd name twelve men, and I was to name twelve. I was to pick six off their list, and they were to pick six of mine. Showed me their twelve and I took 'em all . . . all businessmen, good people. Called 'em the dozen raw." [18]

There followed a series of conferences between Schmidlapp, the spokesman for the Dozen Raw, and Cox. But they failed to agree on a slate. The Dozen Raw, according to Hickenlooper, made the ridiculous proposition that Cox and the machine surrender and "let them have everything."

Apparently willing to risk losing his Hilltop backers, Cox decided that no further attention be paid to insurgents. He set the regular machine in operation and refused to endorse the nominees of the Dozen Raw. The county convention, nonetheless, ratified the legislative slate recommended by the twelve and named but two Cox men to the county ticket.[19]

At four o'clock on election day, Cox released a public letter. "Now that the great battle of 1897 is over," it read, "I voluntarily . . . step down and out as a leader, or so-called 'boss.'" He asked only "the privilege of serving as a private in the ranks of the Republican party, the grandest political party on earth." [20]

The Republican county ticket went down by 4000 votes, and the fusionists elected all but two of their candidates for the state lower house, and two of the three state senators. This made the Republican margin in the state legislature very narrow. So narrow, in fact, that it appeared that Governor Asa Bushnell, a Foraker Republican, might, by joining forces with the Democrats, defeat Hanna's bid to get elected to the full six-year term in the U. S. Senate. In one blow, then, he could detour Hanna's rise in Ohio politics and take revenge for having had to appoint him to Sherman's vacated seat the previous spring.

The votes of the Hamilton County fusionists became critical to Hanna. To get their support, his forces in the state legislature agreed to help pass legislation which would prevent Cox from making a comeback. The fusionists particularly wanted a bill to eliminate Herrmann's board of administration, the tenure of which had been extended through 1899 by the previous legislature.

When Hickenlooper heard of this arrangement, he noted with alarm that, if successful, it meant that "Cox is out sure." He, the Cincinnati Consolidated Street Railway, and the telephone company set up a fund on a "3,000–6,000–3,000" basis to save the board of administration. The fight was unsuccessful, and, in the course of it, the General's admiration for Cox waned. Hickenlooper concluded that Cox was "dead, knows nothing, and cares nothing. We should shake him." On May 6, 1898, he "notified Geo. B. C. that our relations with him terminated on the first." [21]

Cox, meanwhile, faced more than Hickenlooper's displeasure. Cincinnati friends of Senator Foraker believed that, in the spring of 1898, Hanna was making promises in the city to the old gang in an effort to weaken Foraker on his home grounds. Consequently, the Foraker people urged the senator not to appoint any of Cox's friends to federal posts and tried to build up an organization free from his influence that could effectively control the affairs of Hamilton County in the interest of the senator.

Foraker himself was not so willing to forfeit whatever influence Cox might still retain. The senator recruited Herrmann to restore relations, and sent him to Cox. Herrmann was sure the task could be done, and he reported that while Cox might remain in the background, he was coming back stronger than ever.[22]

Cox was, in fact, rebuilding his coalition, and the Cincinnati Gas and Electric Company stood high on his list of recruits. Hickenlooper learned that others had offered to employ Cox. The news came from Cox himself through a gas company official. The General interpreted it as a threat of blackmail and was uncertain what to do. Affairs took an even more ominous turn, from Hickenlooper's point of view, when the Cox organization unhorsed the Eshelby fusionists at the September 1898 GOP convention and carried Hamilton County in November by 10,000 votes. That, concluded the General, "put Cox back in the saddle again."

Still, Hickenlooper hesitated to return to Cox. Then, in 1899, Hickenlooper's attempt to contain the Edison Company failed. The General attributed the defeat to Cox and to treachery upon the part of Mullen. According to Hickenlooper's intelligence, Mullen had been employed permanently by Edison, but Cox had undertaken only this job.[23]

Hickenlooper next faced a "raid" by the so-called Dietrick Gas Combine, another of Foraker's clients, which was seeking a franchise to supply the city with natural gas. The General counterattacked by offering to cut gas company rates, by enlisting the aid of Bernard in the board of legislation to block the ordinance, and by making Cox a proposition. Days of anxiety followed. On April 27 Hickenlooper called on Herrmann, who reported that Cox was still a doubtful quantity. Two days later, however, Cox, "cool, collected and reserved," paid the General a visit. He seemed, Hickenlooper recorded, to be out for blood and feeling his way to a big demand. No agreement was reached.

The General intensified his efforts to stop the Dietrick franchise. He persuaded Eshelby to help set up a "stock scheme" benefiting members of the board of city affairs, which also had to pass on the Dietrick ordinance. In June he held a series of mysterious nighttime meetings during which "great political considerations" were discussed. In mid-July, he deposited $8500 in Cox's account at a local bank. Finally, on July 31 the arrangements were completed. The melodrama ended the next morning when the board of legislation defeated the natural gas ordinance and accepted Hickenlooper's rate-reduction offer.[24]

Cox's comeback was also aided by Foraker's refusal to have a final showdown with Hanna for the control of politics in Ohio. Cox worked both sides, apparently choosing to regard Hanna's alliance with the fusionists in 1897 as a temporary affair. At the 1899 state convention Cox's delegates voted twice for Foraker's gubernatorial candidate, then switched to George K. Nash, Hanna's man and the eventual nominee.[25]

The 1899 gubernatorial campaign and election, moreover, revealed that the Hilltop revolt against Cox had subsided. A handful of fusionists, to be sure, supported the Democratic ticket, which was headed by John McLean. And Cox himself felt he could not carry Cincinnati, in part because of a shortage of local campaign funds. Hanna, too, was worried, and denounced Cincinnati as a "stingy" city. It was a shame, Hanna observed, that with Cincinnati's vast wealth, they would ask for outside help.[26]

Yet the wealth of Cincinnati voted Republican. Nash, who carried the state, won every Hilltop ward, but lost the city to McLean by a scant 1414 votes. McLean carried sixteen of the thirty-one wards, running strongest in the Circle, where he lost only Mullen's Fifth and Kraft's Eighteenth. He took everything in the Zone except two Over-the-Rhine wards and four in the upper West End between the Mohawk-Brighton district and Cumminsville.[27]

The Republican organization approached the spring 1900 city elections in a confident mood. Cox was back at the helm, the Hilltops had re-enlisted, the Hanna-Foraker feud had subsided, the gas and Edison companies had, for the moment, taken their fight out of the political arena and were engaged in a rate war, and the Negro insurgents, disappointed after receiving only a half-dozen jobs in the fusion administration, lost their enthusiasm for independence and returned to their old allegiance. And the Tafel administration, while promising much, had accomplished little.[28]

Nonetheless, the Democrats and independent Republicans managed to put up a Citizens' party ticket in 1900. But they found it difficult to agree on a candidate for mayor. The spot finally went to Alfred Cohen, a fusion state senator and a successful forty-year-old Democratic lawyer with experience on the board of legislation.[29]

The Republican convention went smoothly. As the meeting approached, Hickenlooper held frequent conversations with Herrmann, Cox, and his supporters and spent a busy week selecting Republican candidates. By March 16 their labors were completed. Not a soul but Cox, Herrmann, Kenan, and himself, asserted the General, had any idea who was to be nominated.[30]

The Republicans, welcoming anyone previously associated with the party, met and ratified the slate designed by this quartet. They nominated Julius Fleischmann for mayor and the *American Israelite* expressed amazement that both parties had selected Jews, something which had never before happened in Cincinnati.[31] Fleischmann was, however, virtually the perfect candidate, chosen apparently for his strong appeal to both Zone and Hilltop voters.

Fleischmann was born of German Jewish parentage but belonged to no congregation. At twenty-eight he was a successful and civic-minded businessman who was favorably regarded by union labor. An ardent joiner, Fleischmann belonged to the Commercial Club, the Queen City Club, the Optimist Club, and the Young Men's Business Club. He was also a member of the board of governors of the Queen City Club and held a seat on the board of the Phoenix Club, a German Jewish social organization. And he was an honorary member of the Friendly Sons of St. Patrick.

His Zone credentials were equally impeccable. He was known as a sporting man and a liberal on the liquor and Sunday-closing issues. He contributed generously not only to the United Jewish Charities and Hebrew Union College, but also to a host of local philanthropic institutions, Catholic, Protestant, and nonsectarian. This wide-ranging record of charity, according to Hickenlooper, would be an invaluable asset in the Catholic wards.

With a broad range of political affiliations, Fleischmann was, the *Volksblatt* noted, not controlled by any single "clique." He was a vice president of the Blaine Club and a director and former treasurer of the Lincoln Club. He had, moreover, succeeded his father as an aide-de-camp on Governor McKinley's military staff. Governor Bushnell, a Foraker man, reappointed him to the same post, as did Governor Nash, a Hanna protégé.

But most importantly, he was regarded as a businessman who, as mayor, could get Cincinnati back on the reform track and restore the city's prestige. His occupation, claimed the *Times-Star,* was particularly significant, because it was not suitable that lawyers should continually occupy the mayor's chair.[32]

Fleischmann, moreover, promised a business administration. The phrase, he explained, meant more than just selecting honest and competent men to conduct the branches of city government. The mayor should also see to it that Cincinnati kept pace with the times, "holding out inducements for more manufactories, securing to the city more workmen—the very backbone of all cities and all governments—bringing in more money and establishing a healthy and steady increase of population." [33]

The Republicans elected every man on the ticket and won twenty-two of thirty-one seats on the board of legislation. Cohen carried all the Circle wards except Five, Nine, and Eighteen. In the Zone, he won only Price Hill and the border Zone-Circle wards in the lower West End. He failed to carry a single Hilltop district. Fleischmann, with over 5500 more votes than Cohen, carried twenty wards, seventeen of them in Zone and Hilltop districts. The periphery of the city had once again united against the center.[34]

11

Changing Patterns of Politics, 1900–1905

Julius Fleischmann gave Cincinnati two terms (1900–1905) of his version of an ideal business administration. In many respects, it differed little from the business administration of other GOP governments after 1885. Yet, by 1905 it was clear that it had responded to all elements in the expanding Republican coalition in a positive and productive way. Indeed, in these years the coalition took a new and broader form. But it contained a fatal weakness.

Many of the administration's achievements were due to the activity of Cox and his allies. In 1900, for example, the cold war between Hickenlooper and the Edison Company once again escalated into a political fight. In June 1900 Senator Foraker, counsel for Edison, appeared in the city. This disturbed the General, who confessed that he was unsure of Cox and Herrmann, for although he employed them, they appeared too intimate with Foraker. "Could they be playing double," he wondered.

They were. On August 31 Cox called on the General, said that he had had a conference with Foraker about the Edison matter and intended to introduce two ordinances into the board of legislation, one to extend their franchise for private lighting and another for the laying of conduits. Both were passed, and the General concluded that Cox had been paid a fee of $12,000 by Edison. Of that, Hickenlooper estimated, $3000 went to Herrmann.[1]

The co-operation of Cox and Herrmann with Edison on private lighting placed Hickenlooper at a disadvantage in the contest over the street-lighting contracts. And in January 1901 the North American Company, representing J. P. Morgan, who also controlled the Cincinnati Edison Company, stood ready to lease the gas company and guarantee 8 per cent dividends on the current stock. This arrangement had been worked out by a group of gas company stockholders who had gone east for the purpose of concluding the lease of the Cincinnati Consolidated Street Railway Company—now the Cincinnati Traction Company—to the Widener-Elkins syndicate, a group regarded as closely allied to the North American Company.[2]

These pressures convinced Hickenlooper that he could hold out no longer against the incursion of bigness. He dropped his opposition to the leasing of the street railway, and agreed to a merger of the gas company with the Cincinnati Edison Company and the lease of the Cincinnati Gas and Electric Company to the North American Company. The General served as president for two years and then, fatally ill, resigned.[3]

Bringing Hickenlooper to terms was not the only unpleasantness which marred the early years of Fleischmann's administration. In 1902 anarchy came to the city, at least briefly, because, as Charles P. Taft put it, Mark Hanna was a "selfish hen" who refused to accept the Rogers Law of 1896 and take his street railroads out of politics in Cleveland. As a result, he got into a long fight with Mayor Tom Johnson of Cleveland, in the course of which the Ohio supreme court declared all special legislation for cities unconstitutional. The decision, Fleischmann explained, was so sweeping as to completely nullify the acts of the legislature bearing upon city governments.[4]

Yet the Republicans salvaged something for Cincinnati. That summer a special session of the legislature eased the crisis by enacting a new municipal code. Although the assembly made no radical change in the form of the city's government, it did pass the Longworth Act authorizing city council to issue bonds up to 1 per cent of the assessed value of real property for each of the succeeding four years. This bill provided much of the backbone for the body of positive achievements which Fleischmann described in 1904 as wide-awake and progressive measures which were always in the best interests of all the people.[5]

Perhaps the most ambitious of these came in the field of transportation. The need for a broad program was intensified when, in 1903, Fleischmann's annexation scheme brought Hyde Park, Evanston, Bond Hill, Winton Place, and a strip of land near Avondale into the city. Subsequently, bond issues financed an extensive street-resurfacing program as well as the beginning of work on viaducts and the elimination of dangerous railway grade crossings.

At the same time, negotiations between President Samuel Spencer of the Cincinnati Southern, assisted by his lawyer, Senator Foraker, and various businessmen's organizations, culminated in the extension of the Southern's lease and the issue of $2,500,000 in municipal bonds for the construction of a terminal in the bottoms. The Louisville & Nashville, moreover, quickly followed suit and acquired land in the bottoms for its terminal.[6]

Most of these policies amounted to little more than adopting long-proposed solutions for long-recognized problems which bore heavily or obviously on the Hilltop population. But the Fleischmann administration was not averse to attacking old issues from a new angle.

Delos F. Wilcox, a close student of American urban affairs, remarked in 1906 that Cincinnati occupied a peculiar position in regard to the problem of vice. Since 1900, he noted, a policy of examination and licensing of prostitutes had been adopted and publicly proclaimed, although officials frankly admitted that it was outside of and contrary to the spirit of the law.[7] Under this system, the city tried to examine every prostitute once a week. The uninfected received a certificate of health, and the rest were sent to the hospital for treatment. The owner or manager of a house had to report to the police the arrival of a new girl, pay the hospital bills for those who required medical care, see that no music was played after midnight, and assist the police in preventing robberies and murders. Liquor was permitted in the houses and an occasional attempt to collect the saloon license was made. Prostitution, however, continued to be illegal, which provided officials a weapon to help them keep order in the profession.[8]

Most of the new programs of Fleischmann's business administration, in fact, were related in one way or another to the health or general welfare of Circle residents. The mayor regarded the new hospital as an institution to care properly for the needy sick of the city. Similarly, he defended a park-expansion bond issue by arguing that the park would weed out foul tenements and serve as a resting place for the sick and the weary and a playground for children who often had to play on the streets. He was especially pleased when city council established athletic fields and playgrounds in the parks and expressed the hope that the ordinance would be only the beginning of a movement to give Cincinnati a park system in keeping with the people's requirements.[9]

Fleischmann recommended, too, that the city provide free public baths, as a matter of both cleanliness and hygiene. In 1904 the first one opened. The customer received a towel and soap, had hot and cold water, and was allowed thirty minutes in either tub or shower. It was not free, however. A fee of five cents was charged "as a guard against abuse" and to "remove the taint of charity to sensitive patrons." [10]

The mayor also tried to keep the city abreast of the educational renaissance. He felt the time had come for the free kindergartens in the city, formerly supported by private donations, to be made part of the public school system. As for primary and secondary schools, he thought it manifest that even "the present standard of efficiency" could not be maintained without the addition of new buildings and modern equipment. It was discouraging, he scolded, to know that there were private schools better equipped, especially with laboratory appliances, and that the public-school teaching staff was numerically so small that the average number of pupils to each teacher was forty.[11]

On finances, too, Fleischmann departed from the tradition of his predecessors. He thought that a low tax rate was an effective method of attracting residents and business enterprises. But, he cautioned, while warning of the dangers of excessive bond issues, the needs of a growing city could not be overlooked, and tax revenues were at all times to be consistent with "good, modern and progressive city government."[12]

In 1903 Fleischmann ran for re-election as a reformer. He blasted his opposition, the Citizens' party, as made up of three groups. The first was a mutual admiration society which dispensed a great deal of "twaddle" about divorcing municipal issues from state and national politics. The other consisted of the men of '97 who had given the city a wretchedly bad and palpably inefficient administration. The third was the radical ministers of the Evangelical Alliance. Vote, the *Volksblatt* advised, for Fleischmann, *Freiheit und Ordnung*.[13]

But there was more to the Citizens' party than politicians, the men of '97, and preachers. At its heart was the familiar alliance of Hilltop Democrats and independent Republicans led by a lawyers' committee of twenty-six. The ticket was nonpartisan, made up equally of Democrats and Republicans. The new party planned to set up a complete and permanent political organization, from precinct workers to a city executive committee. Its platform promised "honest, efficient and progressive government," and it was supported by its own weekly newspaper, the *Citizen's Bulletin*.

The ticket won the support of a varied crowd of reformers. The regular Democratic party announced its conversion, as a permanent position, to municipal reform and nonpartisanship in city elections and endorsed the reform slate. The Bigelow-Keifer "radical Democrats" associated with Bryan and Mayor Tom Johnson of Cleveland came along, as did the *Enquirer*, the German Catholic *Volksfreund*, and Fred Tuke of the Taxpayers' Association. In addition, W. P. Dabney and his friends and allies from the Walnut Hills Negro community joined the movement.

The nominees reflected this Zone-Hilltop alliance. The ward city council posts went largely to the regular Democratic organization. For the five Council-at-Large seats the Citizens' party put up a German Catholic, a German Protestant, a German Jew, and two

Anglo-Saxons from the Hilltops. The top executive and judicial nominations included Edward J. Dempsey, a Price Hill Catholic and Bryan-Bigelow Democrat, two long-time independent Republicans, and a representative of the old Pendleton or Kid-Glove Democratic faction. For mayor the party ran Melville E. Ingalls, a New England-born railroad executive and anti-Bryan Democrat.[14] There were no Negroes on the slate, however.

Ingalls built his campaign on the promise to eliminate bossism, gambling, prostitution, and the saloon evil, though he tried to avoid being pinned with a Puritan or anti-German label.[15] His contention that the gang was utterly depraved was given an unexpected boost by Moses Goldsmith's wedding reception for his son. Goldsmith invited the major figures in the Cox circle, including Cox and his wife, to the party at his Walnut Hills home. They were greeted at the door by two "Sisters of Charity" who, after the guests were seated, reappeared and, "throwing off their churchly robes, sprang forth as ballet dancers" in flesh-colored tights.[16]

The affair set off a furor. The *Catholic-Telegraph* denounced the Republican organization as a gang of debauchers. The Knights of Columbus demanded the resignation of all GOP public officials and linked the "orgy" to the city's corrupt politics. The *Volksfreund,* moreover, reported that priests had lectured their congregations on the immorality of "the Republican Ring politicians" and advised all good citizens who possessed any self-respect that they must vote against "the Gang."

The Citizens' party made the most of it. On March 31 two German Catholic priests appeared on the speakers' platform with Ingalls. And an independent Republican, haranguing a Central Turner Hall audience, denounced the spectacle of the most prominent office-holders of the city and their leader attending an orgy that was a disgrace to civilization. "We cannot and will not tolerate a Sodom and Gomorrah in our midst." [17]

Nonetheless, Fleischmann was re-elected with a plurality of 15,000 votes and the Republicans took all but four city council seats. Fleischmann won twenty-one wards, losing only the Fifth, Seventeenth, and Twentieth, all located in heavily Catholic areas of

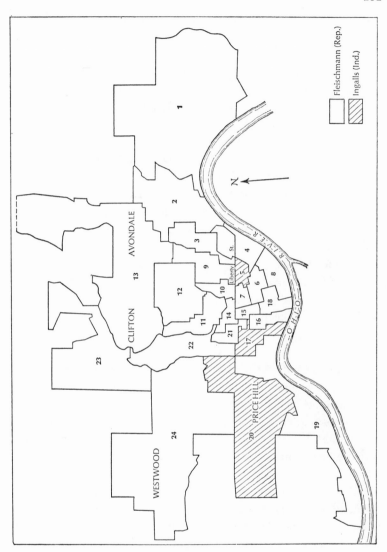

8. Election of 1903

the Zone. He polled his biggest vote in the Circle and in the German wards of the Zone, winning by lesser margins in the Hilltop districts.[18]

The *Citizen's Bulletin,* despite the loss, saw the election as one of the most significant in recent years. It pointed to Ingall's Hilltop strength and the surprisingly large Republican gains in Colonel Bob O'Brien's Sixth, Mike Mullen's Eighth, and Lew Kraft's Eighteenth, all of them Circle wards. There, the Republicans gained 914, 782, and 1128 respectively, and the Democrats lost 429, 266, and 105 from their 1902 totals (see Table 4).

The election had introduced a new pattern in local politics. Cox's strength now lay in the Circle, where the Democrats had traditionally been strongest. The *Citizen's Bulletin* estimated that 80 per cent of the Negro vote, most of it in the Basin, went to Fleischmann. And, it concluded, the evidence of a significant Democratic loss in the center of the city was too obvious to escape attention.[19]

During the final two years of the Fleischmann administration Cox was hard put to keep his state and national alliances in order. Yet he managed to co-operate with the Theodore Roosevelt forces, including Charles P. Taft, in reducing the influence of Senator Foraker in Ohio without irrevocably alienating Foraker and his Cincinnati supporters. The Republican organization approached the 1905 city election with a unified front.

The convention named a slate described by the *Post* as "very gangy" and devoid of the usual sprinkling of businessmen. The Citizens' party scrutinized the GOP candidates, found all of them "under boss domination," and announced its support of the Democratic ticket, headed by Edward J. Dempsey.[20] His running mates included a German-American Protestant candy manufacturer from Clifton, a German-American Protestant pickle processor from Clifton, a German Jewish lawyer from Avondale, and an English-born Mason from Price Hill who had been educated at Xavier University in Cincinnati. None of them, except Dempsey and the Mason, had ever held public office.

This combination resulted from an "entente cordial" among the factions within the Democratic party. The Zone and Hilltop reformers had united and snatched control of the party from what was left of the Circle faction after the depredations of Cox. As Dempsey put it, the anti-Bernard coalition demanded and got candidates who had high social, political, moral, and commercial status and were free from undesirable political affiliations.[21]

The state Democratic ticket was headed by an anti-boss gubernatorial candidate, John M. Pattison, the president of the Cincinnati-based Union Central Life Insurance Company and a staunch Methodist who was well known as a temperance man. But he planned to direct his campaign at the cities. "We should," he wrote, "stand squarely against Coxism and Bossism and all that these imply. . . ." Then "the people in the cities will join the procession and help us to over-throw the 'organization' and aid us in restoring simple, economical and honest administration everywhere." [22]

One of the most valuable allies of the Democrats in 1905 was the *Cincinnati Post*, which, after several years of political equivocation, launched a vicious campaign against Cox. According to the paper's owner, E. W. Scripps, the *Post's* manager, Milton A. McRae, had concluded that he must either make terms with Cox and the "interests" or be put out of business. When Scripps heard of this, he decided that he would rather lose the *Post* as a business than possess it as a "fat, greasy, prosperous prostitute." But Charles P. Taft, from the vantage point of the *Times-Star* business offices, regarded Scripps as something less than a pure altruist. Taft claimed that reform was being used for business purposes by the *Post*. Taft had been informed by his advertising department that the *Post* had "supplanted the *Times-Star* on the hill tops" and had become the real medium for ads.[23]

Whatever his motives, Scripps contributed heavily to the campaign fund. He also sent Homer Davenport, the cartoonist, to Cincinnati, and he, Scripps recalled, cartooned William Howard Taft, and Governor Herrick as bootblacks shining Boss Cox's shoes. John Vandercook, the editor, concentrated his fire on the local situation. The lodging houses, dives, and saloons in the Sixth, Eighth, and Eighteenth wards, he asserted, were packed with illegal voters. And when the city needed laborers, he noted, "you know very well

that Cox prefers Kentucky Negroes, who are also willing to register
and vote early and often." [24]

The anti-Cox crusade of 1905 also differed from that of two years

Table 4

PLURALITIES IN WARDS SIX, EIGHT, AND EIGHTEEN
1897–1913 [*]

WARD SIX

Year	Republican	Democratic	Plurality
1897	1436	1669	233 Dem.
1900	1579	1456	123 Rep.
1903	2493	1027	1466 Rep.
1904	2752	596	2156 Rep.
1905	2174	1214	960 Rep.
1906	1959	968	991 Rep.
1907	2352	577	1775 Rep.
1908	2373	1221	1152 Rep.
1909	2006	790	1216 Rep.
1910	1735	1053	682 Rep.
1911	2037	1301	736 Rep.
1913	2160	1133	1027 Rep.

WARD EIGHT

Year	Republican	Democratic	Plurality
1897	1189	1337	148 Dem.
1900	1524	1215	309 Rep.
1903	2306	949	1357 Rep.
1904	2707	604	2103 Rep.
1905	1848	1225	623 Rep.
1906	1752	1059	693 Rep.
1907	2052	740	1312 Rep.
1908	2327	1127	1200 Rep.
1909	2043	832	1211 Rep.
1910	1817	1038	779 Rep.
1911	2126	1132	994 Rep.
1913	2335	1033	1302 Rep.

[*] "Criminal Rule—Cincinnati's Greatest Menace," The *Citizen's Bulletin*, November 15, 1913, p. 1.

185

Table 4 (continued)

WARD EIGHTEENWARD EIGHTEEN

Year	Republican	Democratic	Plurality
1897	1990	1747	243 Rep.
1900	1811	1198	613 Rep.
1903	2939	1093	1846 Rep.
1904	3657	706	2951 Rep.
1905	2829	1416	1413 Rep.
1906	2796	1055	1741 Rep.
1907	3275	739	2536 Rep.
1908	3366	1259	2107 Rep.
1909	3028	907	2121 Rep.
1910	2810	1042	1768 Rep.
1911	2918	1061	1857 Rep.
1913	2817	869	1948 Rep.

COMBINED PLURALITIES IN THE SIXTH, EIGHTH, AND EIGHTEENTH WARDS

Year	Plurality
1897	138 Dem.
1900	1045 Rep.
1903	4669 Rep.
1904	7210 Rep.
1905	2996 Rep.
1906	3425 Rep.
1907	5623 Rep.
1908	4459 Rep.
1909	4543 Rep.
1910	3229 Rep.
1911	3587 Rep.
1913	4277 Rep.

earlier in that the Evangelical Alliance remained in the background. But other clerics, including Archbishop Moeller, Episcopal Bishop Boyd Vincent, and Rabbi David Phillipson, worked against Cox through the Honest Elections Committee, a new organization chaired by James N. Gamble. It claimed to possess information, gathered from credible sources, of widespread election frauds, including false registration, illegal voting, and tampering with the count and the returns in the Circle wards.[25]

The *Citizen's Bulletin,* of course, supported the Democratic ticket. It hammered away at the idea that prominent men and public officials should set standards for social behavior and citizenship. Under the label "apostate to the cause of good government" it published case histories of educated and wealthy men who had joined forces with Cox for profit and prestige. Charles P. Taft bore the brunt of this attack. Was he not, the paper wondered, co-operating with the system in order to protect his Cincinnati and Cleveland utilities investments and to secure Cox's help in boosting one Taft into the White House and another into Congress in 1908? [26]

The paper also drew upon Lincoln Steffens's muckrake job on Cincinnati. Steffens found apathy everywhere, for in Cincinnati apathy was corruption. The population was awake and teeming with life "like that in a dead horse, but it is busy and it is contented." Everybody, according to Steffens, from criminals to beer-drinking Germans to jobless relatives to small businessmen and traction-company magnates, benefited under Cox's system. "It is terrible. The city is all one great graft." [27]

Steffens's familiar truths were given other and equally sensational airings by outsiders. One was delivered by Secretary of War William Howard Taft, speaking for the Roosevelt administration. Early in August, anti-Cox Republicans began to fear that the President would indirectly support the system in Cincinnati by intervening at the state level to help re-elect Governor Herrick. Vandercook, the editor of the *Post,* told Steffens about these fears. Steffens gave the editor a letter of introduction and sent him to see Roosevelt. [28]

Yet Steffens and Vandercook were not heeded. The state GOP campaign was going badly, and Senator Charles Dick requested Secretary of War Taft to come to Ohio and defend the governor. Because Foraker had been opposing the policy of the President on railway regulation, Roosevelt wanted Taft to answer Foraker. Taft reluctantly agreed to Dick's request, but warned that he could not go to Ohio and make a speech for Herrick without defining his attitude toward Cox and his machine, stating the facts as he knew them and, further, that he was anti-machine. Dick cheerfully agreed, and Herrick, too, was pleased. Cox's co-operation with Dick and Herrick in weakening Foraker was being grandly repaid.

But it was not an easy assignment for William Howard Taft. On some things, he wrote Charles P. Taft before the speech, "you and I may differ and it gives me great pang for I love you . . . as I love no one except my wife and children. I might perhaps have avoided defining my position in reference to Cox in this campaign but it was certain to . . . come up sooner or later." The secretary of war regretted, moreover, that the "bitterness and insane attitude of some of our friends in Cincinnati . . . may accentuate your feeling of pain toward my action." [29]

In the speech Taft admitted the existence of a state organization. But he denied that it possessed the cohesiveness of the Hamilton County machine. That, he argued, was "The result of 15 to 20 years' labor by George B. Cox, a man of great executive talent and political sagacity," and it operated very smoothly. It could be broken only by the people of Cincinnati, and, Taft asserted, if he were in the city for the election, he would not vote for the GOP municipal ticket.[30]

Cincinnati Democrats, then, commanded a powerful coalition in 1905. Yet they feared that the liquor issue might alienate the personal liberty advocates in the Zone and throw the election to the Republicans. The *Volksblatt*, for instance, conceded that Coxism might be bad, but compared with it, Pattison's fanaticism was a calamity.[31]

The anti-Cox forces did what they could to offset this. Theodore Horstmann and a group of sucessful first- and second-generation German businessmen issued an appeal to Republicans to vote for Dempsey. The Democrats assigned Germans—including German Jews—to accompany Dempsey into German districts and deliver speeches in German. Judge Rufus B. Smith, moreover, spoke before the assembled German societies on German Day, praising the influence of Germans on American life and denouncing all sumptuary legislation. He declared the German-American's love for the Fatherland entirely consistent with loyalty to his adopted country.

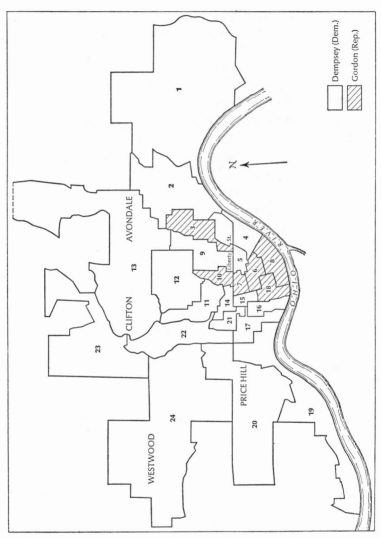

9. Election of 1905

"The practical question," asserted Smith, "is: Do the Germans who live here and the descendants who follow become good American citizens? The answer is emphatically yes." [32]

The election once again pitted the periphery against the center. Dempsey swept the Hilltops and carried every Zone ward but one. The Circle went solidly for the GOP. Dempsey polled 40,865 votes to his opponent's 34,335.

Moreover, while Pattison carried the state by some 40,000 votes, he lost by just over 2000 in Cincinnati. Herrick took all the Circle wards, all but four of the Zone wards, and none of the Hilltop wards.[33] Had the Democrats run a wet Catholic for governor he most probably would have carried enough votes in the Zone and Hilltops to offset the GOP majorities in the Circle.

On election day Cox announced his retirement from active participation in politics and prepared to move his office from above the Mecca saloon into the Cincinnati Trust Company building. That night a group of two hundred men and women dining at the Business Men's Club hissed at the mention of his name.[34] The system was defeated, Herrick was out, and Cox, unless he could revive his alliance with Foraker, was isolated at both the state and national levels. He seemed trapped in the Circle. Winning it had a high price.

12

Factions and Reform, 1905–1909

Mayor Dempsey was determined to show Cincinnati that boss rule was actually as unbusiness-like and inefficient as he and his allies had claimed. This could be done either by conducting a model administration or by using city records to expose the sins of boss rule. Dempsey and his men, with little success, tried both. A series of investigations turned up little that was not already known.[1] And most of their policy innovations were obscured in a cloud of controversy. By the end of the term the anti-machine coalition was shattered. The Republicans took advantage of the respite to patch up and refurbish the old organization.

One of Dempsey's key objectives was to dispel the old notion that an administration ought to be endorsed by the people because it kept down the tax rate. Guided by Dempsey's desire to promote the public good, it rose from $22.38 per $1000 valuation in 1905 to $29.16 in 1907.[2]

The increase was due, first, to an expansion in the services of the city and, second, to an attempt to improve the quality of government by raising wages, enlarging staffs, and hiring the advice of experts. During the flood of 1907, for example, Dempsey appointed a committee composed of the heads of the various city boards and the directors of the major private charities to distribute funds, including $10,000 appropriated by city council, for relief work among the people in the bottoms. After the waters receded the surplus $4000 was given to prominent city charities doing general relief work, the first time that private charities had received a major city subsidy.[3]

Dempsey approached the park question in a similar fashion. He persuaded the board of public service to appoint a commission to adopt a plan for a park system and supported a $15,000 bond issue to provide it with funds to hire George E. Kessler as an expert consultant. Meanwhile, Dempsey boosted the budget of the park department to enable it to put public comfort stations at one end of Fountain Square and to equip the Hunt Street athletic grounds with swimming pools for both women and men and wading pools for children as well as baseball diamonds, children's playgrounds, and parking space.[4]

Dempsey thought, too, that the health department, perhaps more than any other department deserved an increase in expenditure. One of the department's new programs was school medical inspection. It also launched what the *Citizen's Bulletin* described as the city's first continuing, well-planned campaign to clean up the milk supply. Attention was given to the tuberculosis problem. The department established a dispensary on West Ninth Street, where doctors gave free examinations and treatment. Nurses were provided to visit patients in their homes. And in line with Dempsey's belief that the best remedies were the preventive ones, the department printed and distributed literature on tuberculosis and co-operated with the leading philanthropic associations which were already engaged in giving public lectures and demonstrations.[5]

But Dempsey regarded tenements as the chief breeders of consumption. As early as 1904 city council had considered regulating tenement buildings but had bogged down when architects and builders objected that the law would make the cost of new construction prohibitive. Dempsey sought to break the impasse by introducing an ordinance to set up a commission to revise the entire building code. That, however, was promptly bottled up in the

Committee on Law. He had to be content with an ordinance which merely increased the number of fire escape and elevator inspectors.[6]

Dempsey's love of expertise and efficiency was most nearly fulfilled in the street repair and cleaning departments. The mayor removed control of street repair from the board of public service, consolidated repair and cleaning into one department, picked Joseph S. Neave, the former president of a Norwood electrical manufacturing firm, to run the bureau, and doubled its budget. In addition, Neave got the support of the Associated Organizations and Business Men's Club in pushing through a $250,000 bond issue for street repairs.[7]

Everything else Dempsey touched, however, turned into a squabble. When he attacked the police and fire departments for turning civil service into "a farce and a fraud," Max Burgheim, a member of the board of public safety and editor of the *Freie Presse,* immediately accused him of injecting politics into the conduct of the departments. Worse still, in the summer of 1906, the Hilltops were hit by a water famine. A group of angry prominent women petitioned the board of public service to "get rid of the incompetents" appointed by the Democrats to the water department. The women, without water, they said, for four months, complained that they had been forced to use drippings from ice boxes and had even stopped bathing. An acrimonious debate as to who was responsible preoccupied city council for the rest of the month.[8]

Dempsey also created anxiety among the personal liberty advocates. The mayor, to be sure, wanted to put the lid on, but not so tightly as to cause an explosion. He wanted police regulations only to protect the public against any excess of crime. He insisted, therefore, upon a strict closing of saloons at midnight, the elimination of gambling "as far as it can ever be eradicated," and a Sunday-closing policy which "guarantees every one his liberty, and at the same time insures the outward decorum and respect due to the church-going people of the city."

Many, nonetheless, complained that he was too strict. Dempsey replied that he had upheld their interests even in the face of the demands of the clergy and advised them to leave well enough alone.[9]

To make matters worse, Dempsey feuded with the board of public service. The mayor claimed it had covered itself with ridicule and contempt by removing Dr. Christian Holmes from the new hospital commission. The board had such broad administrative powers, he grumbled, that it made the mayor just a figurehead.

Dempsey, moreover, quarreled endlessly with city council. Part of this was due to the 19–10 Republican majority. But Dempsey also thought the election of councilmen by wards constituted a great obstacle to establishing a consistent and economical method of making city improvements. It prevented the drawing up of a master plan and accounted for the ill-timed improvements in some wards and the excess received by others.[10]

Part of the contention which shrouded Dempsey's administration was due to factional fights within the Democratic party. Dempsey was associated with the Bigelow-Kiefer-Lawson reform element. This coterie not only relied pirmarily upon the Zone for voter support, but was also pro-Bryan, and thus clashed with Pendleton and the old Cleveland Democrats. Pendleton and his group, virtually all of them from the Hilltops, were heavily represented on the Citizens' party executive committee, a body in which there were no Bigelow-Kiefer-Lawson Democrats. Tom Noctor served this uneasy alliance as chief lieutenant in charge of party reorganization and helped to carry out their plan to purge Bernard and his adherents who, although pro-Bryan, were tainted with bossism, were strongest in the Circle, and were often accused of being Cox-Democrats.[11]

Not surprisingly, as the fall 1907 city election approached, the Democratic reform coalition disintegrated. The Municipal Voters' League published a list of desirable candidates which did not include the mayor's name. A joint meeting of Irish patriotic societies called for the nomination of a "distinctive and representative Irishman" such as Dr. Thomas P. Hart, editor of the *Catholic-Telegraph*. Elliott Pendleton, moreover, threatened to have the Citi-

zen's party, in co-operation with the Voters' League, put up a separate slate. And the Taxpayers' Association endorsed Frank Pfaff,
the vice mayor, for the top spot.[12]

At the Democratic convention both Dempsey and Pfaff were
placed in nomination, but the mayor won easily, 169–64. The decision set off an uproar. The day after the convention, nine of the
twenty nominees, two of them Republicans, resigned from the
ticket. They announced that they would not fight one Republican
boss with the machinations of another and declared that the convention had been dominated by Dan Kiefer and Tom Noctor.[13]

Subsequently, a meeting of about 125 citizens, most of them independent Republicans, convened to name an independent slate.
They decided to put up a City party ticket and gave a committee of
fifty the task of designing the slate. At first glance the fifty seemed
to have little in common. It included a rabbi, three Protestant
preachers, Hart, and the editor of the *Catholic Knights of America
Journal*. A mixed group of businessmen, including a contractor and
a wholesale grocer, a Negro physician, and a bevy of lawyers, were
also members. Only organized labor and women were unrepre-
sented. The committee was predominantly, but not overwhelmingly, Republican. All of its members lived in the periphery of the
city, most of them on the northeastern hilltops.

They agreed on a ticket which, although more evenly divided
between Republicans and Democrats, reflected the membership of
the committee. It was headed by Pfaff, with Albert Bettinger, a lawyer who had represented twenty-two building associations, as vice
mayor, and included Dr. Frank Cain, a Negro, who was endorsed
for city council in the Eighteenth Ward.[14]

After the bolt, the Democrats reorganized their ticket. They filled
two of the vacancies with members of the Central Labor Council,
welcomed the support of the Bernardites, appointed a new campaign committee, and made overtures to the Negro vote. Yet administration supporters, and especially Dempsey, were far from
happy with the situation. The mayor publicly berated his former
allies. He referred to City party members as autocrats and ridiculed
an official in his administration who defected to the City party as a

smoker, a drinker, a member of the Queen City Club, and a man who did not know his business.[15]

Clearly, although the Dempsey Democrats included some eminently respectable Hilltop residents, part of the bitterness of the falling out rose because of the social chasm which separated Hilltop and Zone. But the question which precipitated the split was strategic, for it was about the nature of nonpartisanship, or the kind of political organization, which could best serve the cause of municipal reform. Daniel Kiefer made this explicit when, shortly after the election, he advocated party responsibility in city, state, and national affairs. He contended that organization was necessary and claimed that the City party was founded on a fallacy that confused organization and leadership with gangs and bosses.[16]

The Republicans, meanwhile, searching for new leadership to fill the vacuum created by Cox's retirement, were also embroiled in an internal Donnybrook. For a time Charles P. Taft, co-operating with Julius Fleischmann, jockeyed with Senator Foraker for a position of dominance. So, too, did Judge Howard Hollister, the creator of still another Hilltop reform organization, the Roosevelt Republican Club. And William Howard Taft boosted its stock by accepting an honorary membership. In his letter of acceptance, Taft condemned bossism and machine politics and endorsed the club's emphasis on municipal reform. But he also urged it to follow a course of common sense and practicality and to accept those who had once worked for Cox but were now glad to see him go.[17]

But the Cox organization now seemed more odious than ever owing to the findings of the Drake Committee, a state legislative committee which in 1906 set out to investigate political corruption in Cincinnati. Although the process was cut short by court action, the committee did reveal that past county treasurers, Rud Hynicka among them, had been pocketing the interest on county funds deposited in Cincinnati banks. Hynicka, however, protested that he was merely following ancient custom. He and two other offenders returned $214,998.76, but because his actions were not, in fact, illegal, he was not indicted. Cox testified that he had received none of the funds.

The scandal seriously complicated the task of reorganizing and reunifying the local party in order to forward the presidential aspirations of William Howard Taft. Charles P. Taft started the movement by co-operating with the local Foraker people, Hynicka and Herrmann, in Cincinnati affairs. The next move was to get the 1907 state convention to endorse William Howard Taft for President. But Foraker balked. He believed that the attempt to eliminate him from the Senate at the 1906 state convention had originated in the Cincinnati Taft camp and feared that it might be repeated. To protect himself, he let the Foraker-for-President boom continue without lending it public or private encouragement. At the same time, he tried to block the Taft campaign in Ohio.

At that point Cox re-entered the picture. He agreed privately with Foraker, Congressman Longworth, and Roosevelt that Taft should get the support of the organization as presidential candidate, and that Foraker was to be returned to the Senate in 1909. Charles P. Taft reluctantly went along. But William Howard Taft refused to be associated with any arrangement by which he was to endorse or use influence to secure the election of anyone, and particularly Foraker, to the Senate in return for support of his candidacy for the Presidency.[18]

Cox, nonetheless, confidently announced the arrangement. He favored, he declared, Taft for President, Foraker for senator, and George A. Harris, the former lieutenant governor who became governor on the death of Pattison, for governor. On June 1, 1907, "Mr. Hooley" of the *Citizen's Bulletin,* unaware of the backstage deal, explained to "Mr. Fennessey" why he thought Cox made this move.

> George had raytired so many times, an' always come back, that he thought he cut do it ivry time. But . . . there were no calls f'r George twenty-threed, th' grand old man in th' mecca. So t'was whin George said . . . "I, George th' twenty-threed, do hereby ordain . . . that Taft shall be Prisident," he says, "Four-flusher, Sinator," he says, "an' th' Honest Farmer c'n be governor," he says, "whereby," he say, "I will either get a riputation f'r lovin' me enemies," he says, "or else all th' pickins," he says.[19]

William Howard Taft, however, still refused to budge, to the displeasure of Roosevelt. Finally, Charles P. Taft broke the impasse. Working with Hynicka and Herrmann, he persuaded the state central committee to endorse William Howard Taft for President without mentioning the forthcoming senatorial election, thus leaving Foraker's fate in the hands of the 1908 state GOP convention.

The settlement was both final and ambiguous. Foraker was virtually eliminated as a presidential candidate, but retained a chance for the Senate. Charles P. Taft and Roosevelt had William Howard Taft launched on his road to the White House without involving him in any distasteful deals with machine politicians and without having to wreck the Hamilton County organization. Herrmann and Hynicka had co-operated with Taft without irrevocably breaking with Cox. And Cox, inadvertently, had remained loyal to Senator Foraker without antagonizing Charles P. Taft. The stage was set for the GOP city convention and the election of 1907.

Before the convention Longworth and Julius Fleischmann issued statements against one man rule and declared themselves in favor of an open convention and a "new deal" in the party. The only major difficulty arose in connection with the mayoralty nomination. It was felt that a German should be selected—perhaps, Charles P. Taft suggested, George Puchta, a self-made businessman not prominently identified with any faction of the party.

William Howard Taft, however, preferred "a more distinctly reform candidate." In any event, he hoped that Charles P. Taft would be able to work out a satisfactory solution of the municipal ticket. He apparently did, for just before the convention the editor of the *Times-Star* wired Charles P. Taft: "Puchta out of race, Fleischmann will be asked to run—expected to decline and Markbreit [sic] will be nominated. Chiefly compliment to you."

At the convention, Leopold Markbreitt, to the surprise of most local observers, was nominated for mayor, and John Galvin, a Foraker man, for vice mayor. Congressman Longworth delivered the keynote address. He declared that the day had passed when any political party could nominate unfit men to public office with any hope of success, and announced that the Republican party of Cincinnati had put its house in order.[20]

Foraker, doubtless considering his chances of being returned to the Senate, agreed. When the Colored Baptist Alliance asked if it should bolt, he replied that he did not consider the party management or city slate hostile to him. Nevertheless, as the *Enquirer* asserted, it did not require any particular discernment to see that the organization had deferrred to the wishes of the Roosevelt-Taft element. The Roosevelt Club, however, was not satisfied. It endorsed the platform and candidates of the City ticket. The Club requested Roosevelt to do the same, a suggestion, he remarked, which must have originated with "an outpatient of bedlam." [21]

The *Citizen's Bulletin* (in a not altogether accurate analysis) thought the whole process highly instructive. The secret of the "boss-made ticket," the paper explained, was that men who claim to be respectable "go down into the gutter and accept office from hands that are reeking with the filth of the slums." In "this alliance of the hosts of iniquity with the greed of special privilege and ambition for power and place . . . we find the rottenness and the shame of our cities." The alliance constituted, the paper asserted, "a legally recognized conspiracy of the arrogant few against the many who by their toil are compelled to bear the entire burden." And the cunning few played so successfully on the prejudices and superstition of the many that wrong is often espoused by those who were victims of it.[22]

"The many" in 1907 voted for Markbreitt. Pfaff failed to carry a single ward. In only six, all of them Hilltop or predominately Hilltop, did he receive more than 500 votes. He ran strongest in the Thirteenth, comprised of Avondale and Bond Hill, "the hot bed of the City Party," where Professor Gotthard Deutsch of Hebrew Union College was elected as a reform candidate to the board of education. Dempsey took only four wards, all of them regular Democratic wards in the Zone. Markbreitt, in sweeping the Circle and Hilltops, got over 8500 more votes than the 1905 Republican candidate, picking up most of them in former Democratic strongholds.

Markbreitt's total was 43,841, Dempsey's 23,566, Pfaff's 10,508.[23]
After the election Cox described the landslide as an accurate measure of his strength in Cincinnati. The victory, he boasted, was won without the endorsement of the local Taft organization (the Roosevelt Republican Club), and state and national issues had no influence on the outcome. He described Foraker as being in good health and claimed that he had not heard any talk of eliminating the senator for over a month.[24] Cox believed, apparently, that he had brought order to the feuding elements of the party by establishing a Taft-Foraker-Cox axis.

The illusion was momentary. Less than a week after Cox's statement the Ohio League of Republican Clubs, a Foraker organization built around his Cincinnati Stamina League, endorsed Foraker for President. In Cincinnati, Foraker supporters began to seek out allies for the spring of 1908 state convention. Exploiting the competition between the *Post* and *Times-Star*, they secured a pledge from the *Post* that it would publish items favorable to Foraker's candidacy as news, but not, for the sake of credibility, as editorial statements of the paper. At the same time they scoured Cox's organization for Foraker men. Out of this developed a crossfire between Foraker and Taft for Negro support which threatened to wreck the machine's Circle foundation.[25]

Cox, however, stuck with the Tafts. At a Blaine Club meeting on the eve of the state convention Charles P. Taft, in a eulogistic speech, named Cox as chairman of the delegation, and announced later that Cox reciprocated by offering a resolution to support Taft for delegate to the national convention. On his arrival at the state convention Cox declared that the best man should win and, with Charles P. Taft, received a bouquet of American Beauty roses from Mike Mullen and the Cincinnati GOP. The convention, without mentioning Foraker, came out for William Howard Taft for President.[26]

By this time, a host of competitors for the senator's seat had appeared. Beside Foraker, these included Theodore Burton, Warren G. Harding, and Charles P. Taft. But Foraker still did not know where Cox stood. He did not believe Cox would aid Burton, but supposed he might help Charles P. Taft and could understand why he and his organization might prefer Taft. Late in December, after conferring with Roosevelt, Charles P. Taft confessed that he had long been ambitious to be a senator from Ohio but would retire from the contest for the best interests of the party. On January 1 Foraker followed suit. On January 2, with the approval of the Hamilton County GOP, Burton was chosen candidate for the Senate by the Republican caucus.[27]

The same day, Charles P. Taft explained the details of the settlement to the President-elect. "My job," he said, "was to clean out Foraker." Having heard that the nomination could be purchased for $25,000, he "shut this off" and agreed with Burton to withdraw. "We also agreed," Taft added, "that I should be consulted on all federal appointments in southern Ohio. He is to keep his hands off Hamilton County." In return, Hamilton County voted solidly for Burton.[28]

Cox, then, did not have the final say. William Howard Taft could sleep with an easy conscience. He had kept faith with the reformers by not dealing with Cox. Foraker was eliminated. And, after three years of confusion, the Cincinnati machine was reunified under the joint direction of Charles P. Taft and George B. Cox.[29]

13

The Syndicate Rejected, 1909–1911

The reconstructed Republican organization received its first test in the fall 1909 city elections. By that time it had patched up the wounds opened in the Foraker elimination fight and the "Peerless Leaders," as the *Post* dubbed the new GOP hierarchy in the Taft age, had raised the cry of reform from within. A "strong purgative" had also been applied to cleanse the machine of some of its more offensive elements. Louis "Snoddy" Trosky of the Fourth Ward was relieved of his responsibilities after his arrest for participating in a brawl in which one man was fatally wounded, another lost an eye, and a third seriously beaten. And two councilmen, notorious as proprietors of gambling dens, voluntarily retired.[1] After these readjustments, harmony prevailed. It was so complete, according to the *Citizen's Bulletin,* that the city's first GOP nominating primary was a farce because there was "not manhood enough to make a contest." The veneer of respectability on the GOP ticket was supplied by Dr. Louis Schwab, the mayoralty candidate, whom the *Volksblatt* applauded as the banner carrier of progressive citizens. He had been county coroner, an associate of Dr. Christian Holmes on the new hospital commission, and had been endorsed by the educational reformers when he ran for a place on the board of education in 1904.[2]

The *Citizen's Bulletin,* however, refused to accept the sincerity of the GOP's reform from within campaign. Declaring that the election would be either a farce or a revolution, it endorsed Democrat John Weld Peck for mayor. Uniquely qualified, claimed the paper, Peck was manly and cultured, a Mt. Auburn resident who was practical, had ideals, and was not a vulgar office-seeker.[3]

Peck tried to draw the scattered anti-Cox forces together. He retained all twenty-four of the old ward captains who had opposed him in the primary and persuaded Lewis Bernard to read a statement of support for the ticket before a Duckworth Club meeting. He brought in Governor Judson Harmon to speak for the City ticket. A Citizens' Peck club comprised solely of Germans was also organized. And A. K. Nippert, a prominent German lawyer, Lester Rothschild of the Jewish Settlement House, Fred Tuke of the Taxpayers' Association, and Rabbi David Philipson took the lead in forming an Independent-Republicans-for-Peck committee. The Bigelow-Dempsey-Kiefer faction of the party co-operated but played an inconspicuous part in the campaign.[4]

The *Post* also joined the Peck forces. It struck hardest at alleged vote frauds in Circle wards. As part of this campaign the *Post* featured a story about a Republican rally in Mike Mullen's precinct in the Eighth Ward. The meeting was attended by about one hundred white men, around one hundred Negro women, and some three hundred Negro men. Negro Deputy Sheriff William Copeland opened the meeting by announcing that Negroes used to have to defer to white men, but they were gaining status and white men would have to defer to them.

Councilman Mullen also addressed the throng. "If you get into trouble, send for Uncle Mike. . . . If you need a bondsman, Uncle Mike will get you one. If you need a lawyer, Uncle Mike will furnish one." Although Mullen was talking about defending against alleged voting irregularities, one white businessman feared the "cocaine and drink-crazed men" might take his remarks as a license to commit crime.[5]

Peck tried, however, to make the "exorbitant" tax rate the major issue of the campaign. Bossism, he asserted, was not only unrepublican, undemocratic, and un-American, but also expensive. His ideal administration would not add new functions or offices to city government, but would simply carry into public affairs the homely virtues that good businessmen exercise.[6]

The election went to Schwab. He had a plurality of just under eight thousand votes and carried eighteen of the twenty-four wards. As expected, Peck ran well on the Hilltops, though he carried none of those districts. He took only the "old" Democratic wards—Four, Fifteen, Seventeen, Nineteen, Twenty, and Twenty-one—all of which formerly lay on the inner edges of the Zone but now, because of the continuing expansion of the Circle, rested precariously on the Zone-Circle border.[7]

Yet the pattern of the returns created confusion among political observers. The *Enquirer* noted that the "old reliable Tenth and rock-ribbed Eleventh," Republican personal liberty wards Over-the-Rhine, almost went Democratic. In addition, other GOP strongholds on Mt. Auburn and in Cumminsville, areas which in 1880 had been Hilltop but which now had been absorbed by the outward push of the Zone, also fell short of past GOP majorities. Peck, it seems, had gained at the expense of Republican strength in the substantial but changing neighborhoods. Schwab, on the other hand, while holding some of this strength, had gained in those wards which had been almost wholly absorbed by the Circle. He coupled this with huge majorities in the center of the city where he piled up a lead of forty-five hundred votes.[8]

Paradoxically, as the Republican organization increasingly relied on the Circle for votes, GOP administrators steadily took up the new plans and projects emanating from the Zone and Hilltop philopolists. They pushed for more annexations, established a park commission and secured funds to carry out Kessler's plan, enacted a new building code regulating both billboards and tenements, set up a municipal lodging house, made the board of health an autonomous body, improved the tuberculosis hospital, instituted the rural cottage system at the house of refuge, strengthened the federal system of local government by bolstering the powers of the mayor, created a civil service commission, continued the drive to improve intraurban transportation for passengers and freight, and protected the regulated monopoly utilities. The Markbreitt and Schwab administrations, in short, adhered to the GOP strategy which dated to the 1890's and was implemented most successfully under Mayor Fleischmann.[9]

Like Fleischmann, moreover, they found it difficult to keep their pledges of economy in the face of the city's growth and the expansion of municipal services. With the tax rate inflated to $31.11, the Markbreitt administration sought to pay for improvements with bond issues. Under new state tax law, however, the city could issue bonds only to 4 per cent of the assessed value of real property. After consulting the civic and business organizations, the administration decided to submit nine bond issues to a referendum as a means of deciding which projects should be adopted. All nine received more than a majority vote, but only those for street improvements, sewers, and hospital construction and equipment got the necessary two-thirds. The park, house of refuge, grade-crossing, viaduct, and police issues were all defeated.[10]

The situation worsened under Schwab. He managed, in 1910, to cut the tax rate to $29.94, but in 1911 the state legislature further complicated matters by passing the Smith Act limiting the city tax rate to 1 per cent of the tax duplicate. More could be assessed only if approved in a referendum. Schwab, in order to meet his proposed budget for 1912, had to request a referendum for the fall of 1911, the date of the city elections.

Despite the financial crisis, the *Citizen's Bulletin,* looking back over a decade of Republican domination, was not pessimistic. It admitted that public opinion had too long been characterized by a social psychology which permitted the community's dominant figures to rule "with autocratic power." [11] But indifference regarding city affairs began to disappear at the turn of the century. Cincinnatians then decided that good city government would be attained through a process of education. That was the mission of the new voluntary organizations, and they were responsible for the civic progress so far achieved.

Equally encouraging to the *Citizen's Bulletin* was the spread of a "New Politics." Its adherents stated that their concerns were with problems of economic efficiency and the preservation and protection of the rights of the common citizen, and they demanded civic patriotism, love of righteousness, pity, and sympathy on the part of the strong toward the weak—in short, "common morality." No longer would they be content merely with freedom from graft or a high rate of bank clearings or industrial product. The paper was confident that the new politicians could now destroy Cox's alliance of "sordid business interests" with the "syndicate" which, through its control of prostitution, gambling, and the voters in the Circle, sustained "despotism" in Cincinnati.[12]

Other Democrats had reached the same conclusion about the nature of Cox's power and had decided that it could readily be turned against him. The reformer and his fellow students, asserted one, might evolve high principles for action, but the people would not be led by those principles unless there was a dramatic setting, and their favorite dramatic setting was the slaying of a dragon. Since people of all kinds love the dramatic, all that was needed was a situation which would enable the right man "to bring the boss himself to book."[13] Between 1908 and 1911 the proper conditions developed.

In 1908 Democrats in the state legislature secured a continuation of the legislative investigation of Cincinnati and Hamilton County which had produced such sensational revelations two years earlier. One of the witnesses claimed that as an assistant in the county treasurer's office he had carried interest on public funds to Cox. Before the investigation could proceed any further, however, it was quashed in circuit court as an unconstitutional exercise of the power of the legislature.[14]

Then, in the fall 1908 elections two "new politicians" were elected to strategic county posts. One, Frank Gorman, was sent to the common pleas court. According to the procedure of that body, he would become judge of criminal court in the winter of 1911. The other, Henry T. Hunt, won the race for county prosecutor. He spent his two-year term running down vote fraud allegations and closing up "vicious resorts." But he did not touch the Cox case. In the fall of 1910 he was re-elected by a margin of six thousand votes, a majority which doubled the one he received in 1908. In the winter of 1911, then, Hunt was county prosecutor and Gorman was judge of criminal court. The new politicians were in a position to investigate and prosecute the alleged misdeeds of the "syndicate." [15]

The winter-spring session of the grand jury lasted forty-five days, examined over 1000 witnesses, and indicted 123 persons. And two former county treasurers, John H. Gibson and Tilden R. French, told the jury that Cox had been given $65,000 of the interest on public funds. Since Cox had told the 1906 grand jury that he received none of that money, he was in 1911 indicted for perjury and tried.

Cox denied the charge. His 1906 testimony, he said, was absolutely correct, and to prove it he needed nothing more than did the humblest citizen—a fair trial. Cox and his defenders, moreover, claimed that the grand jury had been packed with men of the City Club type. The indictment, Cox believed, was a political indictment.

That infuriated the *Citizen's Bulletin*. Boss Ruef of San Francisco, the paper noted, had not resorted to a "Baby Act." Perhaps, the paper suggested, "our Lord Paramount" was neither so fearless nor so honest as claimed. One of Cox's lawyers immediately protested that this kind of attack constituted prosecution without due process of law.[16]

To help clear the atmosphere of political prejudice, Cox gave the New York *World* an interview in which he explained his role in Cincinnati politics. Cox claimed he had been boss of Cincinnati for almost thirty years and that he had been a good boss. He called Cincinnati the best-governed city in the United States. It had, he said, less graft and less dishonesty among its office-holders than any of the larger cities in the country because he had prevented graft. Indeed, he maintained, the boss is most successful only when he sees that the city has honest and efficient servants, for, after all, the people do the voting.

As for crime, he denied that Cincinnati was wide open in the usual usage of the term. However, a liberal policy was observed. It was possible to get a drink on Sunday, he explained, because more than one-third of the population was composed of Germans, and they demanded that privilege. But gambling houses had been driven out many years ago, and the social evil was regulated as much as possible. Not much more could be done, he thought, because Cincinnati had all the problems of the large cities of America and, of course, was plagued by a certain amount of vice and crime.

Cox felt there were two main reasons for the attacks made on him. First, most people supposed a boss was dishonest. Second, he had been successful. "Success," he added, "is one thing disappointed office-seekers can never forgive in a boss."

Although Cox was satisfied with his political accomplishments, he felt others should seek their opportunities elsewhere. He would, he concluded, strenuously advise young men not to enter politics. There was no money in it for honest men, only abuse, whether one was successful or unsuccessful. "Politics as a profession doesn't pay." [17]

The validity of Cox's contention that he was an honest boss was never ascertained. The perjury trial was removed from Judge Gorman's hands when defense argued that he was prejudiced against Cox. The litigation lasted into the summer. Hunt quarreled with the judges and taunted and defied them. Finally, the indictment was quashed on the grounds that Cox's constitutional rights had been violated in 1906 when he testified before the grand jury on matters which might have incriminated him. Hunt protested, but failed to get a reversal.[18]

The affair, nonetheless, jeopardized Cox's position in the GOP. President Taft, in 1910, had already indicated his dissatisfaction with Cox's continued participation in politics. Without Cox's knowledge, he had conferred with Hynicka, complaining that Cox exhibited a swelled head in feuding with Senator Burton. Taft clearly wanted to shrink Cox's stature, and when Theodore Roosevelt attended a reception at Congressman Longworth's home with Cox and others, Taft noted that it was "one of those little inconsistencies which you wish Roosevelt would not commit." [19]

In 1911 Charles P. Taft began to revive the old talk of having Cox, Herrmann, and Hynicka pull out. Taft proposed, however, that Herrmann and Hynicka should continue to help manage the practical part of the organization behind the scenes. They, he thought, could hold the organization together without Cox by advancing men like Frederick Bader, who had extensive acquaintances through his building association activities and who, according to Taft, was an honest man affiliated with the organization yet not depending on, or owing his appointment to, Cox.

Cox, meanwhile, had agreed with Hermann and Hynicka that the Republicans could not win the fall 1911 elections if he headed the organization. Cox admitted he was tired of politics, but refused to step down unless Herrmann and Hynicka also retired.[20]

After the indictment, however, Cox seemed more reluctant to withdraw. In the *World* interview he claimed that "this boss-ship" had become such a part of his life that he could not voluntarily give it up. He said the question of retiring had never entered his mind and pledged to continue as the leader of the Republican party in Cincinnati as long as the Republican party wanted him.[21]

By that time, however, the party's Hilltop faction was determined to dump Cox. And Charles P. Taft and Julius Fleischmann were now able to persuade the Zone bonifaces to reorganize the GOP without Cox. One week after the *World* interview Cox announced his retirement. An epoch, declared the *Times-Star,* had come to an end. The paper called for new leadership which would preserve the existing organization while permitting "other Republicans with political ideas or aspirations" to exercise more influence within the party. No single successor, the *Times-Star* emphasized, should be chosen.[22] The confidence of the periphery in Coxism had been shattered.

The GOP ticket for the fall 1911 city election was selected by the Republican Advisory Committee headed by Hynicka and Herrmann. They were assisted by Julius Fleischmann, Charles P. Taft, and the President. Since Schwab was reluctant to run again, the slate-makers cast about for a new man to head the ticket. At the request of Fleischmann, the President asked Albert Bettinger, "a very high-toned German Republican" and a past president of the Business Men's Club, to make the race. When he refused, the President turned to Joseph T. Carew, the owner of a large downtown department store. Carew also declined the offer. The problem was solved when Schwab agreed to stand for re-election.[23]

On November 4 the *Commercial-Tribune* ran a public letter to Fleischmann from the President. Taft announced that he expected to be in Cincinnati on election day to vote for the Republican ticket. He believed the candidates were "competent and worthy," and he added that the conditions under which he had made his 1905 Akron speech had substantially altered.[24]

The Democrats, meanwhile, were searching for a candidate acceptable to all factions in their party who would also appeal to independent Republicans. The muddle was finally resolved when Peck suggested Hunt. He protested that he had not sought the nomination, but he ran unopposed in the Democratic primary.[25] The coalition was rounded out when a group of Hilltop independent Republican businessmen and professional men endorsed Hunt.

In the campaign Hunt virtually ignored Schwab. Instead, he ran on his record as prosecutor of the syndicate. An "alliance most dangerous to order and decency and the lives of our citizens," he charged, "now exists between the vicious and criminal classes and the so-called Republican organization." Hunt emphasized his attempts as county prosecutor to drive the social evil back into isolation, and he stressed his attacks on bookmakers and druggists who illegally sold cocaine. But he tried to make it clear that he was not an advocate of strict blue-law enforcement.

Hunt also vowed, if elected, to conduct an efficient and democratic administration. He would, he said, call a conference of civic groups, city council members, and all interested citizens to formulate a plan for making the lives of men, women, and children "happier and brighter." Although an advocate of efficiency and economy, he promised to carry out a long list of improvements. He wanted to improve river transportation, encourage the development of both interurban and intraurban railways, secure a union passenger terminal, build a Mill Creek Valley sewer, eliminate grade crossings, and constuct a canal boulevard. He thought, too, that the public utilities should be forced to meet all their franchise obligations. And, as mayor, Hunt claimed, he would see that public contracts were let by competitive bids, that specifications for city work were drawn "scientifically," and that the streets were kept clean.[26]

The Republicans launched a counterattack to neutralize Hunt's appeal to Hilltop voters. Fleischmann claimed that Hunt's reform program had already been put into effect by GOP administrations, and charged that the whole Democratic campaign in Cincinnati was part of a scheme to help Governor Judson Harmon get the presidential nomination in 1912. The *Commercial-Tribune* denounced the Smith 1-per-cent law as a pet measure of Harmon's which had crippled the city just as the Schwab administration prepared to move forward.

The *Commercial-Tribune* also had an urgent message for its readers in the Zone. Hunt, the paper asserted, had entered into a cabal with "ministerial representatives" to enforce Sunday closing. The *Volksblatt* took a similar approach. It called Hunt a modern Judas for declaring for personal liberty when, as a state legislator, he had voted for two temperance laws. The *Freie Presse* also distrusted Hunt. It suggested that Luther Burbank, who had grown a rose without thorns, would have performed a greater service if he had developed a reformer without prohibitionist and nativist tendencies. If Hunt won, it claimed, "the Dutch [would] get it in the Neck!" The *Freie Presse*, like the *Volksblatt*, defended Schwab's administration and argued that it was a reform principle to re-elect a man who had done a good job. Both papers asserted that Schwab should be given two more years to carry out his program.[27]

Nonetheless, Hunt and all his running mates on the top of the ticket were elected. In addition, all the special financial questions passed by overwhelming margins, including bond issues for the tuberculosis hospital, jail, and courthouse improvements. The vote on

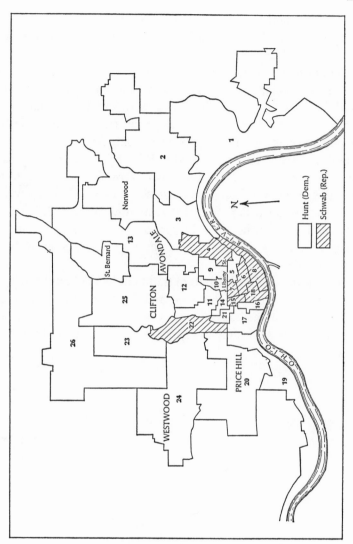

10. Election of 1911

the tax levy increase was closer, but only four wards, the Second, Ninteenth, Twenty-fourth, and Twenty-sixth—one Hilltop and three Zone districts—voted it down.

Most observers were surprised by the size of Hunt's plurality over Schwab—43,673 to 39,771 votes. The Zone German wards which had left the GOP in the 1910 gubernatorial race—the Ninth, Tenth, Eleventh, and Twelfth—all went for Hunt and elected Democratic councilmen. Schwab carried only seven wards. Five of these—the Sixth, Seventh, Eighth, Fifteenth, and Eighteenth—were in the Circle. The other two were the Twenty-second, Schwab's home ward in Cumminsville, and the Fourth, which encompassed Eden Park and that section of Walnut Hills to the north and east of the park. It had been gerrymandered in the spring of 1911 by the addition of three precincts from Mullen's Eighth ward.[28]

Hunt, in the established reform tradition, had united the periphery against the center. The Zone and Hilltops had rejected the GOP's formula of moderate reform, with or without Cox. It seemed that they meant to destroy the gang, or syndicate, regardless of its leadership.

14

Progressives in Power, 1911–1913

Henry T. Hunt's business administration differed markedly from any which had preceded it. In February 1912 a prominent independent Republican, a resident of the city for about forty years, claimed that in Hunt Cincinnati had for the first time a mayor who had a genuine appreciation of his duties and the courage to perform them. He made Cincinnati, according to the *Christian Science Monitor*, one of the most progressive cities in the West.[1]

Yet Hunt possessed no unique qualifications. A Methodist and a resident of Clifton, he had been born in 1878 into the family of a prominent lawyer associated with the Pendleton "Kid-Glove" Democrats. He graduated from Yale in 1900, studied law at the University of Cincinnati, and was admitted to the bar in 1903. Although described as a "college insurgent" at Yale, he took no active interest in urban politics until he returned to Cincinnati.[2]

Hunt claimed that he became a dedicated anti-Cox man during the spring 1903 city elections. He and another law student spent the day watching, with interest and curiosity, the democratic machinery in action at the Silver Moon, where Negroes were paid $2 for voting. The spectacle produced a kind of political fury in Hunt, and his outrage endured. After one term as a state legislator and two as county prosecutor, *The Chronicle* concluded that the initials H.T. stood for "Hell and Trouble." [3]

Men who knew him well as mayor described Hunt as a dark, handsome man with ability, intelligence, energy, courage, and a strong personal appeal. He was not particularly religious, drank moderately, possessed a sense of humor, yet was subject to fits of ill humor. He was something of an adventurist who once tried to interest his friends in investing in Russian gold mines. One associate thought he was an aristocrat who found it difficult to get in touch with the people. All agreed, however, that he was willing to experiment and that he could be stubborn. [4]

Hunt viewed the mayoralty as "an expert job, pure and simple." City government, he claimed, should be a definite profession and, with experts in the various departments, ought to be run as a railroad or a corporation. But Hunt thought it a misconception to suppose that politicians had no value. In the course of a campaign, he noted, every mayor went over the whole city and came in contact with every class in it. As a result, he knew what the people wanted. He knew the city geographically and topographically, and no businessman could have such wide experience or such keen interest. [5]

In Hunt's view, moreover, a great mayor could not be bound by a "pinchbeck economy." Competition among cities in beauty, in cleanliness, in health conditions, in the safety of life and property, and in educational facilities, he claimed, made increased expenditures inescapable. The spending, however, had to be done according to the cult of efficiency, a religion, he asserted, which had "penetrated [the] temples of conservation . . . and is about to displace therein the adoration of the great god Jobs." An efficient government under a strong mayor, Hunt contended, would serve Cincinnati so that its people would be bettered from a social standpoint. [6]

Hunt tried to live up to his concept of urban executive leadership. He relied heavily on a group of experts for advice. His "cabinet" included Safety Director Dennis Cash, a Catholic lawyer who had helped indict Cox, Public Service Director Henry Waite, a former city manager of Dayton, Ohio, and City Solicitor Alfred Bettmann, a German Jew who later became nationally prominent as a city planner. But he also consulted nonofficial opinion. In February Hunt called a meeting of the heads of business and civic organizations—including a representative from the Central Labor Council—to discuss the pressing needs of the city.

These talks were followed by a series of innovations in the conduct of local affairs. First, the mayor demonstrated what he meant by "scientific budget making." The administration drew up a proposal which not only showed the expenses of each department and subdivision but also indicated what the expenditures were for. Some five thousand copies of the proposal were sent to civic organizations and made available to the public along with an invitation to a three-day public hearing. At these sessions city officials answered questions and took note of suggested additions or reductions. Out of this came the final budget. Although $234,935.27 less than that of 1912, it nonetheless covered the costs of several new projects.[7]

Most of the new programs were designed to forward Hunt's ideal of an efficient yet democratic city government. The new budget set aside $100 to start a municipal employment bureau, $2475 for a bureau of information and complaints to help create a continuous dialogue between citizens and city officials, and $10,000 for a bureau of efficiency to make "economy and efficiency surveys" within the administration. The new budget also allotted the city auditor $9794.67 to install a new accounting system. In his budget message, moreover, Hunt emphasized that increased efficiency had enabled him to expand and improve municipal services and reduce the budget without cutting the salaries of city employees.[8]

Despite the budget reduction, however, city revenues under the Smith 1-per-cent law did not cover city expenditures. Hunt, like Schwab before him, had to hold a referendum to secure an increased levy.

To make sure that the voters fully understood the need for the tax increases, Hunt called in Dr. L. D. Upson of the New York Bureau of Muncipal Research to run a "budget" or "municipal exhibit," the first in any major city outside New York. The object, as Upson put it, was to prove that the expenditures of the first eight months of the Hunt administration had been both necessary and efficient.

The exhibit was preceded by a determined advertising campaign to arouse public interest in this new form of city reporting which substituted a "living presentation" for the old volumes of "miscellaneous and inaccurate statistics." Officials made speeches, the city purchased streetcar advertising space, and the water department mailed out promotional literature with water bills. In addition, nearly one-half of the Protestant ministers of the city, persuaded that social work could not be advanced unless the city got more money, agreed to devote at least one sermon to the event. Meanwhile, the board of education, city departments, and major charities, assisted by the Bureau of Municipal Research, prepared charts, photographs, displays, and mechanical models for the exhibit which illustrated the work of the city and the quasi-public agencies.[9]

The exhibit ran for two weeks and attracted an average of 8000 persons per day. The voters were impressed. The tax increase was approved by nearly a 2–1 margin. Schwab's 1911 referendum had gone through by only 6000 votes out of a 67,000 total.[10]

The exhibit was so successful that it was repeated in 1913 as an educational project of "obvious" value.[11] Its goal was to show how

> Mr. Everyman is protected from germs and from burglars and from fires; how he is taught in school to overcome the germs in his mouth by proper toothbrushing, how the food poisoners are detected, how from the moment he gets up until he goes to bed "The City" protects him; how his children are educated so they can get the greatest amount of value out of their education; . . . how Everyman's money, which he contributes to "The City," for what it does for him, is guarded from grafters who beset the body politic.[12]

The Municipal Exhibit was in keeping with Hunt's conviction that no government could be better than the people who elected it and his assertion that the "social work" of his administration was more important to him than its financial success.[13] To help carry out his program of social uplift on a year-round basis Hunt appointed Dr. Otto Geier to direct the new department of charities and corrections.

The problem of social progress, Geier maintained, was one of educating citizens to a full understanding of the functions of citizenship. "The one-half must know how the other half lives and render such service as will assist in their regeneration." To Geier, constructive social work included not only helping the unfortunate —and persuading the unfortunate to co-operate in that task—but also fighting those who preyed on the miserable. It meant, he contended, a constant struggle against the current of tradition, experience, and practice.[14]

Geier did what he could to forward this battle. At the house of refuge, for instance, he had the inmates "scientifically classified," installed a new method of record keeping, and ordered the adoption of the parole system. He eliminated the old regimen of military drill and discipline, placed the educational system under the jurisdiction of the board of education, reopened the manual training shop, introduced courses in domestic science, and let the students write, edit, and print their own paper. For recreation, the institution added new playground apparatus and provided individuals with a flower or vegetable garden. The medical care program was supplemented by the addition of a dental office.

Geier also wanted to separate the dependent from the deliquent children. He adopted a policy of "placing out" dependents in private homes in an attempt to make the house of refuge purely a correctional institution. In connection with that program, the department of charities and corrections acquired land, drew up plans, and submitted a bond issue for the construction of two sets of country cottages, "Boyland" and "The Girls' Farm Training School."[15]

The department secured more publicity, however, from the activities of its new Bureau of Social Investigation and Relief. A bureau investigation led to the clearing of fifty shacks in the Mill Creek bottom shantytown. It also played a decisive role in eliminating the Overseers of the Poor. The bureau charged that they were politically corrupt and turned their duties over to the Associated Charities.

The bureau, in addition, co-operated in Hunt's crusade against loan sharks. It aimed, the bureau explained, to expose the evil of the practice and to teach "the ignorant and the unfortunate" how illegal operators abused garnishee proceedings and charged usurious rates. The administration, moreover, offered the service of the solicitor's office to those seemingly trapped in debts and urged a revision of the state usury laws so that the poor, as well as the rich, could borrow money safely.[16]

This was but one part of Hunt's war on vice and criminal activities in the Circle. City council passed three administration ordinances designed to slam the lid on gambling. The first tightened vagrancy regulations. The second made it illegal to possess a policy slip. And the third, aimed particularly at handbook operators, provided that known gamblers could be arrested and sentenced.[17]

Hunt used a similarly vigorous approach in his attempt to enforce the segregation of prostitution and to reduce crime and disorder in the tenderloin. The police instituted a registration system requiring each girl to report her family members, supply a photograph, and listen to a talk informing her of the error of her ways. Streetwalkers and procurers were picked up. The houses in the tenderloin were closely watched and forbidden to serve intoxicants in an effort to make a visit to the district as unattractive as possible. The health department, however, gave all the registered girls regular medical inspections and sent those who required treatment to the city hospital.[18]

The fight to control prostitution carried over into the effort to banish "dives" which supplied sitting rooms for women customers. By 1912, however, the concept of a dive had expanded to include public dance halls like the Majestic, which the *Post* denounced as a "market place . . . of panderers and the showplace of their women," but which also served as a favorite spot among the residents of the Zone. It was owned and operated by Daniel Bauer, GOP councilman from the Fifteenth Ward. Hunt closed sixty such establishments, including Bauer's. And he temporarily revoked the license of Central Turner Hall after a detective discovered that girls in short dresses were being served drinks at a public dance there.[19]

Hunt, however, refused to touch the saloons open on Sunday so long as they remained orderly. But in July the Hamilton County

Liquor League decided to close the Sunday saloons voluntarily, a tactical maneuver precipitated by the passage of a new state license law which closed permanently the saloon of any two-time violator of state liquor laws.[20]

There were other fields, too, in which Hunt did not cater to blue-law sentiment. He resisted pressure exerted by Protestant and Catholic clergy and lay leaders who favored the establishment of a board of play censors. And he permitted what he called scientific sparring and boxing exhibitions, a policy based in part on the assumption, as one Hunt supporter put it, that "our young are better off at these manly contests than loitering about the Majestic."[21]

Hunt, in fact, based much of his recreational program for the Circle on the deliquency-deterrent idea. The projects were worked out by his Women's Civic Commission. It sponsored twenty-two municipal dances in Music Hall, each of which went on until 11:45 p.m., in the belief that the lateness of the closing hour would prevent youths from entering saloons on their way home. It also put on a children's hour every Saturday afternoon in Music Hall at which folk dances were taught. The commission climaxed its recreation activities in 1913 with a civic Christmas festival. Public-school students gathered around the municipal Christmas tree, performed national folk dances, and sang "O Little Town of Bethlehem" and "God Rest Ye Merry Gentlemen."[22]

Hunt took other steps to alleviate the varied and chronic disorder of the Basin. City council passed a series of administration-backed traffic regulation ordinances, which made it illegal for pedestrians to cross street corners diagonally in the congested district, prohibited U turns, prescribed that all traffic should flow in a single file and keep to the right, defined parking and loading zones, required all motor vehicles to be equipped with night lights visible at twenty feet, outlined the obligations of drivers involved in accidents, and stipulated that horseless carriages had to have a horn, gong, or bell and show two white lights in front and a red and white light in the rear. But a proposal to rip out Fountain Square and replace it with a parking lot failed.

Hunt also launched an attack on the dirt, sanitation, health, and fire hazards emanating from the Circle and Zone. City council enacted his smoke abatement ordinance. Hunt closed twelve theaters as fire hazards, insisted that all large buildings be equipped with fireproof elevator shafts and stairways, have fire doors and walls and fire extinguishers and hoses, and threatened to tear down all public markets that failed to meet health department standards. And Dr. John H. Landis, the head of the health department, herded union officials into a group called the Sanitarians of Organized Labor. Their mission was to discover filthy workshops and persuade labor and management to clean them.

These measures dovetailed with Hunt's program to renovate the entire Circle by eliminating congestion. As a first step, city council passed an ordinance which created a housing division in the health department and gave the chief housing inspector all the powers and duties of the building commissioner. R. E. Todd, a New York housing inspector acting as an advisor to the administration, installed a new system of block inspection and reports and instructed the newly recruited tenement inspectors on the fine points of their jobs. Armed with a more stringent housing ordinance, the department began to crack down on tenement owners and to check all plans for new apartment buildings.[23]

At the same time, Hunt launched a better housing movement which, he told a mass meeting in November 1912, would secure a real home for everyone in Cincinnati, rich or poor, white or colored, healthy or ill. Part of the campaign was designed to encourage private investors to construct model tenements. But Hunt contemplated a program which would go beyond the philanthropists' efforts to provide cheap housing at a 5 per cent profit, a program which, according to Lawrence Veiller, the New York housing expert, would put Cincinnati in step with progressive municipal programs.[24]

Hunt intended to combat all the social ills associated with congestion by decentralizing the city's residential population. Our duty, he asserted, is plain—to provide rapid transit to the suburbs so the people can get to their homes after work, and to provide proper sewer facilities and parks so the people will be attracted

to the suburbs. These projects, he claimed, would relieve congestion below the hills, reduce disease and death rates by removing
workers from the Basin, and would make wasteland in the bottoms of Mill Creek liveable for those who, as yet, could not afford
to move farther out.[25]

Little opposition developed to the comprehensive sewage-system
proposals. Simultaneously, Hunt worked out the details of a project
which would not only improve the rapid-transit system but also
connect it to all the interurban lines which entered the city.

In the spring of 1912 the city leased from the state that part of
the canal which lay within the city limits. Hunt then appointed a
three-man commission to investigate the best way of improving the
city's rail-transportation system. The commission raised $10,320
by private subscription and hired Bion J. Arnold of Chicago to
make the study. He recommended the use of the canal as a backbone for a fifteen-mile terminal belt line circling the city, part of it
underground. A $50,000 bond issue was submitted and approved,
and Hunt hired George F. Swain, the chairman of the Boston
Rapid Transit Commission, to be consulting engineer and to set up
a bureau of subway construction to make the plans and surveys for
the proposed loop.

Enthusiastic Zone and Hilltop supporters of the idea embellished
the project with plans for a $2,000,000 municipal convention hall
and amusement center on the loop in the vicinity of Vine Street and
for a boulevard on top of the subway section of the railroad within
the Basin. Cincinnati, Hunt announced, was going to have the best
urban transportation in the United States.[26]

These steps formed the background for Hunt's traction-company
negotiations. He asked the company to surrender its fifty-year franchise and to accept a permit to operate its streetcar system and the
proposed belt railway as a single unit until the city took over both.
He also offered to appoint a board of valuation, composed of
representatives of the city and company and one neutral, to evalu-
ate the traction company and supervise the management of the
loop railroad. All earnings over 6 per cent of the valuation of the
traction company were to be divided between the city and the com-

pany. Fares were to be six tickets for a quarter or twenty-five for a dollar. Transfers were to be free and valid throughout the entire system. Hunt was not the only Democrat who wanted a showdown with the traction company. The Reverend Herbert S. Bigelow, who had been elected to the state legislature in 1912, introduced a bill which would revoke the traction-company franchise outright and replace it with an indeterminate permit providing a three-cent fare. It also gave the city the right to take over the company.

This angered Hunt, in part because Bigelow had not consulted him before acting. But the mayor also feared that the dubious constitutionality of Bigelow's bill would set off a long court fight. Haggling over the merits of the two proposals continued throughout January of 1913 and into February, but Hunt kept talking with the traction company in the hope of resolving the valuation question. Then the Cincinnati Street Railway Company, which had been leased to the Cincinnati Traction Company, announced that it, not the traction company, held the franchise and that the street railway company had not been negotiating with the city. Hunt, for the moment, was blocked. Bigelow's bill, meanwhile, died in a Senate committee.

Bigelow then decided to escalate the battle by taking the issue into the campaign for a new city charter. According to the home rule amendment of 1912, the Ohio state constitution permitted a city, if it so desired, to write its own charter. In September 1912 Charles Sawyer, a Democratic councilman from Hyde Park and a strong municipal ownership advocate, began to agitate for the immediate election of a commission to write a new charter for Cincinnati.

Once again Hunt found himself at odds with one of his own supporters. The mayor believed that the Republican organization would doubtless control the election of a charter commission. Hunt instead asked the legislature to amend the municipal code and give the city a nine-man council elected at large, a short ballot, nonpartisan elections, four-year terms for elected officials, and the initiative, referendum, and recall. But pressure from Bigelow and the

Federated Improvement Association forced him to back down. Early in June, Sawyer, speaking for the administration, introduced a new charter ordinance without, however, raising the question of municipal ownership. The voters were to cast ballots either for or against writing a new charter and to choose men to sit on the charter commission.[27]

At this point Bigelow intervened. He said there was no difference of opinion among the various organizations or governmental reformers because they all favored the measures which Hunt had proposed to the state legislation. But, he added, in comparison "to the one big issue, these are but details. The paramount issue in the coming [charter] election is the immediate ownership and operation of street railways." [28] He and his associates put up a slate of candidates for the charter commission to oppose the administration-backed Citizen's ticket.

The charter question carried by a scant 110 votes. It lost narrowly in every Hilltop ward. The Sixth, Eighth, and Eighteenth in the Circle, voting no by majorities of from 483 to 727, provided the strongest opposition. The Zone voted yes and put the charter across.

The Citizens' candidates for the charter commission swept through with majorities of from 5000 to 8000 votes. But the small council proposition, a remnant of Hunt's reform bill submitted to the voters by the General Assembly, lost by a similar margin. In both cases, the Zone vote provided the decisive margin. A hospital bond issue passed easily.[29]

Throughout the entire charter campaign Hunt remained remarkably silent. He was, in fact, distracted by other matters. The spring and summer of 1913 were enlivened by traction and ice strikes. In both the mayor played an important part and in both the question of municipal ownership appeared. In the traction strike Hunt worked for an arbitrated settlement. At one point, however, the situation seemed so critical that he called for the state militia. Governor Cox refused to send it. The strike continued. Then City Solicitor Bettmann, arguing that the traction company had broken its contractual obligation to provide the city with streetcar service, started condemnation proceedings. When the company agreed to arbitrate, Bettmann dropped the case.

Hunt later denied that he had been hasty in calling for the militia. He contended that it was a tactical move to strengthen the city's case against the traction company. If, in the judgment of the governor, the local authorities had the situation under control, the city could then argue that there was no reason for the company to halt service.[30]

The ice strike created a deeper crisis. "Nowadays," noted the *Citizen's Bulletin,* "ice is no longer a luxury for city dwellers, but a necessary thing, something that everybody who is above the direst poverty buys for himself, something that charity feels must be furnished to the very poor." [31] Hunt pushed for an arbitrated settlement on the basis of a union shop. When the companies refused, he took over the ice plants, running them on eight-hour shifts. The companies agreed to arbitrate, and a settlement was made.

Yet that did not finish the affair. The companies set off another furor by raising the price of ice. Hunt remarked that the situation demonstrated the need for a new charter. Then, he thought, the city could go into the ice business and force the companies to reduce their prices through competition. Within a year, he said, Cincinnati should have its own ice plant.[32]

As Hunt's first term drew to a close, the key program in his plan to revitalize the city still hung in the balance. The city and the traction company remained at odds over the proposed rapid-transit system. To break the impasse, Hunt resorted to the strategy he had used in the ice strike.

In his annual message for 1913 Hunt proposed that the city should not only build but, if necessary, operate the belt railway. He pointed out that the traction-company franchise came up for revision in 1916 and asserted that the possession by the city of an actual or potential competitor would be a potent factor in these negotiations. It would also be a powerful force, he added, for securing a voluntary settlement of the evaluation question. With a municipal belt railway as a club, he predicted, the entire system could be brought under the control of the city on fair terms.[33]

In his first term Hunt demonstrated his willingness to accept the city's existing political and economic institutions. All the policies of the administration—Geier's welfare program, the broad-gauged clean-up crusade, the rapid-transit scheme, and the tinkering with the machinery of local government—served the overriding goal of accommodating the people of the Circle, Zone, and Hilltops to life in the new city. Hunt conceived of the mayoralty as the center of city government which would respond to and appease the boosters, urban gospellers, and experts and serve as an arbiter between them and the other interests and groups within the city. A strong mayor, armed with a program and buttressed by a political organization, Hunt felt, could boss the municipal government, educate the people, and unify the city.

15

The Zone Defects, 1913

After the Democratic victory of 1911, Hilltop Republicans once again began the task of reconstructing and purifying the organization. But Cox's past political and business ventures continued to haunt him, titillate the press and reading public, and frustrate GOP efforts to prove its respectability to the voters of the Zone and Hilltops.

The *Post*, especially, considered him fair game and set out to prove that all his business success was merely the fruit of his political power.[1] Throughout the spring and early summer of 1912, it repeatedly charged that in the past year three banks, the Second National, the Cincinnati Trust, and the Metropolitan Savings, had gone on the financial rocks because of Cox's tenure.

The head of the Metropolitan, the paper asserted, had been for many years the chief of a ring which controlled paving in Hamilton County. The bank failed after making doubtful loans to contractors who were also in the construction supply business and who controlled the brick and granite situation in Cincinnati. Moreover, the Cincinnati Trust and the Second National, claimed the *Post*, had both suffered from manipulations involving the Ford & Johnson

Chair Company which dated back to 1907. The bubble actually floated on public confidence inspired by the knowledge that Cox was behind the two firms. His indictment and the revelations made by Hunt and the grand jury in 1911 apparently burst that bubble. The *Post* demanded that Prosecutor Pogue launch a grand jury investigation.[2]

To protect himself, Pogue asked Charles P. Taft to contact the President and secure a "thoroughly competent . . . federal man" to help dig up the facts so that Pogue could not be accused of a whitewash. President Taft, through Attorney General Wickersham, obliged and sent out a government bank examiner. Negotiations for his employment, Pogue told the *Post*, were conducted by a friend in Washington.[3]

A flurry of indictments and litigation followed. The insurgent stockholders of the Cincinnati Trust sued the directors for mismanagement. That was settled out of court for $150,000, of which Cox paid $70,000. Cox, along with other Cincinnati Trust officers, was indicted by the county grand jury on two counts of misapplying funds. On both counts, Common Pleas Court Judge Caldwell instructed the jury to acquit. The decision on one was appealed, and the Ohio supreme court upheld Caldwell. "This," Cox observed, "restores my good name. This is what I have been contending all my life."[4]

Meanwhile, as the presidential election of 1912 approached, the Tafts intensified their drive to make the Republican organization palatable beyond the Circle. Charles P. Taft and the *Times-Star* tried to persuade Herrmann and Hynicka, the remaining symbols of Coxism, to resign their positions in the organization. Although both men, after a bitter intraparty squabble, publicly announced their retirement from politics, they were so strong among the Blaine Club bonifaces that Charles P. Taft was forced, as the *Post* predicted, to "make a deal, as in the past." The Taft-Cox axis was replaced by a triple alliance of Charles P. Taft, Hynicka, and Herrmann, but only after Mike Mullen intervened to save Taft from an attempted counterpurge by Hynicka. His East End neighbor, Mullen argued, had done a great deal for the organization and had been a valuable aid in running up big majorities in the Eighth Ward.[5]

Thereafter things went smoothly. In June 1912 all eighty-seven of the Hamilton County delegates to the state convention voted to renominate William Howard Taft. Charles P. Taft, Julius Fleischmann, and Herrmann helped to pay the expenses of the Blaine Club contingent at the national convention; William Howard Taft thanked Scott Small, the editor of the *Commercial-Tribune,* and Hynicka, for the backing of the paper; and the County Advisory Committee paid Hynicka $1871 for expenses in connection with the state and national conventions and elections.

Indeed, it was an open secret that Hynicka had not been eliminated. On October 30 County Prosecutor Pogue assured the Taft Club of the Cincinnati law school that Herrmann was out of party politics. So, too, was Cox, whom he described as "an old man, broken down, not a pauper" yet a man who had recently lost a tremendous amount of money. But, Pogue added, "Hynicka has been counselled with many times because of his ability in political affairs." [6]

There were developments in the 1912 presidential campaign, however, which suggested that the Republicans might regain some lost ground in the periphery despite the local scandals and retention of Hynicka. James A. Green, an iron manufacturer, described himself as a progressive who thought that conditions in this country were steadily working toward the best. But he disliked Roosevelt because of the "Populistic radicalism" he advocated and feared what Wilson and a Democratic Congress might do to the tariff. Green joined the Cincinnati Prosperity League, a group of two hundred business "barons," who replaced the Citizens' Taft League of 1908, and was soon up to his neck in the Taft campaign.[7]

The religious issue, in addition, tended to neutralize whatever negative effect Taft's stand on the tariff may have had on Zone workingmen. Many Catholics were convinced that there existed a systematic, organized, financed movement to influence Protestants to vote against President Taft. And Joseph B. Foraker, who had let

bygones be bygones and was working for Taft, noticed a similar
development. For some reason, he wrote, every Catholic he knew
in Cincinnati intended to vote for Taft. That included his tailor,
"who always votes Democratic top to bottom in presidential years,"
his gardener, and all his friends, former Mayor Dempsey, and General Michael J. Ryan, a wealthy Democrat.[8]

Foraker also noted that the Roosevelt movement was weakening.
A Progressive rally at Music Hall drew only twelve hundred, he
observed, and there were very few TR men among businessmen.
The leadership of the Progressive party in Cincinnati, moreover,
contained no spokesman for organized labor. Its local leader was
Otto C. Lightner of Price Hill, the president of the Associated
Trade Press Company. Lightner and his associates comprised a
motley group of small businessmen and professional men, including three Negroes, from the Zone and Hilltops. And virtually none
of the eighteen most prominent Progressives had been influential in
Cincinnati society, business, labor, politics, or philanthropy. President Taft was not far wrong when he claimed that Roosevelt's
urban support came from "an intelligent class of discontented persons . . . who seek to place their lack of success upon the system"
and "feel crushed or embarrassed by the small salaries they earn." [9]
Such a crowd posed no threat to the reunified local Republicans.

Yet, as in the 1911 city contest when the Tafts also played a
prominent part, the Democratic coalition in the Zone and Hilltops
held up in 1912. In the gubernatorial race Democrat James M. Cox
beat his Republican opponent 47,319 to 42,700 in the county. Governor Cox, moreover, carried seventeen city wards, leaving but nine
to the GOP candidate, Robert A. Brown. To the solid Circle, Brown
had added only the western or Zone sections of Walnut Hills, the
Avondale-Clifton districts on the Hilltops (by narrow majorities),
and the Twenty-second, a Zone ward in Mill Creek between
Mohawk-Brighton and Cumminsville.

The pattern of the presidential vote was similar. Woodrow Wilson also carried both the county and the city by a smaller margin
than Governor Cox. In the city Wilson had 31,221 votes to Taft's
30,588 votes. Wilson carried the entire western half of the city from

the Ohio to College Hill except the Twenty-second Ward. All but two of these nine wards lay in the Zone. To these he added the First and Second, the two Hilltop districts farthest east of the Basin. Roosevelt failed to carry a single ward. Taft carried the other fifteen wards, eight by less than 150 votes. But if Wilson's and Roosevelt's vote is combined, Taft is left with merely six wards. The GOP organization, in short, produced victories only in the Sixth, Eighth and Eighteenth, the Seventh, an Over-the-Rhine ward just north of the notorious triad, the Fourth, the Walnut Hills district which included the Zone Negro community, and the Hilltop Thirteenth.[10]

In addition, the voters approved the Hunt administration's request for a 2.16 mill increase in the tax levy and for $4.5 million in bond issue for sewers, parks, playgrounds, a new convention hall, and hospital improvements. The voters, the *Post* concluded, apparently did not regret the civic revolution of 1911, when they put in "popular government, efficiency and honesty," and a "good-government administration." [11]

In 1913, however, a year of social, economic, and political tension and deep confusion rivaling the turbulence of the worst years of the decade of disorder, the strong sense of satisfaction faded. By March, claimed the *Citizen's Bulletin,* Hunt's detractors were criticizing the mayor with "unscrupulous vehemence that betokens a malice born of hatred." [12]

Little went well for Hunt during his second year in office. Through the heavy floods of January and February, as one advisor put it, "he pitched into the work of salvation and rescue with . . . enthusiasm, dispatch and skill." But his Flood Relief Committee, according to Mike Mullen, grossly insulted good, honest citizens made unfortunate through no fault of their own by doling out supplies as if it feared the victims might overfeed themselves. In the spring and summer, moreover, the Cox perjury and bank trials terminated without a conviction, raising the suspicion that Hunt had conducted a political vendetta against the alleged boss.[13]

Then came a series of feuds over public service corporations. When the Democratic majority in city council referred the applica-

tion of the Cincinnati, Newport & Covington Street Railroad to the
Committee on Street Railroads, several members protested that the
committee was partial to traction companies. The imbroglio between Hunt and Bigelow over the municipal ownership of the Cincinnati Traction Company was more divisive. Hunt got disgusted
with Bigelow, Bigelow became suspicious of Hunt, Kiefer turned
violently against the mayor, and the *Post* danced from one side to
the other. The whole affair, grumbled the *Citizen's Bulletin*, was
filled with sensationalism, demagoguism, and hysterics.[14]

It was in 1913, too, that the slogan "three strikes and you're out"
was applied to Hunt. In January a needle trades' strike was in its
eleventh week and one manufacturer, when his request to "borrow"
the police force was rejected, threatened to bring in sluggers of his
own. In May the Building Contractors' Association locked out eight
thousand men. Then came the traction and ice strikes, and in August the city was disturbed by half a dozen different strikes, of
which the Teamsters' strike was particularly irritating. James A.
Green thought that Hunt's handling of the strikes displeased everybody because he was afraid to keep order and by a process of vacil-
lation had let labor leaders "overrun" the town. Another businessman nostalgically recalled the days of Mayor Fleischmann and
Chief Milliken who "had a way of their own" in dealing with labor
agitators.[15]

Yet organized labor did not always come down on Hunt's side.
During the Teamsters' strike the Central Labor Council protested
that associations of businessmen, commercial bodies, and the like
could get the ear and sympathy of public officials, while organizations of men in the lower walks of life were ignored and condemned.[16]

As leader of his party, Hunt, furthermore, antagonized many of
the regulars. His patronage policies created rumblings in Circle and
Zone precincts. The workers claimed that Hunt had been friendly
in 1911, but once elected had gone "high hat," closed his office to
them, and told job and favor seekers he was busy. And one Central
Labor Council member accused the administration of playing fa-
vorites by advocating a salary raise which constituted "discrimina-

tion in favor of men already drawing high salaries, the bloated aristocrats of favor and partiality." [17]

Hunt also offended ex-Mayor Dempsey. He complained that the administration was ignoring the Western Hills and denying those "suburbs" needed improvements. While the old organization might have been moderately bad, he snorted, what they did happened in the open, not in secret. "I hold such people above [the current] mob of hypocrites and dissemblers." Hunt and his associates, Dempsey recalled, were the same "deceitful hypocrites" who had stabbed him in the back in 1907.[18]

Hunt was also caught up in the furor over the new state liquor law which provided for state and county licensing boards. These bodies were to apportion the number of saloons according to population on the basis of one for every five hundred people. That meant that the thirteen hundred or so saloons in Cincinnati would have to be reduced to about eight hundred. A rumor soon circulated that only Republican saloons in wards Six, Eight, and Eighteen would be closed by "the Democrats." [19]

But that was not the only prominent question related to public morals raised in 1913. Subjects related to sexual behavior received increasing attention in the press. The *Post* grumbled that too many magazines had tossed aside the muckrake. Instead, their "covers in twenty out of thirty instances are covered with a woman, or part of a woman," and "the contents devoted largely . . . to sex relations" and suggestive stories. The *Post* also came up with a new cure for the saloon "sitting room" problem. With high rents forcing people to pack tenements, parents no longer had parlors at home in which daughter could see her "steady." This, explained the *Post*, was one more reason for supporting the neighborhood social center idea and gave credibility to the suggestion of one preacher that every church should have a "courting parlor" as a substitute for the saloon sitting room.[20]

Some of Hunt's other allies devoted time to discussing the merits of teaching sex hygiene in the public schools.[21] And the *Citizen's Bulletin* complained that moving-picture theaters, "a titanic engine for public education," ran too many sensational and vulgar films.

This kind of talk by men around the mayor, plus Hunt's war on concert halls, gambling in saloons, and prostitution, led the *Volksblatt* to brand him a moral reformer, an unpatriotic mayor who slandered the city and did little to further its material progress and physical improvement.[22]

The tension generated by the agitation of emotionally packed issues such as municipal ownership, patronage, strikes, saloons, Sunday closing, and sex was accompanied by increasing sensitivity to ethnic, racial, religious, political-ideological, class, and sexual identities. This latent sense of clan, apparently chronic in the new city, was expressed in increasingly strident terms in 1912 and 1913.

The dimensions of the fear and distrust in any one expression of tribalism varied. The Business Men's Club, for instance, thought that the local National Guard needed moral support and encouragement from businessmen, manufacturers, and all other employers of labor. But Socialists, labor agitators, and the discontented, unruly elements of society were all bitterly opposed to military organizations, and many of the best people, possessed by the "universal peace" idea, were seconding their efforts to abolish all militarism.[23]

In August of 1913 Common Pleas Judge Wade Cushing gave another twist to the spreading sense of insecurity. He claimed that the increase in the number of criminals in the city was due to an increase in socialism. He asserted, too, that Socialists were behind the woman's suffrage movement. And women, he warned, citing the mothers who sat on streetcar tracks with babies in their arms during the traction strike, were just as radical as men.[24]

Women were also prominent subjects of interest in other manifestations of tribalism. A certain Julius Anglos deluged the *Post* with letters complaining of Negro crime, especially against white women. Anglos suggested that Cincinnati needed a Klan and that all Negroes, Japanese, and Chinese should be deported. In addition, three of the four proposed state constitutional amendments which failed in the city in 1912 were related to the sex and race question. One granted woman's suffrage, another permitted women to hold state and local offices, and the third struck the word white from the suffrage clause in the Ohio constitution.[25]

The *Citizen's Bulletin* put the nuances of race, class, sex, and morality together to fit its particular bias. Noting that the *Times-Star* condemned the Negro suffrage vote as blind prejudice, the *Bulletin* claimed that it was well enough to decry a prejudice which was but another name for race hatred, but better to denounce one that kept the better half of the white race in subjection by denying women the vote and the right to hold office. If the Anglo-Saxons were masters of the world, asserted the paper, it was because of the women of that race whose example and influence led men on to progress in civilization and enlightenment. Our friends, the paper added, who are so afraid that the ballot will degrade women are woman's worst enemies.

> They have a way of idealizing woman, so that she is made to appear as something created only to please and amuse. . . . And yet these men are the very ones who lend themselves to produce economic conditions that make it necessary for great numbers of women to get out into the world where they have to battle in competition . . . for a livelihood.[26]

The surge of anti-Catholicism which began in 1907 also reached its peak in 1913. One audience of Zone workingmen gave the editor of *The Menace*, a national patriotic and anti-Catholic weekly, several minutes of intense applause when his presence was announced. Bigelow, the speaker for the evening, was incensed. He claimed that religious bigotry had reached the point that he could speak to a packed house every Sunday if he would only guarantee to attack the Catholic Church. He denounced the sentiment as a divisive issue and urged the Guardians of Liberty, an anti-Catholic and anti-monopoly group, and all workers to forget religious differences and unite for social justice.[27]

The Junior Order of American Mechanics, long a dormant organization in Cincinnati, also increased its activities.[28] According to the *Catholic-Telegraph*, the prominence of Director of Public Safety Cash and City Treasurer William E. Kenney, both Catholics, aroused the religious hatred of the Order and "kindred spirits of the dark-lantern type." The bigotry became so fierce and anti-administration talk became so prevalent that several Masons in the police department became alarmed. Determined to offset rumors that city offices were loaded with Catholics, they conducted a religious census. Their report showed that the detective bureau contained twenty-six Protestants and eleven Catholics, and that Cash had put fifteen Masons on the police force and appointed Masons to nine major and five lesser posts in the city administration.

This list was given to Catholics. They decided that Cash was a traitor and sent out a circular to Catholics urging them to vote against Hunt. The *Freie Presse* picked up this story and announced that, for the first time in the history of the city, an official had published a campaign document showing the religious affiliation of his subordinates.[29]

The rising tide of nativism also cut into the confidence of the defenders of Germandom, men already strained by the gradual dissolution of the German community. Their spokesmen feared that the board of education was going to restrict, and perhaps abolish, the teaching of their language. And, on November 1, the *Volksblatt* published a list of ten school-board candidates who would support German-language instruction in the schools, only three of whom were backers of the Hunt administration.[30]

As the fall city campaign got under way, the two daily German papers launched a vitriolic attack on the policies of the mayor and his associates. Since both papers were Republican, much of their approach was geared to the GOP theme that Hunt could not be trusted, that he was a sham reformer. He promised economy and efficiency, they claimed, but raised taxes; he denounced bossism but used his patronage power politically and co-operated with bosses Peck and Noctor; he boasted of his clean-up crusade yet Democratic saloons and dives flourished; he professed to be a booster yet unpatriotically slandered the city; he planned large improvements but started few and completed fewer.[31]

The German papers, however, added significant variations. Hunt's welfare program, they noted, was inhumane and brutal and increased the suffering of the poor. Germans, the papers said, helped elect Hunt in 1911 because they believed what he said about his interest in Germans, yet in the past two years they had to "take a back position" in the city's life. And among Hunt's admirers, the *Freie Presse* observed, was *The New York Times*, which was constantly attacking Germany and German politics, and *Collier's Weekly*, the worst enemy of the drinking industry.

Nor was that all. Hunt, by harrassing the *Vereins*, had displayed a disrespect for personal liberty. He sent "snoopers" to *Verein* dances who reported "awful happenings" which slipped past the censors and got into the papers. He did not realize, announced the *Volksblatt*, that Germans regarded *Verein* balls as private affairs, not under the jurisdiction of the police force. The mayor, charged the *Freie Presse*, if he had his way, would replace *Verein* balls with municipal dances.[32]

The papers emphasized that now was the time to return to the old party, for the GOP had nominated six personal liberty candidates for city posts. In fact, every GOP candidate for a major office had a German name. Most important, however, the mayoralty candidate was Frederich S. Spiegel, a Prussian-born German Jew from Avondale who had once lived in the Fifteenth Ward and who had held one local elective office or other since 1881. He was an especially welcome nominee, claimed the *Volksblatt*, because he had always been a member of the German circle, believed in personal liberty and progress, and was a former president of a number of *Vereins* who knew "on what high moral grounds" they stood. A progressive, he had, moreover, studied the government of the great cities of Europe and was an advocate of the "German system." [33]

Others were not so impressed. Professor Gotthard Deutsch of Hebrew Union College thought that the politicians forgave Spiegel his religion because he was "a willing tool." The *Post* dismissed him as "one of the pitiful, surviving figures of an age in which the minds of many good men were, politically speaking, atrophied by the tyranny exercised by the Gang." [34]

Indeed, James A. Green complained that the election was a contest of Hunt against the Republican gang. The slate, however, evoked even more pungent language. It represented, the *Post* said, "a slimy company, consisting of privilege-seeking corporations, dive keepers, gambling house owners, loan sharks, the owners of vile tenements—all the horde that break the law and yearn for the protection of which they were deprived two years ago." [35]

Nonetheless, many former Hunt allies seemed eager to stay clear of the campaign. *The Chronicle* remained quiet, and Typographical No. 3 issued a statement denying that it had endorsed anyone. Both the Municipal Ownership League and the Progressive party considered and then rejected running a third ticket. And while Bigelow publicly repudiated a rumor that he opposed the re-election of Hunt, he refused to say anything else.

Yet Hunt preserved some of his coalition. Governor Cox issued a statement of support, and both Democratic congressmen toured the city and shared the platform with Hunt. Some 102 prominent Republicans representing every type of business interest, all the professions, the three major religions, and virtually every branch of philopolistic work endorsed him, and some of them backed it up with campaign contributions. The *Citizen's Bulletin, Post,* and *Enquirer* all provided him unequivocal backing.[36]

The mayor, however, ran scared. From his opening speech in North Cincinnati Turner Hall Hunt not only defended his record but, as in 1911, viciously condemned the "new Gang." It was, he said, headed by Herrmann, Hynicka, and Kraft and "an army of divekeepers, gamblers, touts and procurers." Hunt also attacked those who criticized his vice- and crime-suppression program. The "slanderous Gusweiler," the mayor charged, "the pussy-footed Pogue and the lying Commercial are trying to alibi the Gang for its alliance with the vicious by attacking us." [37]

Hunt would win, predicted the *Citizen's Bulletin*, because the issue was not dollars and cents, but decency against indecency, morality against immorality. Spiegel, however, carried thirteen of the twenty-six wards and was elected with a plurality of just over 3000 votes. From the point of view of the *Citizen's Bulletin*, the Circle Sixth, Eighth, and Eighteenth were responsible. There, the GOP plurality increased by 710 votes over the 1911 margin.[38]

Yet the returns suggest that the turbulent events of 1913 had shaken the periphery's confidence in Hunt. Although all his wards lay in that section of the city, his total vote dropped in every Zone and Hilltop ward from its 1911 level, and six of these districts, only two of them in the Hilltops, went to Spiegel. The Socialists also increased their total, all the gains coming in Zone and Hilltop districts.

More significantly, the Democratic councilmanic candidates increased their majorities in every Hilltop ward except the Twenty-fifth. But in the Zone, as in the mayoralty race, the party vote tailed off. The Democratic progressive coalition had been broken, but not shattered. Apparently, the rise of issues related to morality, race, sex, labor, and religion sparked the Zone defections. Given the tense atmosphere of 1913, it is a wonder the revolt was not on a larger scale.

Post-election interpretations of the meaning of Hunt's defeat varied. But virtually no one suggested that the new administration had a mandate to reject the new methods, concepts, and positive programs introduced by Hunt. Spiegel told the Avondale Improvement Association that the city was on the path of sociological advancement and that he intended to follow the steps made in the past. He assured the Business Men's Club that he would "look to where the dollar goes," but added that he favored progressive government and had made a special study of social service and executive government. And Julius Fleischmann remarked that "in many things done during the Hunt administration, a lead was given that must be followed. . . . There must be no going backward to old conditions," he observed, "for times have changed." [39]

That announcement was "gratifying" to the *Citizen's Bulletin*. It buttressed the paper's contention that reforms, like revolutions, never go backward, and convinced Pendleton that his labors had not been in vain. "Even Mr. Fleischmann, though he be a local Republican leader, is now something of a reformer." [40]

16

Bossism and Reform

The central problems facing reformers after 1897 was like that of the 1880's and 1890's: how to get and retain power to do what was felt necessary to hold the dividing city together. The response in both instances was strikingly similar.

Despite the disorder of the earlier period,[1] George B. Cox, rising from the unique vantage point of the Eighteenth Ward, helped to create a voluntary political action organization which united the Zone and Hilltops and eventually proved capable of bringing the Circle into the coalition. Through this instrument, he and his allies were able to bring positive government to Cincinnati and to mitigate the chaos which accompanied the emergence of the new city. But the machine was a mediator, feeding on the discord it sought to dispel. Its development and the feeling of social and political security it fostered eased the sense of crisis which made it so attractive. Continued success left it increasingly vulnerable.

With the crisis atmosphere muted, "philopolists" developed more sophisticated programs and, eschewing Cox's methods but not his strategy, could educate, discipline, organize, and coalesce without arousing the divisive, emotional, and hysterical responses which helped immobilize municipal statesmen in the 1880's. Their efforts gave residents of the periphery new outlets for their emotions, new avenues to action, and new sources of power and social control.

These circumstances forced the GOP organization into a steady reliance upon the Circle as a power base. The machine, now more susceptible than ever to attack on moral and social grounds, was pilloried not only as expensive and inefficient, but also as ineffective and decadent. It could not heal, or regenerate. It began to look like a menace, a malignant force pulling the whole city down to the level of the Circle. The periphery, responding to these appeals, abandoned the "new order" in 1897, rejected "the system" in 1905, and revolted against "the syndicate" in 1911. And, after the revelations of 1911 and 1912, harried Republicans from the periphery presided over the elimination of Cox.

Not surprisingly, voters in the periphery—especially those in the Zone—felt torn between bossism and reform. Perplexed by the appearance of a complex knot of emotionally colored issues, they failed to rally to the reform coalition in 1913. But by then, bossism was virtually dead. The insistent battering at the boss-slum-special-privilege nexus had gradually shattered the bonds of confidence which, in the final analysis, linked the bonifaces—the colorful assemblage of Circle and Zone politicians—and the Republicans of the Hilltops and Zone to Coxism. Cox said more than he realized when, in 1893, he remarked that a boss was "not necessarily a public enemy." [2]

Although the contests between the machine and its organized competitors were fought for power in the periphery, the Circle was neither ignored nor intentionally scorned. Indeed, slum dwellers acquired not one but two powerful sets of spokesmen, both of them new forces in the city's affairs.

One was, of course, the Republican organization. The other consisted of the shifting coalitions of "philopolists." Despite a chronic inability to win Circle votes, they nonetheless developed programs which, they insisted, would benefit the Circle as well as the Zone and Hilltops. Because of their diversity, their vision of the new city was not monolithic. But they intransigently held that they had undertaken a long-term campaign to secure an outwardly mobile and democratic community which would produce, as they would have said, good and moral citizens. Machine supporters could and did make the same claim with equal zeal. The two sides, to the extent that two sides were involved, differed over the permissible speed, thoroughness, and cost of the transformation as well as over political methods and techniques.

The battle between bossism and reform, moreover, had a remarkable effect on voter participation. In 1889 and 1891 approximately 65 per cent of the eligible voters went to the polls. The figure rose to 72 per cent in 1900, 79 per cent in 1903, and 81 per cent in 1909. It peaked in 1911, when 88 per cent turned out to cast their votes for or against Hunt.[3] The alienated voter was rare in Boss Cox's Cincinnati.

Finally, the pattern of politics suggests that residence rather than race, religion, or ethnicity provides the touchstone to the city's social and political experience. Politics mirrored the conflicts created by the process of urbanization.[4] Throughout the years, and despite the heterogeneity within and among the Circle, Zone, and Hilltops, the contest between the changing populations of the center and periphery persisted. Cox and the *Times-Star* were only half correct, then, when they asserted that the boss evolved with the modern city.[5] If bossism was inevitable in the divided and mobile new city, so too was reform. They were interlocking parts in the new system of urban politics.

Note on Sources

The footnotes accompanying the text are intended as a general guide to the sources. Students who wish to consult a more extensive list will find a forty-three page bibliography in Harper Library at the University of Chicago. Harper Library also has a copy of the three-volume, typed manuscript from which this book derives. It includes additional evidence buttressing interpretations and assertions which may seem here to rest on scant documentation.

The student of recent urban history possesses a mass of sources. The proliferation of agencies and institutions and the impact of the dramatic changes in the city on individuals produced a flood of commentary and a passion for factual collection. None of it can safely be ignored.

Such a study would be virtually impossible without statistical materials. The volumes of the United States census contain a mine of information on American city life. The reports of the Cincinnati city departments include not only statistics, but explanatory comments on the state of the city as well. Although this information must be used with care, its compilers were, for the most part, quite candid. The archives of state agencies, too, contain some useful data. Returns for all elections from 1887 to 1914 are available at the Hamilton County Board of Elections, and its staff gladly dug out the volumes, provided assistance in their use, and permitted them to be microfilmed.

Manuscripts, letters, unpublished diaries, memoirs, and reminiscences abound. Without them the human dimension of the city would have been most difficult to recapture. They contain information on practically every aspect of urban life, including significant nuances and subtleties unavailable elsewhere. The Andrew Hickenlooper Collection at the Cincinnati Historical Society was especially helpful. Hickenlooper was a conscientious diarist and sensitive man who apparently used his avocation as a kind of emotional therapy. The Joseph B. Foraker Papers, also at the society, the William Howard Taft Papers at the Library of Congress, and the David Philipson Papers at the American Jewish Archives in Cincinnati were only slightly less revealing. The forty other items in this category were briefer and varied considerably in usefulness. All are in Cincinnati repositories except the John Sherman and Brand Whitlock collections, both at the Library of Congress. Most professional urban politicians, unfortunately, relied on the spoken rather than the written word.

The number of extant addresses, articles, monographs, and pamphlets written by contemporaries is overwhelming. The Public Library of Hamilton County and Cincinnati and the Cincinnati Historical Society both have rich collections of these. Like statistics, they must be read with care. Frequently they constitute more of an accurate reflection of the author's biases than a description or analysis of what was happening. As such, however, they serve as an index to the intellectual history of the period, a convenient atlas of the city's mood.

The reports and records of private organizations are not only numerous but especially significant. They contain descriptions, analyses, and statistics of all segments of the city. Their authors were committed and perceptive individuals who spoke freely and with enthusiasm in the jargon of their clique. They greatly simplified the task of charting the social, intellectual, and political geography of the city.

The last remark also applies to the books and directories of the period, as well as to interviews. There was a book on almost every subject, and a variety of directories which mirrored the density of the city's institutional life. Interviews served as valuable supplements to the printed materials. Most of those consulted were sophisticated, knowledgeable men and women with remarkable memories. Curiously enough most of the surviving politicians were anti-Cox men. The discussions were not taped for fear of inhibiting the conversation on both sides of the table, but a written memorandum was made immediately following each session.

Newspapers, newspaper scrapbooks, and periodicals furnish the most complete accounts of daily life in the city. The remaining files of twenty-five local daily and weekly papers and journals were culled systematically. All except *The Chronicle*, housed at 1015 Vine Street, Cincinnati, are available in local libraries. Among the ethnic groups, unfortunately, only the Germans had a local press.

The last category of primary materials used were visual. Maps and pictures of all kinds are particularly important for a study of this sort. There are twenty-two maps, including fourteen of election returns, in the Harper Library manuscript mentioned above, and the Cincinnati Historical Society possesses an impressive collection of graphic materials. It is impossible, moreover, to write confidently of the city without spending some time there. Much of the physical, social, and political configuration of Boss Cox's Cincinnati remains intact, despite the great changes which have occurred since the 1930's.

The most useful secondary materials have been cited in the footnotes. For a lengthier list the student should consult Charles N. Glaab, "The Historian and the American City: A Bibliographic Survey," in Philip M. Hauser and Leo F. Schnore (eds.), *The Study of Urbanization* (New York, 1965). Robert H. Wiebe, *The Search for Order, 1877–1920* (New York, 1967) is a distinguished interpretive introduction to the general history of the period.

Notes

PART I

1. Charles Cist, *Sketches and Statistics of Cincinnati in 1851* (Cincinnati, 1851), pp. 20, 269–70.
2. *Citizen's Bulletin* (Cincinnati), January 28, 1911, p. 1.
3. Cincinnati Bureau of Governmental Research, *A Survey Defining the Boundaries of the Cincinnati Region, Report No. 43* (Cincinnati, April 1933), pp. 6–8.
4. For a general discussion of the idea of the new divided city see Samuel B. Warner, Jr., *Streetcar Suburbs: The Process of Growth in Boston, 1870–1900* (Cambridge, Mass., 1962), pp. 1–14.; Oscar Handlin, "The Modern City as a Field of Historical Study," in Oscar Handlin and John Burchard (eds.), *The Historian and the City* (Cambridge, Mass., 1963), pp. 1–26.

CHAPTER 1

1. *Cincinnati Post*, May 8, 1897, p. 2.
2. *Cincinnati Times-Star*, January 20, 1892, p. 4. Also see *The Illustrated Building, Business, and Property Owners' Directory of Cincinnati, 1892*, Vol. I (Cincinnati, 1892), pp. 20–127.
3. *Citizen's Bulletin*, March 5, 1904, p. 4.
4. Rev. John Howard Melish, *The Moral Aspect of the Political Situation in Cincinnati* (Cincinnati, 1903), p. 7.
5. *Citizen's Bulletin*, November 13, 1909, p. 5.
6. Oscar Ameringer, *If You Don't Weaken . . . The Autobiography of Oscar Ameringer* (New York, 1940), p. 49.

7. For the quote see Frank Y. Grayson, *Pioneers of Night Life on Vine Street* (Cincinnati, August 1924), pp. 63–65, 123–25.
8. *Cincinnati American*, October 2, 1913, p. 4.
9. *Citizen's Bulletin*, June 6, 1908, p. 5.
10. Ibid., July 3, 1909, p. 4.
11. *The Chronicle* (Cincinnati), September 30, 1911, p. 4.
12. Willard Glazier, *Peculiarities of American Cities* (Philadelphia, 1886), p. 128.
13. Cincinnati, "Annual Report of the Inspector of Buildings," *Annual Reports of the City Departments . . . 1890* (Cincinnati, 1890), pp. 129–30; Bert L. Baldwin, "Proposed High Pressure Fire System," *The Optimist* (Cincinnati), Vol. II, (October 1912), p. 19.
14. In 1880 there were 13,562 Southerners in Cincinnati. In the next decade the city received 18,891 more from the same source. The figure rose to 26,434 in 1900 and 33,165 in 1910. More came from Kentucky than from any other single Southern state, though an increase in the numbers from the Deep South is discernable after 1900. The Negro population rose from 8179 in 1880 to 11,655 in 1890; to 14,482 in 1900; and to 19,639 in 1910.
15. *Cincinnati Enquirer*, March 27, 1897, p. 5.
16. Frederick T. Bastel, *Report on the Foreign Population in Cincinnati: Made for the Continuation Committee of The World in Cincinnati* (Cincinnati 1912), p. 5.
17. *Citizen's Bulletin*, May 3, 1913, p. 1.
18. E. N. Clopper, "Children on the Streets of Cincinnati," *Annals of the American Academy of Political and Social Science*, Vol. XXXII (July 1908), Supplement, pp. 113–23; *Charities Review* (Cincinnati), Vol. I (February 1909), pp. 10–12.
19. William C. Smith, *Queen City Yesterdays, Sketches of Cincinnati in the Eighties* (Crawfordsville, Indiana, 1959), pp. 32–34, 54–62, contains a brief description of the small businessmen in the West End, including a good account of saloons, saloonkeepers, and peddlers. Smith points out that chain stores began to appear in the eighties and that they were already delivering groceries to suburbs. Smith, born in 1872, grew up in the West End and later became a prominent local bookseller. His memory of Cincinnati in this period was encyclopedic and quite accurate.
20. United Jewish Charities of Cincinnati, *Fourteenth Annual Report, 1910* (Cincinnati, n.d.), p. 59.
21. Smith, op. cit.; Ameringer, op. cit. pp. 48–51.
22. The white Southerners and the non-Irish immigrants from the British Isles present a special problem because of the difficulty of identifying them. They constituted the invisible section of Circle life. The census statistics and local sources suggest, however, that some members of all immigrant groups in this period began their lives working and living in this section of the city.

23. *Charities Review* (Cincinnati), Vol. I (April 1918), p. 8.
24. United Jewish Charities of Cincinnati, *Fourteenth Annual Report, 1910* (Cincinnati, n.d.), p. 59.
25. United Jewish Charities of Cincinnati, *Eighteen Annual Report, 1914* (Cincinnati, n.d.), pp. 7–8.
26. The total number of homes in the wards under discussion were: Three, 2077; Five, 1398; Six, 1509; Eight, 880; Nine, 1440; Eighteen, 1741; Nineteen, 1814. In 1900, in the Fifth, Sixth, Eighth, Ninth, and Eighteenth fewer than one hundred families owned homes free of debt. The Third, Seventh, and Nineteenth, each encompassing large segments of Circle territory, had only 112, 103, and 144 such families. Ward boundaries did not conform precisely to Circle boundaries so this is not an exact account of the situation. United States Bureau of the Census. *Twelfth Census of the United States Taken in the Year 1900: Population, Part I* (Washington, D.C., 1902), p. 708. In 1910 Negroes, foreign-born, and second-generation immigrants comprised over half the population in each of these nine wards. In 1910 the wards with the fewest home owners were the Sixth (50), the Eighth (99), and the Eighteenth (108). The lowest in the homes encumbered rubric were the Sixth (4), the Eighth (14), and the Eighteenth (44). United States Bureau of the Census, *Thirteenth Census of the United States Taken in the Year 1910, Vol. I, Population* (Washington, D.C., 1912), pp. 632–33, 1362.
27. United States Bureau of the Census, *Report on Vital and Social Statistics in the United States at the Eleventh Census: 1890, Part II, Vital Statistics* (Washington, D.C., 1896), pp. 182–97; *Thirteenth Census of the United States Taken in the Year 1910, Vol. III, Population* (Washington, D.C., 1913), pp. 426–27.
28. "How Shantytown Went Out With the Flood," *The Survey*, Vol. XXX (August 2, 1913), pp. 558–59; *Cincinnati Post*, June 27, 1911, p. 1; Joseph D. Emery, *Thirty-Five Years Among the Poor and Public Institutions of Cincinnati* (Cincinnati, 1887), pp. 370–71.
29. Dudley Ward Rhodes, *Creed and Greed* (Cincinnati, 1879), pp. 122–34.
30. *The Civic News* (Cincinnati), Vol. I (September 1910), p. 10.
31. Cincinnati, "Report of the Board of Administration," *Annual Reports of the City Departments . . . 1896* (Cincinnati, 1897), p. 1482.
32. *Citizen's Bulletin*, October 2, 1912, p. 12.
33. Ibid. January 18, 1913, p. 7.
34. Cincinnati Anti-Tuberculosis League, *Sixth Annual Report, 1912* (Cincinnati, n.d.), p. 19.
35. S. C. Ayres, *Civic Medical Inspection of School Children . . .* (Cincinnati, 1911), p. 4.
36. First, or Walnut Hills District Society of the Associated Charities of Cincinnati, *Fifth Annual Report* (Cincinnati, n.d.), p. 3.

37. *Cincinnati Post,* February 21, 1912, p. 4.
38. Smith, op. cit. p. 46.
39. Cincinnati Juvenile Protective Association, *Recreation Survey of Cincinnati* (Cincinnati, 1913), p. 14; United Jewish Charities of Cincinnati, *Fourteenth Annual Report, 1910* (Cincinnati, n.d.), p. 55.
40. For lists and dates of establishment of churches see Erastus Burnham, *Directory of the Cincinnati Protestant Churches, Young People's Societies, Sunday Schools, Missionary Societies, Charitable and Beneficient Organizations, 1895* (Cincinnati, n.d.); William A. Spencer (comp.), *Cincinnati Social Service Directory, 1914* (Cincinnati, 1914), pp. 123–50; Rev. John H. Lamott, *History of the Archdiocese of Cincinnati, 1821–1921* (New York and Cincinnati, 1921), pp. 332–36; *Catholic-Telegraph,* September 23, 1897, p. 4; Barnett R. Brickner, "The Jewish Community of Cincinnati: Historical and Descriptive" (unpublished Ph.D. dissertation, University of Cincinnati, 1935), pp. 108–12.
41. Bastel, op. cit. pp. 9, 12.
42. *American Israelite* (Cincinnati), January 23, 1896, p. 6; June 11, 1896, p. 4.
43. For the residences of supporters and history of the Orthodox Home for the Aged, see Cincinnati, *First Annual Report of the Orthodox Jewish Home for the Aged* (Cincinnati, 1918), pp. 3, 6–9, 17, 33–55.
44. Maurice B. Hexter, "The Dawn of a Problem," *Jewish Charities,* Vol. IV (December 1913), pp. 2–5; and "Discussion [of Levantine Jews]," *Jewish Charities,* Vol. IV (June 1914), pp. 27–28.
45. Boris D. Bogen, "Politics in Jewish Settlements," *Jewish Charities,* Vol. II (September 1911), pp. 10–11.
46. United Jewish Charities of Cincinnati, *Eighteenth Annual Report, 1914* (Cincinnati, n.d.), p. 59.
47. There were ten police districts in 1900. Those with the highest number of arrests were: the First, covering the central Basin; the Second, the lower East End; the Fourth, in the lower West End; the Fifth, in the upper West End. Cincinnati, "Annual Report of the Cincinnati Police Department," *Annual Reports of the City Departments . . . 1900* (Cincinnati, 1901), pp. 525, 550–51, 553, 556–57.
48. *Catholic-Telegraph,* October 18, 1888, p. 4.
49. *Citizen's Bulletin,* April 23, 1910, p. 1.
50. *American Israelite,* May 4, 1899, p. 6.
51. *Cincinnati Enquirer,* April 20, 1903, p. 10.
52. *Citizen's Bulletin,* July 9, 1910, p. 4.

CHAPTER 2

1. Graham Romeyn Taylor, *Satellite Cities: A Study of Industrial Suburbs* (New York and London, 1915), pp. 91–92.

2. *Suburbs Scrapbook, Norwood,* Cincinnati Historical Society; Graham Romeyn Taylor, "Norwood and Oakley," *The Survey,* Vol. XXIX (December 7, 1912), pp. 287–89. Cincinnati Historical Society hereafter referred to as CHS.

3. *Cincinnati Times-Star,* August 11, 1886, p. 4.

4. Robert C. Schmitt, "Cumminsville: A Study in Suburban Growth and Structure" (unpublished M.A. thesis, University of Cincinnati, 1944), pp. 104–8; City Planning Commission of Cincinnati, *The Population of the Cincinnati Metropolitan Area* (Cincinnati, 1945), p. 126; Cincinnati Community Chest, Research Department, *Social Work Statistics for Cincinnati and Hamilton County, Bulletin, No. 2, Population Trends in Cincinnati* (Cincinnati, 1939), p. 7.

5. R. W. Harris, *Report on Cincinnati Traffic Conditions to the City of Cincinnati* (Cincinnati, 1912), pp. 20–21.

6. Robert A. Woods and Albert J. Kennedy, *The Zone of Emergence* (Cambridge, Mass., 1962), pp. 31–183.

7. *The Chronicle,* August 26, 1911, p. 4.

8. Because of the overlapping of Circle and Zone wards the figures for immigrants and Negroes in the Zone are doubtless too high. Similarly, because of overlapping of Zone wards and those in the more fashionable districts, the figures for second-generation foreign-born in the Zone are probably too low. The point is, however, that the Zone contained an ethnically and racially diverse population. I have compiled these figures from the 1910 census because it gives the composition of each ward by race and nationality group. Wards Three, Four, Nine, Ten, Eleven, Twelve, Fourteen, Sixteen, Seventeen, Nineteen, Twenty, Twenty-one, Twenty-two, and Twenty-three were used. See United States Bureau of the Census, *Thirteenth Census . . . 1910, Vol. III,* op. cit. pp. 426–27. Similar compilations for Negroes, foreign-born and native-born with foreign or mixed parentage can be made from the 1890 and 1900 census. Also helpful on Negro residential districts were Alfred Segal to Author, Interview, November 2, 1962; William Wabnitz to Author, Interview, December 12, 1963; Yeatman Anderson, III, to Author, Interview, July 27, 1964.

9. *Graphic History of Mt. Adams* (Cincinnati, 1931), n.p.

10. It is difficult to document precisely this section. It was gleaned from a great variety of sources. Especially helpful, however, was Guido Dobbert, "The Disintegration of an Immigrant Community: The Cincinnati Germans, 1870–1920" (unpublished Ph.D. dissertation, University of Chicago, 1965), chs. i and ii.

11. Quoted in Frank U. Quillan, *The Color Line in Ohio: A History of Race Prejudice in a Typical Northern State* (Ann Arbor, Mich., 1913), p. 3.

12. Frank U. Quillan, "The Negro in Cincinnati," *The Independent,* Vol. LXVIII (February 24, 1910), pp. 399–403.

13. United States Bureau of the Census, *Report on the Population . . .*

Eleventh Census, 1890, Part I, op. cit. p. 547; *Thirteenth Census . . . 1910, Vol. III,* op. cit. pp. 426–27.

14. Cincinnati Public Schools, *Sixty-Sixth Annual Report for the School Year Ending August 31, 1895* (Cincinnati, 1895), p. 103; *Eighty-Fourth Annual Report . . . August 31, 1913* (Cincinnati, 1914), p. 252.

15. W. C. Dabney, "Condition and History of the University in 1912 Including a Sociological Study of the Student Body," *University of Cincinnati Record,* Series I, Vol. IX (August 1913), pp. 9–30; *Citizen's Bulletin,* May 11, 1912, p. 1.

16. Taylor, *Satellite Cities,* op. cit. pp. 95–96.

17. *Trades and Labor Directory* (Cincinnati, n.d. [ca. 1896–1900]), p. 87.

18. Taylor, *Satellite Cities,* op. cit. pp. 99–100.

19. Ibid. pp. 100–102; *Cincinnati Enquirer,* September 27, 1909, p. 8.

20. Taylor, *Satellite Cities,* op. cit. pp. 100–101; *Cincinnati Enquirer,* October 18, 1908, p. 3.

21. *The Chronicle,* August 17, 1902, p. 4.

22. Quoted in *The Chronicle,* April 23, 1897, p. 4.

23. In defining the occupational, racial, ethnic, and religious composition of the Zone, the daily and weekly papers were an invaluable source. Particularly useful were ward descriptions and biographical data in the political sections of the papers as well as advertisements. Newspaper accounts of disputes over the routes of proposed streetcar lines were also useful.

24. *Cincinnati Post,* June 11, 1913, p. 4.

25. *The Citizen and Taxpayer,* Vol. I (January 20, 1903), p. 4.

26. "Aiding the Home Builder," *Cincinnati Magazine,* Vol. I (November 1909), pp. 18–19.

27. For the quote see Will L. Finch (ed.), *Cincinnati: Queen City of Industries and the Gateway to the South* (Cincinnati, [1901 or 1902]), p. 35. The building associations were typically organized along ethnic, racial, or neighborhood lines. They were widely, but mistakenly, regarded as peculiarly German institutions.

28. *The Chronicle,* June 13, 1914, p. 5. For the societies see August G. Gorbach, *Deutscher Vereins-Wegweiser von Cincinnati, Ohio* (Cincinnati, 1915), pp. 5–6.

29. Dobbert, op. cit. chs. iv, v, and viii.

30. Charles F. Williams to Joseph B. Foraker, January 29, 1906, Foraker Papers, Box 56, CHS.

31. *Catholic-Telegraph,* March 14, 1889, p. 4; March 21, 1889, p. 4; *Cincinnati Post,* March 18, 1913, p. 8.

32. *Cincinnati Post,* March 29, 1897, p. 2; July 28, 1897, p. 2; *Cincinnati Times-Star,* March 20, 1900, p. 5; "Wendell Phillips Dabney" (unpublished typed ms., undated, in W. P. Dabney Papers, CHS).

33. Spencer, op. cit., pp. 123–50; Burnham, op. cit.; Carl Wittke, *Wil-*

liam Nast: Patriarch of German Methodism (Detroit, 1959), pp. 78–79, 86, 218–23.

34. United States Bureau of the Census, *Report on the Statistics of Churches in the United States at the Eleventh Census: 1891* (Washington, D. C., 1894), pp. 98–99; United States Bureau of the Census, *Religious Bodies, 1916* (Washington, D.C., 1916), pp. 29, 124; Gorbach, op. cit. p. 217.

35. *Catholic-Telegraph*, April 4, 1889, p. 4.

36. Ibid. January 3, 1889, p. 4.

37. Ibid. October 4, 1900, p. 4.

38. Cincinnati Public Schools, *Eighty-Fourth Annual Report . . . April 13, 1913*, op. cit. p. 252. Also see *Catholic-Telegraph*, February 4, 1897, p. 1.

39. Cincinnati, Juvenile Protective Association, *Recreation Survey*, op. cit. pp. 25–42.

40. Quillan, "The Negro in Cincinnati," op. cit. p. 400.

41. *Cincinnati Post*, November 16, 1912, p. 3.

42. *Cincinnati Enquirer*, March 13, 1905, p. 10; October 28, 1905, p. 8.

43. *Cincinnati Post*, October 18, 1913, p. 1. Religious differences also created problems in the Zone. See, for example, *The Chronicle*, Vol. III (October 1894), p. 2. There is also evidence that nativist organizations drew heavily upon the Zone population, principally the Germans, for leaders and members.

44. *Catholic-Telegraph*, April 18, 1907, p. 4.

45. Quoted in Joseph Stacy Hill, "Further Chats With My Descendents" (Cincinnati, unpublished typed ms., ca. 1933, CHS), p. 42.

CHAPTER 3

1. James Albert Green, *History of the Associated Charities of Cincinnati, 1879–1937: A Record of Service* (Cincinnati, n.d.), pp. 18–19.

2. Thomas Stanley Matthews, *Name and Address* (New York, 1960), pp. 3, 8, 26–27.

3. Glazier, op. cit. p. 128.

4. Mrs. Joseph Deistler to Mrs. Eleanor [Hulbert] Taft, August 19, 1958, in CHS.

5. *Citizen's Bulletin*, December 6, 1913, p. 4.

6. United States Bureau of the Census, *Report on Vital and Social Statistics . . . 1890*, op. cit.; Cincinnati, "Annual Report of the Health Department," *Annual Reports of the City Departments . . . 1910* (Cincinnati, 1911), pp. 997, 1010.

7. Ishbel Ross, *An American Family: The Tafts, 1678–1964* (Cleveland and New York, 1964), p. 109.

8. Cincinnati Public Schools, *Sixty-Sixth Annual Report . . . 1895*, op. cit. p. 103; *Eighty-Fourth Annual Report . . . 1913*, op. cit. p. 252.

9. *Citizen's Bulletin,* January 21, 1911, p. 3.
10. *Cincinnati Post,* February 15, 1897, p. 8.
11. *American Israelite,* November 23, 1899, p. 6.
12. Ibid. *American Israelite,* October 26, 1899, p. 6.
13. Matthews, op. cit. p. 104–7.
14. This section is based primarily upon *The Cincinnati Society Address Book: Elite Family Directory—Club Membership, 1898* (Cincinnati and Buffalo, 1898), pp. 1, 115–67, which lists "prominent families" by street residence, and *Dau's Blue Book of Selected Names of Cincinnati & Suburban Towns for the Year 1908* (New York, 1908), pp. 137–84, which includes suburban towns.
15. For the quote see Charles Frederic Goss, *The Philopolist, or, City Lover* (Cincinnati, 1898), p. 119.
16. Taylor, *Satellite Cities,* op. cit. p. 120.
17. William Howard Taft to Mother, January 6, 1884, Taft Papers, Family Correspondence, Box 23, Library of Congress.
18. Clara Longworth de Chambrun, *Cincinnati: The Story of The Queen City* (New York and London, 1939), p. 271.
19. Alice Roosevelt Longworth, *Crowded Hours: Reminiscences of Alice Roosevelt Longworth* (New York and London, 1933), p. 229. Also see Ross, op. cit. p. 86.
20. Ross, op. cit. p. 85.
21. Longworth, op. cit. p. 117.
22. *Cincinnati Post,* January 13, 1897, p. 7. I found no evidence that the arrests were made.
23. de Chambrun, op. cit. pp. 275–76.
24. *American Israelite,* August 7, 1913, p. 6.
25. New England Society of Cincinnati, "Record, 1845–1914" (handwritten unpublished ms., CHS), pp. 40–41, 51–95, 143–45; *Year Book, 1904–1905* (Cincinnati, n.d.), n.p.
26. For the quote see Andrew Hickenlooper, "Reminiscences" (typed unpublished ms. in Andrew Hickenlooper Papers, CHS), p. 672.
27. *Cincinnati Enquirer,* May 3, 1893, p. 4; Charles P. Taft to William Howard Taft, January 17, 1903, Taft Papers, Family Correspondence, Box 35, Library of Congress.
28. *American Israelite,* July 1, 1897, p. 4; July 15, 1897, p. 5; September 22, 1898, p. 6.
29. Hickenlooper, "Reminiscences," op. cit. p. 672.
30. James A. Green to Joseph C. Green, September 20, 1909, James A. Green Papers, CHS.
31. de Chambrun, op. cit. p. 274.
32. Charles Dudley Warner, "Sketches of the Great West, Cincinnati and Louisville," *Harper's Magazine,* Vol. LXXVIII (August 1888), p. 430.
33. *Catholic-Telegraph,* October 17, 1901, p. 4.
34. James A. Green to Joseph C. Green, March 3 and March 6, 1908, James A. Green Papers, CHS.

35. *Cincinnati Times-Star,* March 12, 1891, p. 4.
36. *Cincinnati Post,* October 17, 1905, p. 1.
37. *Cincinnati Commercial-Tribune,* May 1, 1905, p. 2; *Cincinnati Times-Star,* May 3, 1910, p. 6.

CHAPTER 4

1. *Cincinnati Enquirer,* March 9, 1884, p. 9. The story was illustrated with the pictures of twenty-three of the city's murderers, six of them Negroes and the remainder of German or Irish extraction.
2. Ibid. March 25, 1884, p. 8.
3. *Cincinnati Volksfreund,* March 25, 1884, p. 4.
4. The signatories all resided in the fashionable East End and West End or Hilltop districts. They comprised an ethnically and religiously mixed group.
5. *Cincinnati Enquirer,* March 29, 1884, p. 1; *The Great Cincinnati Riots! Being the Only Correct History of That Most Lamentable Outbreak in Ohio's Largest City, Because of the Villanious Verdict of the Berner Jury!* (Philadelphia, 1884), pp. 6–7, 11, 17. This account is based primarily on Halstead's reports of the meeting and ensuing riots as printed in the *Cincinnati Gazette.* The casualty totals are from Cincinnati, "Annual Report of the Department of Police," *Annual Reports of the City Departments . . . 1884* (Cincinnati, 1885), p. 311.
6. *Catholic-Telegraph,* October 16, 1884, p. 1; Cincinnati, "Annual Report of the Department of Police," *Annual Reports of the City Departments . . .* op. cit. pp. 287–88, 311.
7. Ameringer, op. cit. pp. 44–45.
8. *Cincinnati Times-Star,* May 3, 1886, p. 5; May 6, 1886, pp. 4–5; May 9, 1886, p. 4.
9. Ameringer, op. cit. p. 47; *Cincinnati Times-Star,* May 15, 1886, p. 4.
10. For the term "beer bosses" and their anti-union campaign see *Cincinnati Times-Star,* March 29, 1889, p. 8. For a description of the functioning of the old "patriarchal" brewers' societies and the effect of the union on that structure see *Cincinnati Freie Presse,* January 23, 1921, p. 4.
11. *Cincinnati Times-Star,* March 29, 1889, p. 4; December 2, 1889, p. 4.
12. *Catholic-Telegraph,* June 5, 1884, p. 4.
13. Rev. T. H. Pearne, *What Shall Be Done with the Cincinnati Sunday Saloon? . . .* (Cincinnati, 1887), p. 7.
14. *Cincinnati Times-Star,* February 13, 1889, pp. 4, 6; February 14, 1889, p. 4.
15. *Sam, the Scaramouch,* Vol. II (February 6, 1886), p. 387.
16. *Address of the Bund fur Freiheit und Recht* (Cincinnati, 1886),

pp. 3, 4, 5, 6–7. The Law and Order League, as well as other Sabbatarians, sought to abolish all commercial entertainment on Sunday. The league's membership was not primarily clerical, nor solely white Anglo-Saxon Protestant. It was a Hilltop organization, religiously and ethnically mixed. See The Citizens' Association To Promote the Observance of Law and Order in Cincinnati, *List of Members, November 21, 1885* (Cincinnati, n.d.), p. 1.

17. Jno. Pearson to Gov. Joseph Benson Foraker, July 26, 1889, Foraker Papers, Box 38, CHS.

18. Governor Joseph B. Foraker to John B. Mosby, July 26, 1889, Foraker Papers, Box 29, CHS; Cincinnati, "Report of the Non-Partisan Board of Police Commissioners," *Annual Reports of the City Departments . . . 1889* (Cincinnati, 1889), pp. 199–200; Joseph B. Foraker, *Notes of a Busy Life*, Vol. I (Cincinnati, 1916), pp. 411–16.

19. William Christie Herron, *Immigration* (Cincinnati, 1892), pp. 10–11.

20. *Cincinnati Times-Star*, May 6, 1886, p. 4; February 28, 1887, p. 4; September 19, 1888, p. 4; March 29, 1889, p. 4.

21. Ibid. December 2, 1889, p. 4.

22. *Sam, the Scaramouch*, Vol. II (November 21, 1885), p. 198; ibid. Vol. II (November 28, 1885), p. 214.

23. *Catholic-Telegraph*, April 6, 1893, p. 4.

24. Ibid. March 9, 1893, p. 4; March 23, 1893, p. 4; September 16, 1893, p. 1; September 28, 1893, p. 4. Judging from the reaction of the *Catholic-Telegraph*, the A.P.A. reached its peak strength in 1893. It is doubtless more than coincidental that the urban expansion which created the Circle, Zone, and Hilltops in Cincinnati occurred at the same time as the crisis atmosphere to which John Higham attributes the national resurgence of nativism. See John Higham, *Strangers in the Land: Patterns of American Nativism, 1860–1925* (New York, 1963), pp. 35–67.

25. For the development of municipal services by date see Cincinnati Municipal Reference Bureau, *The March of City Government, City of Cincinnati (1802–1936)* (Cincinnati, 1937), *passim*.

26. Cincinnati, "Report of [the] Fire Department," *Annual Reports of the City Departments . . . 1886* (Cincinnati, 1887), p. 646; ibid., *1888* (Cincinnati, 1889), pp. 926–27; *Cincinnati Times-Star*, April 6, 1887, p. 4.

27. Cincinnati, "City Waterworks Report," *Annual Reports of the City Departments . . . 1888*, op. cit. pp. 700–71.

28. For the crisis atmosphere generated by an epidemic see Associated Charities of Cincinnati, *Third Annual Report* (Cincinnati, 1883), pp. 12–13; *Eighth Annual Report* (Cincinnati, 1888), p. 8. For the hysterical reaction to the approach of cholera see *Cincinnati Times-Star*, August 18, 1892, p. 1.

29. Cincinnati, "City Work-House Report," *Annual Reports . . . 1886*, op. cit. pp. 312–17; ibid. *1894* (Cincinnati, 1895), p. 505.
30. Cincinnati, "City Infirmary Department Report," *Annual Reports . . . 1884*, op. cit. pp. 625, 635–36; ibid. *1886*, op. cit. pp. 446, 449, 474–75, 477; ibid. *1888*, op. cit. pp. 398, 400.
31. Cincinnati Public Schools, *Fifty-Sixth Annual Report . . . August 31, 1885* (Cincinnati, 1885), pp. xii, xiii.
32. Cincinnati, "Mayor's Annual Message," *Annual Reports . . . 1890*, op. cit. pp. xxiii–vi; ibid. *1893* (Cincinnati, 1894), p. xxiii.
33. *Report of the Standing Committee of the Cincinnati Chamber of Commerce, April, 1885, Terminal Facilities* (Cincinnati, 1885), pp. 5, 7–17.
34. *Address of Melville E. Ingalls on Finance and Taxation before the Commercial Club of Cincinnati, March 19th, 1892* (Cincinnati, n.d.), pp. 24–26; *Commercial Gazette* April 13, 1894, p. 9; *Cincinnati Tribune*, March 19, 1894, p. 4; March 21, 1894, p. 4; Charles B. Wilby, "What Is the Matter with Cincinnati?" *Extracts of a Paper Read before the Young Business Men's Club, Nov. 30, 1896* (Cincinnati, n.d.), p. 7.
35. *Cincinnati Times-Star*, October 29, 1885, p. 4; March 31, 1887, p. 4; *Catholic-Telegraph*, January 20, 1887, p. 1.
36. *Catholic-Telegraph*, November 2, 1892, p. 4.
37. For the details of this fascinating story and still other gas battles see Hickenlooper, "Reminiscences," op. cit. pp. 608, 622, 706, 713–14, 778–85; Andrew Hickenlooper, "Diaries" (unpublished handwritten ms. in CHS), January 10, 1887–April 26, 1887.
38. *Cincinnati Post*, January 9, 1890, p. 2.
39. "Constitution of the Committee of One Hundred" (unpublished ms. in Julius Dexter Papers, Scrapbook, CHS), pp. 1–8. The organization was open to all for a $5 initiation fee and $5 annual dues. The original committee, however, was initially composed of an Executive Committee of forty, half Republican and half Democratic, which in turn chose ten additional members. They then selected fifty more to complete the Executive Committee of One Hundred. The constitution bears 450 signatures.
40. *Proceedings of the "Committee of One Hundred" of Cincinnati, At the First Annual Meeting Held in the Odeon, Tuesday Evening, October 5th, 1886* (Cincinnati, 1886), pp. 1–11; Alphonso Taft to William Howard Taft, August 14, 1886, Taft Papers, Family Correspondence, Box 27, Library of Congress; *Committee of One Hundred to the Legal Voters of Cincinnati March 13, 1886*, Flysheet in Taft Papers, Family Correspondence, Box 27, Library of Congress.
41. Horace D. Taft to William Howard Taft, August 4, 1886, Taft Papers, Family Correspondence, Box 27, Library of Congress.
42. *Cincinnati Times-Star*, August 10, 1884, p. 8; July 22, 1886, p. 8.

43. *Cincinnati Times-Star,* September 27, 1890, p. 4; September 29, 1890, p. 4. There is an abundance of sources detailing and decrying the political chaos in this decade.
44. The situation was similar, in many respects, to that described in Stanley Elkins and Eric McKitrick, "A Meaning For Turner's Frontier, Part I: Democracy in the Old Northwest," *Political Science Quarterly,* Vol. LXIX (September 1954), pp. 321–53.

CHAPTER 5

1. William Howard Taft to Mother, March 27, 1885, Taft Papers, Family Correspondence, Box 25, Library of Congress.
2. The Hamilton County Board of Elections has no records of this election. I used the returns given in the *Cincinnati Times-Star,* April 6, 1885, p. 5, complete except for two precincts, and in the *Cincinnati Volksblatt,* April 7, 1885, p. 4. Smith carried wards One, Two, Ten, Eleven, Twelve, Thirteen, Fourteen, Fifteen, Seventeen, Eighteen, Twenty-two, Twenty-three, Tweny-four, and Twenty-five.
3. *Cincinnati Times-Star,* April 8, 1885, p. 4.
4. Ibid. January 12, 1887, p. 2; January 24, 1887, p. 4; March 31, 1887, p. 4; April 4, 1887, p. 1; *Cincinnati Volksblatt,* March 21, 1887, p. 4; April 4, 1887, p. 1; *Catholic-Telegraph,* March 24, 1887, p. 1; April 7, 1887, p. 4.
5. Stevenson carried wards Three, Four, Seven, Eleven, Thirteen, Fourteen, Seventeen, Twenty, Twenty-one, Twenty-two, Twenty-three, and Twenty-four. Of these, Smith had carried Eleven, Thirteen, Fourteen, Seventeen, Twenty-two, Twenty-three, and Twenty-four in 1885. The *Volksblatt* claimed that German workers in the Seventh, Tenth, and Twelfth did not desert the GOP "in large numbers" but that in the Eleventh Republicans and Democrats alike voted Union Labor. See *Cincinnati Volksblatt,* April 5, 1887, p. 4. The vote in the "German" Tenth, which Stevenson lost, was 891 for Smith, 740 for Stevenson, and 294 for Matson, the Democratic candidate. The Seventh, however, which contained a larger German population, went to Stevenson.
6. *Cincinnati Post,* undated clipping in C. W. Woolley to John Sherman, April 16, 1887, John Sherman Papers, Vol. 400, Library of Congress.
7. Cox left no personal papers except a few scattered letters in the Foraker collection. There is, however, no dearth of information regarding his career, much of it reliable, though little of it covers the years before 1885. This brief account of his early career was drawn primarily from newspapers and William Howard Taft to Mother, February 17, 1884, Taft Papers, Family Correspondence, Box 23, Library of Congress; Warner Bateman, "Diaries" (unpublished handwritten ms., CHS), May 23, 1886, p. 43; Henry C.

Wright, *Bossism in Cincinnati* (Cincinnati, n.d.), pp. 7–8, 12–13, 24; Gustave J. Karger, "George Barnesdale Cox: Proprietor of Cincinnati," *Frank Leslie's Popular Monthly*, Vol. LVII (January 1904), pp. 273–78; Murray Seasongood (William Wabnitz, comp.), "Nisi Serenas" (unpublished ms. of autobiography in the offices of Paxton and Seasongood, Cincinnati, Ohio), chs. vii, xx.

8. *Cincinnati Times-Star*, March 19, 1885, p. 1.
9. George B. Cox to Joseph B. Foraker, October 18, 1887; November 8, 1887, Foraker Papers, Box 32, CHS; Joseph B. Foraker to R. A. Alger, November 14, 1887, Foraker Papers, Box 28, CHS.
10. Joseph B. Foraker to Murat Halstead, March 21, 1888, Foraker Papers, Box 28, CHS.
11. *Cincinnati Times-Star*, November 7, 1888, p. 5. The paper presented an analysis of the vote of Harrison, Cleveland, and Cox in twelve wards to prove its point.
12. George B. Cox to J. B. Foraker, December 24, 1888, Foraker Papers, Box 32, CHS.
13. Hickenlooper, "Diaries," op. cit. January 15-November 8, 1888; J. B. Foraker to T. W. Graydon, March 16, 1889, Foraker Papers, Box 29, CHS; *Cincinnati Times-Star*, March 5, 1889, p. 4; Wright, op. cit. pp. 14–15.
14. Hickenlooper, "Diaries," op. cit. March 1, 8, 9, 1889.
15. *Cincinnati Times-Star*, March 9, 1889, p. 1.
16. Wright, op. cit. p. 36.
17. *Cincinnati Post*, March 13, 1889, p. 1; March 18, 1889, p. 1; Wright, op. cit. p. 36.
18. *Cincinnati Times-Star*, March 19, 1889; pp. 1, 7; March 23, 1889, pp. 1, 4; March 27, 1889, p. 1; March 28, 1889, p. 8; *Cincinnati Post*, March 20, 1889, p. 4; March 29, 1889, p. 1; "Hon. John B. Mosby," *Saxby's Magazine*, Vol. I (June 1893), p. 248.
19. *Cincinnati Times-Star*, March 19, 1889, p. 1.
20. Both the *Times-Star* and the *Volksfreund* took the three Republican journals to task for accepting the slate. See *Cincinnati Volksfreund*, March 21, 1889, p. 4; *Cincinnati Times-Star*, March 20, 1889, p. 4. Before the convention the *Times-Star* observed that the Committee of Arrangements divided the thirty vice presidencies equally between the Blaine and Lincoln Club forces. See *Cincinnati Times-Star*, March 15, 1889, p. 8.
21. See *Cincinnati Times-Star*, March 22, 1889, p. 1; March 23, 1889, p. 3; *Cincinnati Post*, March 22, 1889, p. 1; March 23, 1889, p. 2. The *Times-Star* felt that the Democrats had nominated a good ticket except for the mayoral candidate, Thomas J. Stephens, whom it called "The Hero of the Riot" and "The Gambler's Friend." He had been mayor from 1883 to 1885. See *Cincinnati Times-Star*, March 21, 1889, p. 1; March 22, 1889, p. 2. The *Post* and W. H. Stevenson, the former ULP mayoral candidate also supported the

Citizens. Rumors also circulated that German Jews would back Stone because Mosby had given "gross offense to our Jewish citizens." See *Cincinnati Post,* March 27, 1889, p. 1.

22. Mosby took the Hilltops, the fashionable West End, and most of the Zone. He carried the First, Second, Seventh, Ninth, Tenth, Eleventh, Twelfth, Thirteenth, Fourteenth, Fifteenth, Seventeenth, Eighteenth, Twenty-third, Twenty-fourth, Twenty-fifth, Twenty-sixth, Twenty-seventh, and Twenty-eighth. Of these, the *Post* labeled the Seventh and Tenth, on the Circle-Zone border, and the Eleventh and Thirteenth, in the Zone, as "German." Dobbert calculated that these four plus the Third, which went Democratic, and the Twelfth and Twenty-eighth, won by Mosby, could also be called German. They all contained between 18 and 21 per cent German-born and between 47.9 and 53.9 per cent native-born with both parents born in Germany. See *Cincinnati Post,* April 1, 1889, p. 1; Dobbert, op. cit. ch. ii. Stephens, the Democratic candidate, carried the Third, Fourth, Fifth, Sixth, Eighth, Sixteenth, Nineteenth, Twentieth, Twenty-first, Twenty-second, Twenty-ninth, and Thirtieth. Election returns compiled from Hamilton County Board of Elections, "Record of City Elections, Commencing in 1888" (unpublished handwritten ms. in the offices of the Hamilton County Board of Elections, Cincinnati, Ohio), pp. 20–33.

23. *Cincinnati Times-Star,* September 1, 1890, p. 8; September 12, 1890, p. 4; November 1, 1890, p. 4. There were seven contenders for the sheriff's nomination. See *Cincinnati Times-Star,* September 8, 1890, p. 8.

24. Joseph B. Foraker to Murat Halstead, August 18, 1890, Murat Halstead Correspondence, Box 1, CHS; Joseph B. Foraker to [President] Benjamin Harrison, January 2, 1891, Foraker Papers, Box 21, CHS; *Cincinnati Post,* February 5, 1891, p. 1; *Cincinnati Times-Star,* February 6, 1891, p. 4.

25. Hickenlooper, "Diaries," op. cit. January 1, 1891-April 7, 1891; *Cincinnati Commercial-Gazette,* September 18, 1890, clipping in Hickenlooper, "Reminiscences," op. cit. p. 777; *Cincinnati Post,* March 4, 1891, p. 1; March 6, 1891, p. 1.

26. Hickenlooper, "Diaries," op. cit. February 2, February 16, 1891.

27. The outline of this story can be found in *Cincinnati Post,* February 1, 1897, p. 2. Also see Alphonso Taft to William Howard Taft, July 30, 1886, Taft Papers, Family Correspondence, Box 27, Library of Congress.

28. *Cincinnati Post,* March 6, 1891, p. 1. Henry W. Kliemeier, a participant, subsequently claimed that votes went for $500 apiece. *Cincinnati Enquirer,* January 9, 1948, n.p., in Central Turners, Inc., Clipping Collection, CHS.

29. *Cincinnati Post,* March 6, 1891, p. 1. The General suspected as much before the *Post* article appeared and tried, in vain, to find out what happened. He then asked the *Post*'s managing editor for the

name of the reporter. Andrew Hickenlooper to Milton A. McRae, March 26, 1891, Hickenlooper Papers, CHS; Andrew Hickenlooper, "Diaries," op. cit. March 23, 1891; March 25, 1891.

30. *Cincinnati Times-Star*, March 28, 1891, p. 4; April 4, 1891, p. 2; *Cincinnati Volksblatt*, April 6, 1891, p. 4. The *Post*, the building trades' unions, and the Committee of Five Hundred all came out for the Mosby-Horstmann ticket. See *Cincinnati Post*, March 6, 1891, p. 1; March 19, 1891, p. 1; *Cincinnati Times-Star*, March 27, 1891, p. 3; March 30, 1891, p. 4.

31. Ibid. March 23, 1891, p. 8; March 25, 1891, p. 4; *Cincinnati Post*, April 2, 1891, p. 1; April 3, 1891, p. 1.

32. *Cincinnati Times-Star*, March 25, 1891, p. 4; March 26, 1891, p. 4. *Cincinnati Post*, March 31, 1891, p. 1; *Cincinnati Volksfreund*, March 25, 1891, p. 4.

33. Hickenlooper, "Diaries," op. cit. April 7, 1891. The Socialist-Labor mayoral candidate received 318 votes, almost all of them in Zone wards, and the Prohibitionist 112, most in Hilltop districts. Election returns compiled from Hamilton County Board of Elections, op. cit. pp. 44–53. The *Times-Star* was delighted over the split in the German vote. See *Cincinnati Times-Star*, April 7, 1891, p. 4.

34. Hickenlooper, "Diaries," op. cit. May 8, 1891.

35. Clara Longworth de Chambrun, *The Making of Nicholas Longworth* (New York, 1933), pp. 181–82. Longworth believed it better "to board a train going to the spot than to wreck it because the travelers disapprove of the engineer."

36. "Dr. T. W. Graydon," *Saxby's Magazine*, Vol. I (November 1893), pp. 466–67. Also see *Cincinnati Times-Star*, March 3, 1900, p. 2.

37. *Cincinnati Post*, June 20, 1897, p. 4; "Frank S. Krug" in CHS Biographies File; *Cincinnati Enquirer*, January 9, 1948, n.p., in Central Turners, Inc., Clipping Collection, CHS; *Cincinnati Enquirer*, December 9, 1940, n.p.; *Cincinnati Commercial-Gazette*, April 7, 1894, p. 1.

38. For a list of the members of this group and their recreational life see Grayson, op. cit. pp. 63–65. Grayson was a political reporter for the *Times-Star* and a member of this coterie. The term "bonifaces" was used in the Cincinnati Police Department, *Police and Municipal Guide, 1901* (Cincinnati, n.d.), n.p.

39. Wright, op. cit. pp. 63–65; *Cincinnati Post*, May 3, 1897, p. 1; April 26, 1931, pp. 1, 14; *Cincinnati Times-Star*, April 25, 1931, pp. 1, 11; April 28, 1931, pp. 1, 4.

40. Wright, op. cit. p. 65. Also see *Cincinnati Post*, February 1, 1897, p. 2; January 8, 1897, p. 5; George B. Cox to Gov. Joseph B. Foraker, December 24, 1888, Foraker Papers, Box 32, CHS.

41. *Cincinnati Post*, January 8, 1897, p. 5.

42. Wendell P. Dabney, op. cit. p. 116. Stith controlled precincts C and D in the western edge of Walnut Hills in the Second Ward. See *Cincinnati Commercial-Gazette*, April 3, 1894, p. 2.

43. For Leuders see (Cincinnati) *Civic News*, Vol. I (June 1912), p. 7; *Cincinnati Post*, September 13, 1912, p. 8; *Cincinnati Volksblatt*, October 27, 1913, p. 5. For Bode see John B. Shotwell, *A History of the Schools of Cincinnati* (Cincinnati, 1902), p. 570.

44. The *Cincinnati Times-Star*, March 27, 1891, p. 8, and March 30, 1891, p. 8, list all the Republican councilmen, their occupations, and comments on their background.

45. Cincinnati Police Department, op. cit. This description coincides with the account of Frank Y. Grayson in his *Pioneers of Night Life on Vine Street*.

46. *Cincinnati Post*, March 1, 1894, p. 1; *Cincinnati Tribune*, March 2, 1894, p. 1; Hickenlooper, "Diaries," op. cit. March 2, 1894.

47. The Populists were led by veterans of the 1887 ULP campaign. One group, dominated by Anglo-Saxons, nominated a Populist slate which included the first Negro ever put up for justice of the peace. He was not elected. The other wing, composed of a mixture of ethnic groups, endorsed the full Citizens' ticket, though some favored replacing Horstmann with Caldwell, the Republican nominee. *Cincinnati Tribune*, January 27, 1894, p. 3; March 7, 1894, p. 4; March 8, 1894, p. 2; March 14, 1894, p. 4. The *Cincinnati Herald*, the organ of People's party, went defunct in September 1892. I found no copies of it.

48. *Cincinnati Tribune*, January 11, 1894, p. 1; January 25, 1894, p. 1.

49. Ibid. February 25, 1894, p. 1.

50. Ibid. March 8, 1894, p. 2.

51. Ibid. March 28, 1894, p. 2; *Cincinnati Post*, April 2, 1894, p. 3; *Cincinnati Volksfreund*, March 12, 1894, p. 4; *Cincinnati Commercial-Gazette*, March 17, 1894, p. 1. There is no evidence that Hilltop Democrats or McLean knew of Cox's role in setting up the convention. And the evidence that he was primarily responsible is thin.

52. *Cincinnati Commercial-Gazette*, March 24, 1894, pp. 2, 4; March 25, 1894, p. 12; *Cincinnati Tribune*, March 27, 1894, p. 4; March 28, 1894, p. 1; March 30, 1894, p. 3; *Cincinnati Volksblatt*, March 20, 1894, p. 4.

53. *Cincinnati Commercial-Gazette*, March 3, 1894, p. 1; March 30, 1894, p. 2; April 1, 1894, p. 12.

54. Ibid. March 1, 1894, p. 4; March 2, 1894, p. 4; March 12, 1894, p. 4; *Cincinnati Times-Star*, April 2, 1894, p. 1; *Cincinnati Tribune*, April 2, 1894, p. 1.

55. Of thirty prominent supporters of Horstmann listed by the *Tribune* on the eve of the election, three were identifiable German Jews and at least two were Catholic. See *Cincinnati Tribune*, March 30, 1894, pp. 1–2.

56. The Populist candidate garnered only 261 votes, most of them in the Zone wards. Election returns from Hamilton County Board of

Elections, op. cit. pp. 72–81. Also see *Cincinnati-Gazette*, April 3, 1894, p. 1.
57. Frank Parker Stockbridge, "The Biggest Boss of Them All," *Hampton's Magazine*, Vol. XXVI (January 1911-June 1911), p. 616.
58. This attitude toward Cox was repeated endlessly in the various anti-gang campaigns conducted by the *Times-Star, Commercial-Gazette,* and *Tribune*.
59. *Cincinnati Commercial-Gazette*, January 29, 1892, p. 4.
60. Ibid. February 22, 1911, p. 2. Also see *Cincinnati Post*, May 20, 1916, p. 1.
61. *Cincinnati Post*, February 22, 1911, p. 2.
62. *Cincinnati Commercial-Gazette*, January 29, 1892, p. 4; *Cincinnati Post*, February 22, 1911, p. 2.

CHAPTER 6

1. *Cincinnati Times-Star*, April 4, 1891, p. 4.
2. Ibid. March 13, 1891, p. 4; *Citizen's Bulletin*, August 29, 1903, pp. 1–2.
3. *Cincinnati Post*, February 24, 1891, p. 4.
4. Cincinnati, "Report of the Non-Partisan Board of Police Commissioners," *Annual Reports of the City Departments . . . 1891* (Cincinnati, 1892), p. 227.
5. Ibid. *1886*, pp. xi–xii; ibid. *1890*, pp. 198–99, 201–2, 207; ibid. *1893*, pp. 328, 401; ibid. *1894*, pp. 360–61.
6. Ibid. *1892*, p. 252; ibid. *1893*, pp. 387–88.
7. Ibid. *1892*, pp. 197–98, 201–2, 218–21; ibid. *1893*, pp. 393–96; ibid. *1894*, pp. 221, 355–59.
8. Charles B. Wilby, "How To Boom Cincinnati," (unpublished typed ms. in Charles B. Wilby Papers, 1893, CHS); Hickenlooper, "Reminiscences," op. cit. p. 603.
9. Cincinnati, "Report of the Board of Trustees of the University of Cincinnati," *Annual Reports . . . 1890*, op. cit. pp. 1094, 1096–98.
10. Cincinnati, "Report of the Building Inspector," *Annual Reports . . . 1895* (Cincinnati, 1896), pp. 243–49; ibid. *1897* (Cincinnati, 1898), pp. 503–7: Cincinnati, "Mayor's Annual Message," *Annual Reports . . . 1892* (Cincinnati, 1893), pp. lxxvii–lxxxiii; ibid. *1893*, pp. lxxxiii–iv.
11. Ibid. *1890*, pp. xxiii–vi; Cincinnati, "Report of the Board of Administration," *Annual Reports, . . . 1896*, op. cit. pp. 1483–85.
12. *Cincinnati Post*, March 3, 1897, p. 8.
13. G. Bouscaren to John Carlisle, March 18, 1895, G. Bouscaren Letters—Personal, Vol. 9, 1895–1900, CHS, p. 71; Bouscaren to John Scott, April 24, 1895, ibid. p. 74; *Cincinnati Times-Star*, October 15, 1894, p. 1; October 16, 1894, p. 4.

14. Cincinnati, *Board of Legislation, Minutes*, XV, pp. 467, 494, 572–74; *Cincinnati Commercial-Gazette*, March 22, 1894, p. 8.
15. *The Chronicle*, June 19, 1896, p. 2; August 7, 1896, p. 2; *American Israelite*, July 23, 1896, p. 4; *Cincinnati Post*, October 30, 1907, p. 1; Wright, op. cit. pp. 56–57; J. C. Harper to Joseph B. Foraker, July 24, 1896, July 25, 1896, Foraker Papers, Box 35, CHS.
16. The proposition lost in the Third, Seventh, Eighth, Tenth, Twelfth, Thirteenth, Fourteenth, Fifteenth, Twentieth, Twenty-first, Twenty-second, Twenty-third, Twenty-seventh, Twenty-eighth, Twenty-ninth, and Thirtieth wards. See Hamilton County Board of Elections, *Record of City Elections, Commencing in 1888*, op. cit. n.p.
17. Cincinnati, "Mayor's Annual Message," *Annual Reports . . . 1893*, op. cit. pp. xiv–xix, lxxi–iv.
18. *Cincinnati Tribune*, April 11, 1894, p. 4.
19. John Kilgour to A. Howard Hinkle, February 28, 1896, Foraker Papers, Box 27, CHS; Frank M. Coppock to J. B. Foraker, March 20, 1913, ibid. Box 103.
20. Hickenlooper, "Diaries," op. cit. May 8, 1893–July 7, 1893; Cincinnati, "Mayor's Annual Message," *Annual Reports . . .* op. cit. pp. xxxv–vi.
21. Cincinnati, *Board of Councilmen, Journal* [n.v.], pp. 461, 583–84, 595–96, 604–6; Cincinnati, "Report of the Chief Engineer of the Board of Public Works," *Annual Reports . . . 1889*, op. cit. pp. 704–9.
22. At one time there were ten electric companies with franchises to light the city's streets. See Andrew Hickenlooper, *Reply to "Open Letter" of Thos. McDougall, Esq., to Members-Elect from Hamilton County to Seventy-First General Assembly* (Cincinnati, Pamphlet in A. Hickenlooper Papers, Box E, CHS), p. 7.
23. Hickenlooper, "Diaries," op. cit. January 7, 1889–November 21, 1889; February 12, 1891.
24. The major sources for all the maneuvering in the electric street-lighting fight were the *Minutes* of the city council (board of legislation) from 1889 to 1894 and Hickenlooper's "Diaries" from 1889 through 1895.
25. *Cincinnati Tribune*, January 27, 1894, p. 5; Cincinnati "Mayor's Annual Message," *Annual Reports . . . 1893*, op. cit. p. xxxvii; ibid. *1894*, p. xvii; Cincinnati, "Report of the Board of Administration," *Annual Reports . . . 1894*, op. cit. pp. 1430, 1433–36.
26. Cincinnati, "Mayor's Annual Message," *Annual Reports . . . 1889*, op. cit. pp. liv–vii.
27. Cincinnati, *Board of Legislation, Minutes*, XVI, p. 95.
28. Hamilton County Research Foundation, op. cit. pp. 7–9.
29. Cincinnati, *Board of Legislation, Minutes*, XVI, pp. 95, 245–53; *Cincinnati Commercial-Gazette*, April 5, 1894, p. 1; Cincinnati, "Annexation of the Villages of Avondale, Clifton, Linwood, River-

side and Westwood together with the Court Proceedings," *Annual Reports* . . . *1895*, op. cit. pp. 1873–2012.

30. Hamilton County Board of Elections, *Record of City Elections, Commencing in 1888*, op. cit. pp. 72–81.
31. Cincinnati Municipal Reference Bureau, *The March of City Government* . . . op. cit. pp. 15–16.
32. Letter of E. A. Ferguson Accepting [the] Democratic Nomination for State Senator, October 9, 1895, Julius Dexter Papers, CHS.
33. Wilby, op. cit.

CHAPTER 7

1. "The Muckrakers Answered" *Cincinnati Magazine*, Vol. I (December, 1909), p. 10.
2. Wilby, "What Is the Matter with Cincinnati?" op. cit. p. 5; William Howard Taft, "The Proper and Possible Influence of Young Men in Public and Municipal Affairs," *An Address Delivered Before the Young Men's Business Club of Cincinnati, Feb. 22, 1896* (Cincinnati, n.d.), pp. 11–12.
3. Business Men's Club of Cincinnati, *Code of Regulations, Adopted May 18, 1903* (Cincinnati, n.d.), pp. 19–38; Business Men's Club of Cincinnati, *History* (Cincinnati, n.d.), pp. 3, 6–7; *The Optimist*, Vol. II (October 1912), pp. 20–23. Southern and eastern Europeans and Negroes were not represented.
4. Joseph Stacy Hill, "An Intimate Chat With My Descendents, Supplement" (unpublished typed ms., 1933, in CHS), pp. 26–50.
5. The Business Men's Club Co., *Annual Report, 1903–1904*. President's [T. J. Moffett] *Report* (Cincinnati, n.d.), pp. 10, 16.
6. Most of this section is based on the available annual reports of the club and its magazine, *The Optimist*. See especially, however, *The Optimist*, Vol. I (October 1912), p. 19; ibid. Vol. I (December 1912), pp. 9–10; ibid. Vol. II (October 1913), pp. 19–20; ibid. Vol. II (December 1913), pp. 50–51; Alfred K. Nippert to Brand Whitlock, January 8, 1912, Whitlock Papers, General Correspondence, Box 25, Library of Congress.
7. C. R. Hebble, "Cincinnati's Industrial Survey," *The American City*, Vol. XI (December 1914), p. 487.
8. Cincinnati Chamber of Commerce, *Sixty-Fifth Annual Report, 1913* (Cincinnati, 1914), p. 41.
9. Cincinnati Chamber of Commerce, *Sixty-Fourth Annual Report, 1912* (Cincinnati, 1913), p. 24.
10. The committees included new ones on agriculture, annexation, building code, city planning and civic center, city charter, commercial and industrial education, fire prevention, flood prevention, good roads, industrial relations, industrial survey, industrial welfare and housing, interurban terminal, municipal affairs, municipal auditorium, pub-

lic utilities, safe and sane Fourth of July, smoke abatement, social welfare, taxation, and Ohio River improvement. Cincinnati Chamber of Commerce, op. cit. *1913*, pp. xii–xvii.

11. *Civic News*, Vol. I (October 1911), p. 1.
12. Only Negroes, southern and eastern Europeans, and unskilled workers were not represented. For a list of officers of each of the associations in the federation see *Civic News*, Vol. I (October 1911), p. 3; ibid. Vol. II (February 1913), pp. 1, 4.
13. *Civic News*, Vol. I (October 1911), p. 7.
14. Ibid. (November 1911), p. 2.
15. Ibid. (February 1912), pp. 1, 4.
16. Howard C. Hollister to Samuel W. Smith, April 29, 1914, Samuel W. Smith Correspondence, CHS.
17. Charles R. Hebble and Frank P. Goodwin (eds.), *The Citizen's Book* (Cincinnati, 1916), p. 112.
18. Quoted in *Citizen's Bulletin*, February 4, 1911, p. 1.
19. Mary P. Wells Smith to Cincinnati Woman's Club, March 21, 1899, Clara Chipman Newman Papers, Box 2, CHS.
20. Cincinnati Woman's Club, *First Annual Report, 1895* (Cincinnati, n.d.), pp. 35–37.
21. Cincinnati Woman's Club, *Year Book, Reports and Membership List, 1913–1914* (Cincinnati, n.d.), pp. 71–74.
22. Cincinnati Chamber of Commerce, *Sixty-Fifth Annual Report, 1913*, op. cit. p. 35.
23. [Taxpayers' Association of Hamilton County], *Some of the many Reasons Why Every Tax Payer Should Become a Member of this Association* (Cincinnati, 1898), p. 1; *Fourteen Reasons Why Every Real Estate Owner of Hamilton County Should be a Member of the Taxpayers' Association* (Cincinnati, n.d.), pp. 1–2.
24. Taxpayers' Association, *Brief Quarterly Report, August, 1906* (Cincinnati, 1906), p. 3; Taxpayers' Association, *Annual Report, 1906* (Cincinnati, n.d.), p. 3; *Citizen's Bulletin*, November 9, 1907, p. 11.
25. *Cincinnati Post*, November 24, 1913, p. 8.
26. Professionals, especially physicians, dominated the leadership of the organization. Nearly one-third of its members were German Jews. See Cincinnati Anti-Tuberculosis League, *Fifth Annual Report, 1911* (Cincinnati, n.d.), pp. 33–34.
27. Ibid. pp. 14, 22–23. *Cincinnati Post*, June 1, 1912, p. 7.
28. Cincinnati Anti-Tuberculosis League, *Fifth Annual Report, 1911*, op. cit. pp. 18, 19–20, 31.
29. *The Chronicle*, Vol. II (October 1893), p. 3.
30. Ibid. August 10, 1900, p. 2; May 11, 1912, p. 4; November 15, 1913, p. 4.
31. Ibid. July 16, 1904, p. 4.
32. Ibid. March 19, 1897, p. 1; October 1, 1897, p. 1; ibid. October 24, 1903, p. 4; December 26, 1903, p. 1.

33. Ibid. Vol. II (October 1893), p. 2; Vol. III (February 1894), p. 1; Vol. III (March 1894), pp. 1–2.
34. Ibid. January 21, 1911, p. 4.
35. Ibid. December 31, 1897, p. 2; October 14, 1898, p. 2; August 6, 1904, p. 4; April 24, 1909, p. 4; August 17, 1912, p. 4.
36. Ibid. March 11, 1911, p. 4; February 15, 1913, p. 4.
37. Ibid. January 25, 1895, p. 2; August 17, 1907, p. 4; May 1, 1909, p. 4; December 4, 1909, p. 4; June 17, 1911, p. 4; July 20, 1912, p. 4.
38. Ibid. May 24, 1895, p. 4; August 23, 1902, p. 2; January 20, 1906, p. 4; April 10, 1909, p. 3; July 24, 1909, p. 4; September 17, 1910, p. 4.
39. Ibid. December 24, 1897, p. 1; December 8, 1901, p. 2; July 11, 1903, p. 2.
40. *Cincinnati Post,* September 24, 1913, p. 4.

CHAPTER 8

1. I am using the differentiation between "German" Jew and "Russian" Jew common during the period. It had religious as well as cultural significance. Thát is, German Jews were not only "German," but also Reform Jews, and Russian (or east European) Jews were not only "Russian," but also Orthodox Jews. See Oscar Handlin, *Adventures in Freedom: Three Hundred Years of Jewish Life in America* (New York, Toronto, London, 1959), pp. 49, 80–85, 104–5; Nathan Glazer, *American Judaism* (Chicago, 1957), pp. 22–42, 60–78.
2. Borris D. Bogen (in collaboration with Alfred Segal), *Born a Jew* (New York, 1930), p. 72; David Philipson, "Journal, June 2, 1888–Nov. 10, 1892," September 16, 1890, entry (unpublished ms. in American Jewish Archives). American Jewish Archives hereafter referred to as AJA.
3. In 1881 there were between 12,000 and 15,000 Jews of German descent in Cincinnati. Brickner, op. cit. pp. 16, 346.
4. Philipson, "*Journal,*" op. cit. September 16, 1890, November 10, 1892 entries.
5. Glazer, op. cit. p. 132; Brickner, op. cit. pp. 260–61, 281, 285; Lawrence H. Fuchs, *The Political Behavior of American Jews* (Glencoe, Illinois, 1956), p. 488.
6. Charles T. Greve, *Centennial History Cincinnati and Representative Citizens* (Chicago, 1904), p. 939.
7. Isaac M. Wise, *A Defense of Judaism Versus Proselytizing Christianity* (Cincinnati and Chicago, 1889), pp. 3, 5–6.
8. In 1890 there were three Reform congregations in Cincinnati with 3200 members and property valued at $435,000. There were also three Orthodox congregations which reported 525 members and two synagogues valued at $49,000. See H. S. Linfield, *Statistics of*

Jews and Jewish Organizations: A Historical Review of the Census, 1850–1937 (New York, 1939), p. 45. These "old Orthodox" Jews were generally accepted and respected by the Reform Jews. See Bogen, *Born a Jew*, op. cit. p. 73.

9. David Philipson, *My Life as an American Jew* (Cincinnati, 1941), p. 77. Brickner, op. cit. p. 190.

10. Brickner, op. cit. pp. 189–96; Philipson, *My Life . . .* op. cit. p. 18; Greve, op. cit. p. 946; *Cincinnati Enquirer,* September 3, 1899, Newspaper clipping in *Scrapbook,* Moch Family Collection, AJA. Also see *Cincinnati Post,* February 8, 1897, p. 8; United Jewish Charities, *Second Annual Report, 1898* (Cincinnati, 1898), p. 10.

11. "Address by Mr. Max Senior, Annual Dinner, United Jewish Social Agencies, Cincinnati, Ohio, June 1, 1938" (unpublished ms., Max Senior Papers, AJA), pp. 6–7; Bernhard Bettmann, *Some Addresses and Poems by Bernard Bettmann Edited as a Jubelschrift on the Occasion of His Seventieth Birthday, Aug. 7, 1914* (Cincinnati, 1914), p. 17; Philipson, *My Life . . .* op. cit. p. 121; United Jewish Charities of Cincinnati, "Minute Book, 1895–1897" (Cincinnati, unpublished ms. in AJA), p. 50. The federation was originally composed of the Hebrew General Relief Society, the Society for the Relief of Jewish Sick Poor, the Jewish Ladies Sewing Society, the Jewish Foster Home, the Kindergarten Association, the Kitchen Garden Association, the Plum Street Industrial School, and the Industrial School for Boys. The Jewish Settlement, founded in 1899, joined in 1906. United Jewish Charities of Cincinnati, *Minute Book, 1895–1897,* op. cit. p. 50; Brickner, op. cit. p. 213.

12. Bogen, *Born a Jew*, op. cit. p. 72.

13. The Cincinnati Jewish Settlement, *Annual Report, 1904–1905* (Cincinnati, 1905), pp. 4–5.

14. S. C. Lowenstein, "What Does the Jewish Settlement Mean to Us?," *Neighborhood News,* Vol. I (April 1, 1903), p. 2; S. C. Lowenstein, "The Necessity for Resident Workers," *Second National Conference of Jewish Charities in the United States, 1902* (Cincinnati, 1902), p. 292; The Cincinnati Jewish Settlement, op. cit. p. 11.

15. Philipson, *Journal, July 19, 1905–Feb. 22, 1905,* op. cit. July 21, 1905, n.p.; Boris D. Bogen, "Jews of Many Lands," *Jewish Charities,* Vol. III (May 1913), pp. 3–4; United Jewish Charities, *Fourteenth Annual Report, 1910,* op. cit.

16. Jewish Settlement of Cincinnati, *Jews of Many Lands* (Cincinnati, 1913), pp. 3, 6, 9, 18–38; Bogen, "Jews of Many Lands," op. cit. pp. 3–8, 10; Boris D. Bogen, *Jewish Philanthropy* (New York, 1917), pp. 252–57.

17. For a similar but not altogether identical interpretation of the emergence of Jewishness among the German Jews see Glazer, op. cit. pp. 79–105, 146–47. He dates the phenomenon to the twenties and

emphasizes the intellectual or religious vitality of the notion of a holy community.

18. Philipson, *Journal*, op. cit. July 21, 1905.
19. Philipson, *Journal*, op. cit. February 22, 1905; Philipson, *My Life* . . . op. cit. pp. 169–70. Murray Seasongood, in reviewing Philipson's career, recalled that he regarded "citizenship and the fearless discharge of civic duty as a religious obligation."
20. David Philipson, *et al.* (eds.), *Hebrew Union College Jubilee Volume (1875–1925)* (Cincinnati, 1925), p. 39; Kaufman Kohler, *Hebrew Union College and Other Addresses* (Cincinnati, 1916), pp. 46, 207–8.
21. *Williams' Cincinnati Directory, 1897* (Cincinnati, 1897), p. 2114. This paragraph is based primarily on material gleaned from the *Catholic-Telegraph.*
22. For the quote and description of "conservative" Catholicism and its identification with Germans see Robert D. Cross, *The Emergence of Liberal Catholicism in America* (Cambridge, Mass., 1958), pp. 22, 26, 98–99, 174. Also, on Walburg's attitudes, see *Catholic-Telegraph*, March 5, 1891, p. 4. Coleman J. Barry places Elder a bit left of center in the conservative-liberal controversy. See Coleman J. Barry, O.S.B., *The Catholic Church and German Americans* (Milwaukee, 1953), p. 184.
23. *Catholic-Telegraph*, March 5, 1885, p. 4; March 12, 1885, p. 4; April 11, 1889, p. 4.
24. Lamott, op. cit. pp. 189–218; *Catholic-Telegraph*, August 21, 1884, p. 4.
25. Ibid. September 13, 1888, p. 1; August 11, 1892, p. 4; August 25, 1892, p. 4; November 23, 1893, p. 4; January 10, 1895, p. 1; January 17, 1895, p. 4; January 24, 1895, p. 4; September 19, 1895, p. 4; *Cincinnati Times-Star*, January 10, 1887, pp. 4, 5; January 11, 1887, p. 3; February 19, 1889, p. 5; August 12, 1890, p. 5; Lamott, op. cit. pp. 219–20. The *Catholic-Telegraph* in the 1890's did not take sides in feud between the Knights and the Central Labor Council, but supported workers generally and pointed to strikes as an indication that serious wrongs needed correcting.
26. *Catholic-Telegraph*, March 3, 1898, p. 1; *American Israelite*, March 10, 1898, p. 4.
27. For biographical data on Moeller see Lamott, op. cit. pp. 92–94; *Catholic-Telegraph*, November 17, 1904, pp. 1, 4.
28. *Catholic-Telegraph*, February 4, 1897, p. 1; September 21, 1905, p. 4; February 23, 1911, pp. 1, 8; August 31, 1911, p. 4.
29. Ibid. February 10, 1898, p. 4; February 17, 1898, p. 4; August 30, 1906, Sec. 4, p. 6; October 19, 1911, p. 4.
30. Ibid. March 6, 1902, p. 4; November 23, 1911, p. 4; June 19, 1912, p. 4.
31. Ibid. February 24, 1898, p. 1; February 10, 1910, p. 5.

32. Rev. John O'Grady, "Study of Catholic Charities of the Archdiocese of Cincinnati" (Cincinnati, unpublished ms., 1926, in the offices of the Bureau of Catholic Charities, Cincinnati), n.p.

33. Ibid. For the constitution see Bureau of Catholic Charities, *Annual Report, 1918* (Cincinnati, n.d.), p. 1.

34. Bureau of Catholic Charities, *Annual Report, 1916* (Cincinnati, n.d.), p. 1.

35. On this point also see Daniel J. Boorstin, *The Genius of American Politics* (Chicago, 1953), pp. 141–49; John Tracy Ellis, *American Catholicism* (Chicago, 1956), pp. 152–54.

36. Frank H. Nelson (ed.), *The Clergy Club of Cincinnati: Its History and Significance and a Roster of Its Members Past and Present* (Cincinnati, 1934), pp. 17–20, 22–25, 26–28. Also relevant for this chapter is Gibson Winter, *The Suburban Captivity of the Protestant Churches* (New York, 1962). He argues that the rapidity of change in cities after 1870 increased the outwardly mobile middle classes' search for roots. They increasingly turned to the church for solace. But, as we shall see, to 1914 at least, they were frequently greeted by preachers who turned their attention back to the problems of the Circle and Zone, which mitigated the social and political effects of the suburban captivity. In Cincinnati, moreover, annexation kept pace with the urban explosion.

37. W. J. Norton, "An Old Institution Turning Its Work to the Day's Needs," *The Survey*, Vol. XXXII (June 13, 1914), p. 308; Cincinnati Union Bethel, *Eighteenth Annual Report, 1882–1883* (Cincinnati, 1883), p. 6; *Twentieth Annual Report, 1884–1885* (Cincinnati, 1885), p. 6; *Twenty-First Annual Report, 1885–1886* (Cincinnati, 1886), p. 6.

38. Cincinnati Union Bethel, *Thirty-Sixth Annual Report, 1900–1901* (Cincinnati, n.d.), p. 4; Bessie Bruce White, *A Story of the Cincinnati Union Bethel* (Cincinnati, 1912), pp. 55–57.

39. Cincinnati Union Bethel, *Twenty-Second Annual Report*, op. cit. pp. 2, 29–31; *Thirty-First Annual Report, 1895–1896* (Cincinnati, 1896), pp. 15–17; *Forty-Fourth Annual Report, 1909–1910* (Cincinnati, n.d.), pp. 25–27.

40. Cincinnati Union Bethel, *Forty-Fourth Annual Report*, op. cit. p. 9; *Forty-Eighth Annual Report*, op. cit. p. 5.

41. *Cincinnati Enquirer*, March 10, 1903, p. 12; March 16, 1903, p. 5.

42. Quoted in Warren Herrick, *Frank H. Nelson of Cincinnati* (Louisville, 1945), p. 19.

43. Goss, *The Philopolist* . . . op. cit. pp. 1, 7, 10, 18–19.

44. *Cincinnati Times-Star*, February 18, 1889, p. 8; February 23, 1889, p. 6.

45. Edward F. Alexander to Author, Interview, November 13, 1962; Daniel R. Beaver, *A Buckeye Crusader: A Sketch of the Political Career of Herbert Seely Bigelow, Preacher, Prophet, Politician* (Cincinnati, 1957), pp. 1–12. For the charge that he preached

unitarian principles see *American Israelite*, February 3, 1898, p. 4.
46. Alexander, op. cit.; Segal, op. cit. Segal was a *Post* reporter. Alexander was a friend and associate of Bigelow's.
47. Franklin H. Lawson to Author, April 10, 1963 (letter in possession of Author); Alexander, op. cit. For a story on "labor leaders" as "workers" in the church see *Cincinnati Post,* October 5, 1912, p. 7.
48. Brand Whitlock, "Daniel Kiefer," *The American Magazine,* Vol. LXXIV (September 1912), pp. 549–53; Lincoln Steffens, *The Autobiography of Lincoln Steffens* (New York, 1931), p. 642; *Citizen's Bulletin,* December 28, 1912, p. 3; Alexander, op. cit.; Max Hirsch to Author, Interview, March 15, 1963.
49. Herbert S. Bigelow, "Old Institutions and New Ideas," (undated, unpublished ms. in Bigelow Papers, 1900–1912, CHS), p. 21; Herbert S. Bigelow, *The Religion of Inspired Politics* (Cincinnati, 1913), p. 17.
50. Bigelow, "Old Institutions . . ." op. cit.; Herbert S. Bigelow, "The Ideals of a City, Address by Herbert Seely Bigelow, Grand Opera House, Oct. 3, 1909" (unpublished ms., 1909, in Bigelow Papers, 1900–1912, CHS), pp. 1, 4.
51. Herbert S. Bigelow, *A Growing God* (Cincinnati, n.d. [between 1908 and 1912]), p. 7; Herbert S. Bigelow to Brand Whitlock, October 18, 1906, Whitlock Papers, General Correspondence, Box 11, Library of Congress; Daniel Kiefer to Brand Whitlock, December 26, 1911, December 11, 1913, Whitlock Papers, General Correspondence, Box 29, Library of Congress.

CHAPTER 9

1. Associated Charities of Cincinnati, *First Annual Report, 1880–1881* (Cincinnati, 1881), pp. 8, 11–12. Among the groups and individuals whose activities fit this category but are not discussed here were Jacob G. Schmidlapp, who specialized in low cost housing and women's education; William Cooper Procter in housing and profit-sharing; Mrs. Mary Emery, James N. Gamble, Annie Laws and the Charles P. Tafts in Negro education; and W. P. Dabney in anti-tuberculosis work and housing for Negroes.
2. Associated Charities of Cincinnati, *First Annual Report,* op. cit. pp. 4, 12, 19–20; *Second Annual Report, 1881–1882* (Cincinnati, n.d.), pp. 16–19.
3. See Associated Charities of Cincinnati, *Twentieth Annual Report, 1899–1900* (Cincinnati, n.d.), p. 32; *Thirtieth Annual Report, 1909–1910* (Cincinnati, n.d.), pp. 14, 15, 16–19; *Thirty-First Annual Report, 1910–1911* (Cincinnati, n.d.), pp. 21–35.
4. Associated Charities of Cincinnati, *First Annual Report,* op. cit. p. 22. Formally, the Associated Charities was "not a disbursing Society. Its objects were investigation, maintenance of a body of friendly visitors to the poor, registration, prevention of duplicate

giving, counsel, help toward self-support, direction to existing societies for appropriate relief." *Tenth Annual Report, 1889–1890* (Cincinnati, n.d.), p. 1.

5. *A Year's Charity Work in Cincinnati with a Directory of the City Charities,* [1891–1892] (Cincinnati, 1892), p. 4; Associated Charities of Cincinnati, *Twenty-Fifth Annual Report, 1904–1905* (Cincinnati, 1905), pp. 16–17.

6. *Citizen's Bulletin,* February 25, 1911, p. 7.

7. *Citizen's Bulletin,* July 21, 1906, p. 7; Reginald C. McGrane, *The Cincinnati Doctor's Forum* (Cincinnati, 1957), pp. 167–72, 182–86, 205–10, 221–22.

8. Most of the data for this section, including the quote from Cox, came from Martin Fischer, *Christian Holmes: Man and Physician* (Springfield, Ill., and Baltimore, 1937), pp. 21, 25–26, 30–31, 34–37, 40, 42–43, 49, 51–57, 59, 62, 65–66, 70, 88, 93–95, 106. Also see Christian Holmes to the Public, February 5, 1906, in the CHS files; *The Chronicle,* January 12, 1907, pp. 4, 5; *Citizen's Bulletin,* January 5, 1907, pp. 1, 3; May 1, 1909, pp. 1–2; *Cincinnati Commercial-Tribune,* November 5, 1911, p. 5.

9. *Cincinnati Post,* November 1, 1912, p. 4; January 23, 1913, p. 4.

10. Ibid. May 15, 1912, p. 10; July 10, 1912, p. 2; Gilbert Bettmann, "The Movement of the Cincinnati Bar Association for a Non-Partisan Judiciary," *The Optimist,* Vol. I (July 1912), pp. 28–30.

11. *Citizen's Bulletin,* October 19, 1912, p. 4. For the quote see ibid. October 26, 1912, p. 4.

12. J. M. Rice, "Our Public School System: Schools of Buffalo and Cincinnati," *The Forum* (November 1892), pp. 294–95, 303–5; *Citizen's Bulletin,* January 12, 1907, p. 4; *Cincinnati Post,* February 24, 1912, p. 3; Cincinnati Schoolmasters' Club, "Proceedings, 1910–1914," I-IV (Cincinnati, unpublished typed ms. in the Cincinnati Public Library, n.d.) n.p.

13. *Citizen's Bulletin,* December 12, 1903, p. 2; February 2, 1907, p. 1; *The Chronicle,* March 18, 1900, p. 1; Ralph R. Caldwell, "Cincinnati, Why It Does Not Grow, A Paper Read Before the Cincinnati Club, January 14, 1911," reprinted in *Citizen's Bulletin,* January 21, 1911, p. 3; *Cincinnati Post,* October 15, 1904, p. 10.

14. *Citizen's Bulletin,* February 1, 1908, pp. 1–3.

15. Ibid. October 7, 1905, p. 1; December 12, 1908, p. 5; Hebble and Goodwin, op. cit. p. 118.

16. Hebble and Goodwin, op. cit. pp. 117–18, 121–25; J. R. Schmidt, "Cincinnati's Continuation School," *The World Today,* Vol. XVII (November 1909), pp. 1211–12; *Citizen's Bulletin,* March 25, 1911, p. 1.

17. Hebble and Goodwin, op. cit. pp. 118–20; *Citizen's Bulletin,* February 1, 1908, p. 3; June 1, 1912, p. 7; *Catholic-Telegraph,* February 16, 1911, p. 4; *Cincinnati Post,* December 7, 1910, p. 3:

November 20, 1913, p. 2; *Cincinnati Commercial-Tribune*, October 11, 1911, p. 4.

18. *Citizen's Bulletin*, November 26, 1910, p. 1; Hebble and Goodwin, op. cit. p. 128.

19. *Cincinnati Enquirer*, March 12, 1897, p. 7; *The Chronicle*, December 8, 1901, p. 2; Hebble and Goodwin, op. cit. p. 124.

20. *Citizen's Bulletin*, October 9, 1909, p. 3; April 5, 1913, p. 1.

21. *The American Review of Reviews*, Vol. XXVI (September 1903), pp. 262–63; Reginald C. McGrane, *The University of Cincinnati: A Success Story in Urban Higher Education* (New York, Evanston, and London, 1963), pp. 193–96; *Citizen's Bulletin*, January 2, 1904, p. 2.

22. *Citizen's Bulletin*, March 11, 1905, p. 1; December 16, 1905, p. 7; January 12, 1912, p. 1.

23. Ibid. June 6, 1906, p. 15; Charles William Dabney, *The University of the City, Annual Statement . . . at the Commencement Exercises, June 1, 1907* (Cincinnati, n.d.), p. 17; Charles William Dabney, "The University and the City in Co-operation," *The Outlook*, Vol. LXXXIX (July 25, 1908), p. 655; *Citizen's Bulletin*, March 9, 1912, p. 1.

24. Dabney, *The University of the City . . .* op. cit. p. 21; Dabney, "Condition and History of the University . . ." op. cit. pp. 1–10; McGrane, *The University of Cincinnati . . .* op. cit. pp. 206–18; *Cincinnati Post*, September 28, 1912, p. 8; *Citizen's Bulletin*, January 8, 1910, p. 5; Dabney, "The University and the City in Co-operation," op. cit. pp. 660–61.

25. *Citizen's Bulletin*, May 19, 1906, p. 13; *Cincinnati Post*, February 27, 1912, p. 2; E. F. Dubrul, "A Young Instructor and His Big Dream," *The American Magazine*, Vol. LXVIII (May 1909), pp. 17–21; J. R. Schmidt, "Co-operative Courses in Technical Education," *The World To-Day*, Vol. XVII (January 1909), pp. 100–102; J. R. Schmidt, "Coordinating Workshop and School," *The World's Work*, Vol. XVI (July 1908), pp. 10407–8; Clyde W. Park, *Ambassador to Industry: The Idea and Life of Herman Schneider* (New York and Indianapolis, 1943), pp. 31–98, 315–16.

26. Fischer, op. cit. pp. 129–30; *Cincinnati Enquirer*, November 3, 1911, p. 2; Dabney, "Condition and History of the University . . ." op. cit. p. 13; *Citizen's Bulletin*, December 29, 1906, p. 4; March 22, 1913, p. 1; *Cincinnati Post*, March 8, 1912, p. 11.

27. *Cincinnati Post*, September 28, 1912, p. 8.

28. University Settlement, *Annual Report, 1905–1906* (Cincinnati, 1906), pp. 4, 20–22, 29. *University Settlement Review*, Vol. I (Cincinnati, 1906), p. 1.

29. (Cincinnati) Business Men's Club Company, *Annual Report, 1908–1909* (Cincinnati, n.d.), p. 75; *Citizen's Bulletin*, May 15, 1909, p. 1; Cincinnati Bureau of Municipal Research; *The Cincinnati Bureau*

of Municipal Research; Its First Year's Work (Cincinnati, 1910), p. 7; Herbert F. Koch to Author, Interview, November 15, 1962.

30. Quoted in Community Chest and Council of Social Agencies of Cincinnati and Hamilton County, *Ten Years of Progress in Social Service, 1914–1924* (Cincinnati, n.d.), pp. 5–6.
31. Ibid. pp. 3–4; *Citizen's Bulletin*, June 21, 1913, p. 7; *Cincinnati Post*, May 29, 1913, p. 7.
32. Hebble and Goodwin, op. cit. p. 109.
33. Cincinnati Union Bethel, *Fiftieth Annual Report, 1916* (Cincinnati, n.d.), p. 3.

CHAPTER 10

1. *Cincinnati Post*, January 2, 1897, p. 4; January 15, 1897, p. 4; January 20, 1897, p. 4; January 26, 1897, pp. 2, 4; January 30, 1897, p. 4.
2. Ibid. March 1, 1897, p. 1; March 3, 1897, p. 8; March 4, 1897, p. 1; *Cincinnati Enquirer*, March 1, 1897, p. 5.
3. *Cincinnati Enquirer*, March 3, 1897, p. 10; March 4, 1897, p. 12.
4. Ibid. March 5, 1897, p. 5; March 11, 1897, p. 5. The "legitimate perquisites" enjoyed by the police court clerk took the form of fees for making out bonds for those arrested after 4 p.m. weekdays and between noon Saturday and eight Monday morning when the office was officially closed.
5. *Cincinnati Post*, March 19, 1897, p. 3.
6. *Cincinnati Enquirer*, March 7, 1897, p. 4; March 12, 1897, p. 4; March 15, 1897, p. 6; March 20, 1897, pp. 4, 5; March 23, 1897, p. 4; March 27, 1897, p. 8; March 31, 1897, pp. 4, 12.
7. *Cincinnati Volksfreund*, March 8, 1897, p. 4; March 17, 1897, p. 4; March 26, 1897, p. 4; April 2, 1897, p. 4; April 5, 1897, p. 4.
8. *Cincinnati Post*, March 11, 1897, p. 6; March 24, 1897, p. 1; March 27, 1897, p. 3; March 30, 1897, p. 4; March 31, 1897, p. 4.
9. Ibid. March 6, 1897, p. 8; April 3, 1897, p. 5; Gustav Tafel to Julius Dexter, October 19, 1895, in Julius Dexter Papers, CHS, *Scrapbook*, pp. 196–97.
10. *Cincinnati Post*, March 3, 1897, p. 4; March 12, 1897, p. 5; *Cincinnati Enquirer*, March 12, 1897, p. 5.
11. *Cincinnati Post*, February 2, 1897, pp. 1, 7; March 16, 1897, p. 6; Dabney, *Cincinnati's Colored Citizens* . . . op. cit. pp. 123–27.
12. *Cincinnati Enquirer*, March 30, 1897, p. 8; April 1, 1897, p. 7; April 3, 1897, p. 8.
13. *Cincinnati Post*, January 19, 1897, p. 8; March 1, 1897, pp. 4, 6; March 15, 1897, p. 5; *Cincinnati Volksblatt*, March 1, 1897, p. 4; Wright, op. cit. p. 47; Hickenlooper, "Diaries," 1897, op. cit. February 5, 1897; April 5, 1897.
14. Hickenlooper, "Diaries," op. cit. April 5, 1897; April 6, 1897; August 20, 1897; *Cincinnati Enquirer*, April 6, 1897, p. 4. H. P. Boy-

den later claimed that Tafel got "the largest vote a majority candidate had ever received in this city." See *Citizen's Bulletin,* August 29, 1903, p. 1.

15. Election returns from Hamilton County Board of Elections, *Record of City Elections, Commencing 1888,* op. cit. pp. 90–104; *Cincinnati Enquirer,* April 6, 1897, p. 4; April 20, 1897, p. 4.

16. *Cincinnati Post,* April 22, 1897, p. 1; April 7, 1897, p. 1; May 3, 1897, p. 1; Hickenlooper, "Diaries," op. cit. April 17–May 6, 1897. I tried to get the grand jury reports but was told by the county prosecutor's office that all of these records for the period covered by this study had been destroyed.

17. *Cincinnati Post,* April 30, 1897, p. 2; May 1, 1897, p. 1; *Cincinnati Enquirer,* April 11, 1897, p. 6.

18. *Cincinnati Post,* April 8, 1897, p. 6; April 13, 1897, p. 5; Joseph B. Foraker to Theodore Roosevelt, July 28, 1903, Foraker Papers, Box 24, CHS; Jacob Godfrey Schmidlapp to Carl J. Schmidlapp, September 1907 (unpublished typed ms. in CHS), pp. 81–82; J. G. Schmidlapp, "Autobiography" (Cincinnati, unpublished ms., Cincinnati Public Library), pp. 92–98; Steffens, op. cit. pp. 177–78.

19. Hickenlooper, "Diaries," op. cit. September 14, 1897, p. 7; November 2, 1897; Sidney Maxwell to Emma Maxwell, October 10, 1897; October 11, 1897; October 13, 1897; November 2, 1897, Maxwell Papers, CHS; Joseph B. Foraker to Mark Hanna, September 21, 1897, Foraker Papers, Box 27, CHS.

20. Reprinted in Wright, op. cit. pp. 51–52.

21. Hickenlooper, "Diaries," op. cit. January 12, 1898–June 25, 1898; Wright, op. cit. p. 111; Karger, op. cit. pp. 280–81. Hanna was charged with bribery in securing his election, but it was not proven. However, because of a mysterious $2000 check bearing the signature of Charles Dick with a letter requesting that it be cashed and then returned to Hanna's office in Cleveland, Schmidlapp took himself to Mexico City during the state legislature's investigation of the affair. See Jacob Godfrey Schmidlapp to Carl J. Schmidlapp, op. cit. pp. 82–83.

22. J. R. Foraker to J. B. Foraker, February 14, 1898, Foraker Papers, Box 33, CHS; John Galvin to J. B. Foraker, March 21, 1898, ibid. Box 34, CHS; Miller Outcault to J. B. Foraker, March 24, 1898, ibid. Box 38, CHS; August Herrmann to J. B. Foraker, June 11, 1898, ibid. Box 25, CHS.

23. Hickenlooper, "Diaries," op. cit. June 22, 1898–March 21, 1899; George B. Cox to J. B. Foraker, September 3, 1898, Foraker Papers, Box 32, CHS.

24. Hickenlooper, "Diaries," op. cit. April 18, 1899–August 1, 1899. The entries for the nocturnal meetings in June are largely illegible.

25. William S. Capeller to J. B. Foraker, April 26, 1899, Foraker Papers, Box 2, CHS; George B. Cox to J. B. Foraker, June 12, 1899, Foraker Papers, Box 32, CHS.

26. Thomas Beer, *Hanna* (New York, 1929), pp. ix, 304–19. The Central Labor Council also endorsed McLean. See *The Chronicle,* April 1, 1899, p. 4; November 10, 1899, p. 3.
27. Election returns compiled from Hamilton County Board of Elections, "Abstract of Votes Cast from 1896–1899, Incl., Gubernatorial Election of 1899" (Cincinnati, unpublished ms. in the offices of the Hamilton County Board of Elections, n.d.), n.p. Nash carried wards One, Two, Five, Ten, Eleven, Twelve, Fourteen, Eighteen, Twenty-three, Twenty-four, Twenty-five, Twenty-six, Twenty-seven, Twenty-eight, and Thirty-one. McLean took Three, Four, Six, Seven, Eight, Nine, Thirteen, Fifteen, Sixteen, Seventeen, Nineteen, Twenty, Twenty-one, Twenty-two, Twenty-nine, and Thirty.
28. Hickenlooper, "Diaries," op. cit. January 5, 1900–March 2, 1900; George B. Cox to J. B. Foraker, December 10, 1899, Foraker Papers, Box 32, CHS; Dabney, *Cincinnati's Colored Citizens,* . . . op. cit. p. 118; Wright, op. cit. pp. 49–50. The mayor's annual messages also record the futility of the reform administration.
29. Unidentified paper clipping, April 4, 1900, Andrew Hickenlooper Papers, Box E, CHS; Judge Stanley Matthews to Author, Interview, November 20, 1962; *American Israelite,* March 22, 1900, p. 4.
30. *Cincinnati Times-Star,* March 10, 1900, p. 5; Hickenlooper, "Diaries," op. cit. March 2, 1900–March 16, 1900.
31. *Cincinnati Times-Star,* March 17, 1900, p. 1; Hickenlooper "Diaries," op. cit. March 17, 1900; *American Israelite,* March 22, 1900, p. 4. After the election the *Post* guessed that Hickenlooper had played a crucial part in designing the ticket. As concrete evidence it pointed to the sudden return of Kenan to Cox's table at Wielert's and the appointment of the superintendent of the gas company's plants as city electrician. It argued, however, that Hickenlooper was "boss" and made Cox come to him. The reverse, as we have seen, was the case. But Cox was not boss in the absolute sense, for the ticket was chosen in a series of conferences among several men. Indeed, Herrmann, who played a crucial role throughout this period as intermediary among the various factions, did as much as any other single man to reconstitute the coalition. See *Cincinnati Post,* April 23, 1900, in Andrew Hickenlooper Papers, [no box], CHS.
32. *Cincinnati Times-Star,* March 17, 1900, p. 10; March 19, 1900, p. 4; March 31, 1900, p. 4; *Cincinnati Volksblatt,* March 19, 1900, p. 4; March 28, 1900, p. 4; March 29, 1900, p. 4; April 2, 1900, p. 4; Hickenlooper, "Diaries," 1900, op. cit. March 26, 1900.
33. *Cincinnati Times-Star,* March 28, 1900, p. 1.
34. *Cincinnati Volksfreund,* April 3, 1900, p. 4. Cohen carried wards Three, Four, Six, Seven, Eight, Seventeen, Nineteen, Twenty, Twenty-one, Twenty-two, and Twenty-nine. Fleischmann took One, Two, Five, Nine, Ten, Eleven, Twelve, Thirteen, Fourteen, Fifteen, Sixteen, Eighteen, Twenty-three, Twenty-four, Twenty-five, Twenty-six, Twenty-seven, Twenty-eight, Thirty, and Thirty-one. Election

returns compiled from Hamilton County Board of Elections, *Record of City Elections, Commencing 1888: City Elections, April 2, 1900,* op. cit. pp. 122–34. Some GOP fusionists took credit for the defeat of the Citizens' party, claiming that they did not support the ticket. The *Times-Star* disagreed. It said the Republicans won because "their organization was perfect and enthusiastic and brought to the polls the full Republican strength" while the Democratic factional fights prevented "that harmonious action which is necessary on election days." See *Cincinnati Times-Star,* April 4, 1900, p. 4. The total vote, however, was nearly 20,000 below the total registration and 1100 less than the vote of 1897. It seems unlikely that lack of a full Democratic vote accounted for all 20,000 of those who failed to vote, especially since the Democrats did well in the Circle, their traditional source of strength. It is more probable that the Zone did not respond enthusiastically to a campaign dominated by two Jewish reformers.

CHAPTER 11

1. Hickenlooper, "Diaries," op. cit. June 8, 1900–August 31, 1900.
2. Charles P. Taft to William Howard Taft, January 22, 1901, Taft Papers, Family Correspondence, Box 31, Library of Congress. Also see Charles P. Taft to William Howard Taft, May 8, 1903, and May 25, 1903, Taft Papers, Family Correspondence, Box 35, Library of Congress.
3. *Citizen's Bulletin,* May 30, 1903, p. 1. The board of appraisers which evaluated the gas and Edison companies before their merger was chaired by Herrmann.
4. Lincoln Steffens, *The Struggle for Self-Government Being an Attempt To Trace American Political Corruption To Its Sources In Six States of the United States With A Dedication To The Czar* (New York, 1906), pp. 198–199; Charles P. Taft to William Howard Taft, April 18, 1903, Taft Papers, Family Correspondence, Box 35, Library of Congress; Cincinnati, "Mayor's Annual Message," *Annual Reports of the City Departments . . . 1902* (Cincinnati, 1903), pp. ix, xi.
5. Under the new code the mayor appointed the board of sinking fund trustees, the bipartisan board of public safety which controlled the police and fire departments, the board of health, and the University of Cincinnati board of trustees, the latter two of which were formerly appointed by the superior court. The sinking fund trustees appointed the park and hospital boards. A five-man board of health was added and the number of wards was reduced from thirty-one to twenty-four with five additional city council members elected at large. The mayor also got the veto. *Citizen's Bulletin,* March 14, 1903, p. 4; Cincinnati, "Mayor's Annual Message," *Annual Reports . . . 1902,* op. cit pp. x-xi; Cincinnati, "Mayor's Annual Message," *Annual*

Reports of the City Departments . . . 1904 (Cincinnati, 1905), p. iii.
6. Samuel Spencer to Joseph B. Foraker, January 15, 1898, Box 39, CHS; J. G. Schmidlapp and James J. Hooker to Samuel Spencer, December 23, 1897, Foraker Papers, Box 39, CHS; Samuel Spencer to J. G. Schmidlapp and James J. Hooker, January 14, 1898, Foraker Papers, Box 39, CHS; Cincinnati, "Mayor's Annual Message," *Annual Reports . . . 1902,* op. cit. pp. vi-vii.
7. Delos F. Wilcox, *The American City: A Problem in Democracy* (New York, 1906), pp. 128–32.
8. Cincinnati, "Annual Report of the Board of Public Service," *Annual Reports . . . 1900,* op. cit. pp. 1250–51.
9. Cincinnati, "Mayor's Annual Message," *Annual Reports . . . 1902,* op. cit. pp. x-xv, xxi.
10. Cincinnati, "Report of the Bath-house Department," *Annual Reports . . . 1904,* op. cit. pp. 1623–27.
11. Cincinnati, "Mayor's Annual Message," *Annual Reports . . . 1900,* op. cit. pp. xii-iii; "Mayor's Annual Message," *Annual Reports . . . 1902,* op. cit. pp. xxv-vi; "Mayor's Annual Message," *Annual Reports . . . 1904,* op. cit. p. viii.
12. Cincinnati, "Mayor's Annual Message," *Annual Reports . . . 1902,* op. cit. pp. vii-viii; "Mayor's Annual Message," *Annual Reports . . . 1904,* op. cit. p. vii.
13. *Cincinnati Enquirer,* March 5, 1903, pp. 7, 12; March 26, 1903, p. 7; April 1, 1903, p. 12; April 4, 1903, p. 10; *Cincinnati Volksblatt,* April 4, 1903, p. 4.
14. *Cincinnati Enquirer,* March 4, 1903, p. 12; March 18, 1903, p. 12; *Citizen's Bulletin,* March 14, 1903, p. 1; March 28, 1903, p. 5.
15. *Cincinnati Enquirer,* March 8, 1903, p. 8; March 20, 1903, p. 12; March 26, 1903, p. 3; April 4, 1903, p. 8; *Citizen's Bulletin,* March 14, 1903, p. 2.
16. *Cincinnati Enquirer,* March 22, 1903, pp. 3, 6; March 29, 1903, p. 3; March 31, 1903, p. 7. Afterward the guests, except Cox, signed a public letter claiming that the girls were dressed as nurses, not nuns, and that they did not dance. Goldsmith, moreover, disclaimed any intention of offending anyone and described himself as a life-long respector of all creeds. In addition, the dressmaker who made the costumes, F. Szwirschina, a Catholic, issued a notarized statement saying that Goldsmith had placed an order simply for nurses' costumes. That, apparently, is precisely what he got.
17. *Catholic-Telegraph,* March 26, 1903, p. 4; April 2, 1903, pp. 1–2, 4; *Cincinnati Volksfreund,* March 28, 1903, p. 4; March 31, 1903, p. 4; *Citizen's Bulletin,* March 28, 1903, p. 1.
18. Election returns compiled from Hamilton County Board of Elections, *Record of City Elections Commencing 1888 . . .* op. cit. pp. 122–34. The Socialist ticket received but 3751 votes, most of them from the non-Catholic German wards in the Zone.

19. *Citizen's Bulletin,* April 11, 1903, p. 1; May 9, 1903, p. 3; August 29, 1903, p. 2.
20. Ibid. September 22, 1905, p. 1.
21. Ibid. July 15, 1903, p. 1. For the Socialist party slate, dominated by German names, but headed by Edward Gardener, see *Cincinnati Enquirer,* September 2, 1905, p. 16. The *Citizen's Bulletin* did not discuss the Socialists.
22. John M. Pattison to Brand Whitlock, July 6, 1905, Brand Whitlock Papers, General Correspondence, Box 10, Library of Congress. The Hamilton County delegation to the state convention voted against Pattison, but Milton A. McRae of the *Post* persuaded him to make the race. See *Citizen's Bulletin,* August 26, 1905, p. 4; Milton A. McRae, *Forty Years in Newspaperdom* (New York, 1924), pp. 229–30.
23. For the quote from Scripps see Negley D. Cochran, *E. W. Scripps* (New York, 1933), p. 56. Also see Charles P. Taft to William Howard Taft, November 7, 1906, Taft Papers, Family Correspondence, Box 36, Library of Congress. According to Scripps his reform venture cost him the support of the "Interests" but the paper continued to turn a profit. For this and the paper's feeding "from the swill trough of corrupt politics" under McRae, see Charles R. McCabe (ed.), *Damned Old Crank: A Self Portrait of E. W. Scripps Drawn From His Unpublished Writings* (New York, 1951), pp. 162–64.
24. Cochran, op. cit. p. 56; McRae, op. cit. pp. 275–76; *Cincinnati Post,* October 5, 1905, p. 2; October 13, 1905, p. 1; October 23, 1905, p. 3. *The Chronicle* endorsed a labor union candidate on the Democratic ticket, but said nothing else. It did not, however, as it had in the past, publish the ads of Republican candidates. See *The Chronicle,* November 4, 1905, p. 4.
25. *Cincinnati Post,* October 19, 1905, p. 1; *Citizen's Bulletin,* December 1, 1906, pp. 3–4.
26. *Citizen's Bulletin,* September 16, 1905, p. 1; September 30, 1905, pp. 1–2, 4; October 7, 1905, p. 4; October 28, 1905, p. 14.
27. Steffens, *The Struggle for Self Government* . . . op. cit. pp. 200–204; *Citizen's Bulletin,* July 15, 1905, p. 4. Steffens later said that he did not tell all that he learned and that Cox disagreed only with the charge that he tampered with the courts. Steffens also claimed that he told reporters and reformers that Cox could be beaten and that they agreed to nominate a ticket and use Steffens's article to stir up the voters to prove him wrong about the city's satisfaction with bossism. See Steffens, *The Autobiography* . . . op. cit. pp. 485, 488, 490.
28. Howard C. Hollister to Horace D. Taft, October 13, 1905, Taft Papers, Family Correspondence, Box 36, Library of Congress; Lincoln Steffens to Theodore Roosevelt, August 7, 1905, in Ella Winters and Granville Hicks (eds.), *The Letters of Lincoln Steffens* (New York, 1938), p. 169.

29. William Howard Taft to Charles P. Taft, October 21, 1905, Taft Papers, Family Correspondence, Box 36, Library of Congress; Pringle, op. cit. Vol. I, pp. 268–69; Myron T. Herrick to William Howard Taft, October 9, 1905, Taft Papers, Family Correspondence, Box 37, Library of Congress.
30. *Cincinnati Enquirer*, October 22, 1905, pp. 1–2. The *Post* interpreted the speech as a message from Roosevelt constituting part of his fight against business and political graft. It also lumped Cox, Herrick, and Dick together as part of the machine. See *Cincinnati Post*, October 23, 1905, pp. 1, 2. Foraker spoke out for the city ticket after Taft's blast. Herrick and Dick avoided the subject, but Warren G. Harding took pot-shots at Cox. See *Cincinnati Enquirer*, October 27, 1905, p. 3; October 30, 1905, p. 2.
31. *Cincinnati Volksblatt*, October 30, 1905, p. 4; November 4, 1905, p. 4. The *Volksfreund* supported the Democrats.
32. Rufus B. Smith, *The Influence of the Germans of the United States on Its Life and Institutions, An Address delivered by Rufus B. Smith before the German Societies of Cincinnati, on German Day, September 3d, 1905* (Cincinnati, n.d.), pp. 3–10, 12. The *Citizen's Bulletin* noted that "a number of gentlemen of Jewish stock," and particularly Rabbi Philipson, had helped in "arousing our people to a sense of civic duty" in the campaign. See *Citizen's Bulletin*, November 18, 1905, p. 4; December 2, 1905, p. 4.
33. Dempsey carried wards One, Two, Four, Five, Nine, Eleven, Twelve, Thirteen, Fourteen, Fifteen, Sixteen, Seventeen, Nineteen, Twenty, Twenty-one, Twenty-two, Twenty-three, and Twenty-four. Of the wards carried by Dempsey, Pattison failed in Nine, Eleven, Twelve, Thirteen, Seventeen, Nineteen, Twenty, and Twenty-two, all of them heavily German and Catholic districts. Hamilton County Board of Elections, "Abstract of Votes Cast for 1904 to 1907" (unpublished ms. in the office of the Hamilton County Board of Elections, n.d.), n.p.
34. *Cincinnati Enquirer*, November 8, 1905, p. 7; November 9, 1905, p. 12.

CHAPTER 12

1. Cincinnati, *Mayor's Annual Message, 1907* (Cincinnati, 1907), pp. 56–61; *Citizen's Bulletin*, April 7, 1906, p. 7; February 2, 1907, p. 1.
2. Cincinnati, *Mayor's Annual Message*, op. cit. pp. 9–11. Between 1885 and 1897 the tax rate fluctuated from a low of $26.40 to a high of $28.32. Under Tafel it stayed between $25 and $26. During Fleischmann's two terms it dropped steadily from $25.98 in 1900 to $22.38 in 1905. See *Citizen's Bulletin*, August 28, 1909, p. 1.
3. Cincinnati, *Mayor's Annual Message*, op. cit. p. 78; Cincinnati Municipal Reference Bureau, op. cit. p. 16.
4. Cincinnati, *Mayor's Annual Message*, op. cit. pp. 46–51. *Citizen's*

Bulletin, September 15, 1906, p. 12; May 19, 1906, p. 15; April 20, 1907, pp. 1, 5, 10; May 4, 1907, pp. 1, 9; *Cincinnati Commercial-Tribune,* November 29, 1911, p. 10; Cincinnati Park Commission, *A Park System for the City of Cincinnati* (Cincinnati, 1907), p. 49.

5. *Citizen's Bulletin,* March 31, 1906, pp. 3–4; July 20, 1907, p. 4; Cincinnati, *Mayor's Annual Message,* op. cit. pp. 23–26; Cincinnati, "Health Department Report," *Annual Reports of the City Departments . . . 1906* (Cincinnati, 1907), pp. 240–43, 305–14.

6. Cincinnati, *Mayor's Annual Message,* op. cit., pp. 15–17, 26; *Citizen's Bulletin,* September 1, 1906, pp. 1–2; March 2, 1907, pp. 4–5.

7. Cincinnati, *Mayor's Annual Message,* op. cit. pp. 38–43; *Cincinnati Enquirer,* November 21, 1905, p. 12; *Citizen's Bulletin,* April 21, 1906, pp. 12–13.

8. Cincinnati, *Mayor's Annual Message,* op. cit. pp. 20–23; *Citizen's Bulletin,* November 24, 1906, p. 11; December 22, 1906, p. 4; *Cincinnati Enquirer,* September 1, 1906, p. 8.

9. Cincinnati, *Mayor's Annual Message,* op. cit. pp. 7–9; *Cincinnati Volksfreund,* November 18, 1905, p. 4; *Citizen's Bulletin,* January 13, 1906, p. 8. Dempsey discontinued, without arousing criticism, the medical inspection of prostitutes. See *Citizen's Bulletin,* January 20, 1906, p. 15.

10. Cincinnati, *Mayor's Annual Message,* op. cit. pp. 5–6, 62–63, 68–69.

11. Daniel Kiefer to Brand Whitlock, April 16, 1906, Whitlock Papers, General Correspondence, Box 11, Library of Congress; Edward F. Alexander to Author, op. cit.

12. *Cincinnati Enquirer,* September 22, 1907, p. 6; September 25, 1907, p. 6; September 27, 1907, p. 7.

13. Ibid. October 2, 1907, p. 3; *Cincinnati Post,* October 1, 1907, pp. 1, 2. In the voting Pfaff had the backing of wards One, Two, Three, Fourteen, and Eighteen.

14. *Citizen's Bulletin,* October 12, 1907, pp. 1, 4; *Cincinnati Post,* October 8, 1907, p. 1. The City party also endorsed some members of the Democratic ticket.

15. *Cincinnati Enquirer,* October 15, 1907, p. 7; October 17, 1907, p. 12; November 8, 1907, p. 7; *Cincinnati Post,* October 23, 1907, p. 5.

16. See Fenton Lawson to Brand Whitlock, November 7, 1907, Whitlock Papers, General Correspondence, Box 14, Library of Congress.

17. *Citizen's Bulletin,* December 23, 1905, p. 5; March 17, 1906, p. 5. For a list of the first one hundred members of the Roosevelt Club see *Citizen's Bulletin,* October 20, 1904, p. 4.

18. Theodore Roosevelt to Joseph B. Foraker, February 21, 1907, in Elting E. Morison (ed.), *The Letters of Theodore Roosevelt* Vol. V (Cambridge, Mass., 1952), pp. 595–96; John Galvin to Joseph B. Foraker, January 20, 1907, Foraker Papers, Box 64, CHS; Charles P. Taft to William Howard Taft, May 6, 1907, and May 20, 1907, Taft Papers, Family Correspondence, Box 37, Library of Congress; William Howard Taft to Charles P. Taft, May 8, 1907 and May 11,

1907, Taft Papers, Family Correspondence, Box 37, Library of Congress; William Howard Taft to Nicholas Longworth, May 13, 1907, Taft Papers, Family Correspondence, Box 37, Library of Congress.
19. *Citizen's Bulletin,* May 11, 1907, pp. 5, 8; May 25, 1907, p. 16; June 1, 1907, p. 8.
20. Ibid. September 14, 1907, p. 1; October 5, 1907, p. 4; Charles P. Taft to William Howard Taft, September 2, 1907, Taft Papers, Family Correspondence, Box 37, Library of Congress; Joseph Garretson to Charles P. Taft, [date in part illegible], 1907, Foraker Papers, Box 88, CHS. Fleischmann lunched with Roosevelt on August 12. See Theodore Roosevelt to Nicholas Longworth, June 26, 1907, in Morison, op. cit. pp. 695–96.
21. *Cincinnati Post,* October 9, 1907, p. 3; *Cincinnati Enquirer,* September 15, 1907, Main Sheet, p. 3; October 17, 1907, p. 6; Joseph B. Foraker to Charles Dick, September 30, 1907, Foraker Papers, Box 25, CHS; Joseph B. Foraker to J. F. Walker, October 9, 1907, Foraker Papers, Box 61, CHS; Theodore Roosevelt to Alice Roosevelt Longworth, November 10, 1907, in Morison, op. cit. pp. 836–37.
22. *Citizen's Bulletin,* October 19, 1907, p. 4.
23. *Cincinnati Post,* November 5, 1907, p. 9; November 6, 1907, p. 5; *Cincinnati Enquirer,* November 5, 1907, pp. 4, 5; Hamilton County Board of Elections, *Abstract of Votes Cast from 1904–1907,* op. cit., n.p. The Socialist candidate polled 1669 votes, almost half of them in the Seventh, Tenth, Eleventh, and Twelfth, the so-called German wards in the Zone.
24. *Citizen's Bulletin,* November 16, 1907, pp. 1, 4–5.
25. *Cincinnati Post,* November 20, 1907, p. 7; November 21, 1907, p. 6; A. E. B. Stephens to Joseph B. Foraker, November 21, 1907, Foraker Papers, Box 72, CHS; George W. Hays to Joseph B. Foraker, November 22, 1907, Foraker Papers, Box 65, CHS; John C. Gallagher to Joseph B. Foraker, February 13, 1908, Foraker Papers, Box 77, CHS; William Greene to Joseph B. Foraker, February 21, 1908, Foraker Papers, Box 77, CHS; unsigned letter to Joseph B. Foraker, February 29, 1908, Foraker Papers, Box 77, CHS; Dabney, *Cincinnati Colored Citizens . . .* op. cit. p. 119.
26. *Citizen's Bulletin,* March 7, 1908, p. 4; April 11, 1908, p. 4; July 18, 1908, p. 4.
27. Joseph B. Foraker to Warren G. Harding, November 7, 1908, Foraker Papers, Box 48, CHS; Theodore Roosevelt to William Howard Taft, January 1, 1909, in Morison, op. cit. Vol. VI, pp. 1454–55.
28. Charles P. Taft to William Howard Taft, January 2, 1909, Taft Papers, Family Correspondence, Box 38, Library of Congress.
29. For a sample of Charles P. Taft's advice to the President on local politics and patronage see Charles P. Taft to William Howard Taft, April 30, 1909, February 11, 1910, December 16, 1910, and Jan-

uary 5, 1911, Taft Papers, Presidential Series, No. 3, Box 523, Library of Congress.

CHAPTER 13

1. *Cincinnati Post,* October 1, 1909, p. 15; October 26, 1909, p. 9.
2. *Citizen's Bulletin,* July 31, 1909, p. 4; *Cincinnati Volksblatt,* October 19, 1909, p. 4.
3. *Citizen's Bulletin,* July 17, 1909, p. 4.
4. *Cincinnati Enquirer,* September 14, 1909, p. 4; September 23, 1909, p. 3; *Cincinnati Volksblatt,* October 31, 1909, p. 3; *Cincinnati Post,* October 2, 1909, p. 8; October 26, 1909, pp. 1, 9.
5. Ibid. October 19, 1909, pp. 1, 7; October 30, 1909, pp. 1, 7. The Republicans claimed Hunt's honest voter campaign was "merely an attempt to intimidate Republican voters who are poor." See *Cincinnati Enquirer,* October 27, 1909, p. 5.
6. *Citizen's Bulletin,* August 28, 1909, p. 1; September 4, 1909, p. 1; *Cincinnati Post,* October 12, 1909, p. 1; October 23, 1909, p. 9; October 25, 1909, p. 1.
7. Election returns from Hamilton County Board of Elections, "Abstract of Votes Cast from 1908–1911 Inclusive" (Cincinnati, unpublished ms. in the offices of the Hamilton County Board of Elections, n.d.), n.p.
8. *Cincinnati Enquirer,* November 3, 1909, pp. 9, 12; November 4, 1909, p. 7.
9. It bears repeating that the GOP strategy of moderate reform in the 1880's and 1890's rested on voter support from the Zone and Hilltops. After 1897, however, the same strategy was kept, but the base of Republican power shifted to the Circle. All of these administrations were careful to avoid antagonizing the "personal liberty" forces.
10. *Citizen's Bulletin,* March 21, 1908, p. 3; February 13, 1909, p. 4; May 15, 1909, p. 4; August 21, 1909, p. 4; November 14, 1909, p. 4.
11. Ibid. August 29, 1908, p. 4; September 30, 1911, p. 4.
12. Ibid. January 8, 1910, p. 4; August 27, 1910, p. 4; January 8, 1910, p. 4; June 11, 1910, p. 4; September 24, 1910, p. 4.
13. A. Julius Freiberg, "Mayor Hunt's Administration in Cincinnati," *National Municipal Review,* Vol. III (July 1914), pp. 517–18.
14. *Citizen's Bulletin,* February 22, 1908, p. 4; April 4, 1908, p. 4; May 30, 1908, p. 1; August 1, 1908, pp. 1–2.
15. George Kibbe Turner, "The Thing Above the Law; the Rise and Rule of George B. Cox and His Overthrow by Young Hunt and the Fighting Idealists of Cincinnati," *McClure's Magazine,* Vol. XXXVIII (November 1911–April 1912), p. 588; Freiberg, op. cit. p. 518.
16. *Cincinnati Post,* February 22, 1911, p. 2; February 25, 1911, p. 1;

Citizen's Bulletin, February 25, 1911, p. 4. Eight of the fifteen members of the grand jury were City Club members.

17. Reprinted in *Cincinnati Post,* May 15, 1911, pp. 1–2.

18. Freiberg, op. cit. p. 518; Turner, op. cit. pp. 589–90; *Citizen's Bulletin,* March 18, 1911, pp. 1–3; May 27, 1911, p. 4.

19. William Howard Taft to Rud Hynicka, July 15, 1910, Taft Papers, Letterbooks, Presidential Series 8, Library of Congress; William Howard Taft to Joseph Garretson, August 1, 1910, Letterbooks, Presidential Series 8, Library of Congress. For the Longworth reception see *Citizen's Bulletin,* September 24, 1910, p. 4, and Pringle, op. cit. p. 616.

20. Charles P. Taft to William Howard Taft, January 19, 1911, and January 20, 1911, Taft Papers, Presidential Series, No. 3, Box 253, Library of Congress; William Howard Taft to Franklin Alter, January 14, 1911, Taft Papers, Letterbooks, Presidential Series 8, Library of Congress.

21. *Cincinnati Post,* May 15, 1911, p. 1.

22. William Howard Taft to Horace D. Taft, November 1911, Taft Papers, Letterbooks, Presidential Series 8, Library of Congress; *Cincinnati Times-Star,* May 21, 1911, p. 1.

23. William Howard Taft to Horace D. Taft, November 1911, Taft Papers, Letterbooks, Presidential Series 8, Library of Congress; William Howard Taft to Joseph Carew, July 25, 1911, Taft Papers, Letterbooks, Presidential Series 8, Library of Congress.

24. *Cincinnati Commercial-Tribune,* November 4, 1911, p. 1.

25. Max B. May to Judson Harmon, July 20, 1911, Harmon Papers, June–July 1911, CHS; Judson Harmon to Henry T. Hunt, November 8, 1911, Harmon Papers, November 1911, CHS.

26. Henry T. Hunt, *An Account of My Stewardship of the Office of Prosecuting Attorney* (Cincinnati, n.d.), pp. 6, 10–11; Anon., *The Approaching City Election* (Cincinnati, n.d.), pp. 20–21. See *Citizen's Bulletin,* November 18, 1911, p. 2, for a tabulation of Hunt's election promises.

27. *Cincinnati Commercial-Tribune,* October 1, 1911, p. 1; October 9, 1911, p. 7; October 28, 1911, p. 4; October 29, 1911, p. 1; *Cincinnati Times-Star,* November 6, 1911, p. 6; *Cincinnati Volksblatt,* November 2, 1911, p. 2; November 5, 1911, pp. 12–13. For Burbank and reform see *Cincinnati Freie Presse,* November 10, 1911, p. 4. The "Dutch will get it in the Neck" editorial was in German, but the title in English. See *Cincinnati Freie Presse,* November 1, 1911, p. 4.

28. *Cincinnati Post,* March 20, 1911, p. 9; *Cincinnati Times-Star,* November 8, 1911, pp. 1, 12. The Socialist candidate, Lawrence A. Zitt, got only 2648 votes. Zitt ran poorest in the Circle and Hilltops and best in the Zone where he received from 100 to 261 votes in each ward. Election returns from the Hamilton County Board of Elections, *Abstract of Votes . . . 1908–1911,* op. cit.

CHAPTER 14

1. *Citizen's Bulletin,* February 17, 1912, p. 5. For the *Monitor* comment see *Cincinnati Post,* November 29, 1912, p. 15.
2. *Cincinnati Volksblatt,* November 2, 1913, p. 15; Brand Whitlock, "Henry T. Hunt," *The American Magazine,* Vol. LXXIV (July 1912), p. 297; *Cincinnati Post,* May 7, 1912, p. 12.
3. Henry T. Hunt, "Obligations of Democracy," *The Yale Law Review,* New Series, Vol. VI (April 1917), p. 598; *The Chronicle,* January 27, 1912, p. 4.
4. The recollections of Hunt came from Judge John Druffel to Author, Interview, October 31, 1963; Robert Goldman to Author, Interview, February 26, 1963; Robert Heuck to Author, op. cit.; Max Hirsch to Author, Interview, March 15, 1963; Herbert F. Koch to Author, Interview, November 15, 1962; A. J. Murdock to Author, Interview, October 9, 1963; Charles Sawyer to Author, Interview, October 16, 1963.
5. *Citizen's Bulletin,* November 2, 1912, p. 3; June 15, 1912, p. 3.
6. *Cincinnati Post,* February 25, 1913, p. 7; *Citizen's Bulletin,* April 26, 1913, p. 1.
7. *Citizen's Bulletin,* June 15, 1912, p. 4.
8. Ibid. February 24, 1912, p. 7; March 9, 1912, p. 7.
9. L. D. Upson, "Cincinnati's First Municipal Exhibit," *The American City,* Vol. VII (December 1912), pp. 530-32; *Cincinnati Post,* October 2, 1912, p. 4; *Citizen's Bulletin,* August 3, 1912, p. 7.
10. Anon., "Cincinnati's Budget Exhibit," *The Survey,* Vol. XXIX (November 23, 1912), p. 218.
11. *Cincinnati Post,* October 1, 1913, p. 17.
12. Cincinnati, "Budget Exhibit," *Annual Reports of the City Departments . . . 1912* (Cincinnati, 1913), p. 21; *Cincinnati Post,* September 30, 1913, p. 1.
13. *Citizen's Bulletin,* May 10, 1913, p. 1.
14. Cincinnati, "Report of the Superintendent of the Department of Charities and Correction," *Annual Reports of the Offices, Boards and Departments of the City of Cincinnati, 1913* (Cincinnati, n.d.), pp. 306-7, 315-17, 317-18.
15. Cincinnati, "Cincinnati House of Refuge," *Annual Reports . . . 1913,* op. cit. pp. 333-54; *Citizen's Bulletin,* March 16, 1912, p. 7.
16. Cincinnati, "Bureau of Social Investigation and Relief," *Annual Reports . . . 1913,* op. cit. pp. 320-24, 326-32; *Cincinnati Post,* December 18, 1911, p. 10; *Citizen's Bulletin,* January 20, 1912, pp. 2, 6; February 17, 1912, p. 7; April 6, 1912, p. 1.
17. *Citizen's Bulletin,* February 17, 1912, p. 6; March 5, 1912, p. 6; December 14, 1912, p. 6.
18. Cincinnati, "Department of Police," *Annual Reports . . . 1913,* op. cit. p. 212; "Department of Health," *Annual Reports . . . 1913,*

op. cit. p. 490; *Citizen's Bulletin,* April 13, 1912, p. 2; June 28, 1913, p. 6.

19. *Cincinnati Post,* January 12, 1912, p. 12; October 2, 1912, p. 9; December 18, 1912, pp. 1, 13; Juvenile Protective Association, *A Report of Its Second Year's Work* (Cincinnati, 1914), p. 12.

20. *Cincinnati Post,* July 8, 1913, p. 1.

21. *Cincinnati Post,* March 4, 1912, p. 1; March 9, 1912, p. 8; Anon., *An Account of the Administration of Henry T. Hunt and His Associates* (Cincinnati, 1913), n.p.

22. Cincinnati, "Women's Civic Commission," *Annual Reports . . . 1913,* op. cit. pp. 22–23; *American Israelite,* December 5, 1912, p. 6; *Cincinnati Post,* December 31, 1912, p. 10.

23. Cincinnati, "Housing Department," *Annual Reports . . . 1913,* op. cit. pp. 579–93.

24. *Civic News,* Vol. II (December 1912), p. 1; *Cincinnati Post,* November 29, 1912, p. 1.

25. *Civic News,* Vol. II (December 1912), p. 1; *Cincinnati Post,* December 7, 1912, p. 8; Cincinnati, "Mayor's Annual Message," *Annual Reports . . . 1913,* op. cit. pp. 5–6.

26. Cincinnati, "Mayor's Annual Message," *Annual Reports . . . 1913,* op. cit. pp. 7–8; "Canal Subway Division," *Annual Reports . . . 1913,* op. cit. pp. 110–13; *Civic News,* Vol. II (April 1913), p. 1; *Cincinnati Post,* January 31, 1912, p. 8.

27. *Citizen's Bulletin,* May 31, 1913, p. 6.

28. *Cincinnati Post,* June 4, 1913, pp. 1, 7.

29. Ibid. July 30, 1913, p. 1; July 31, 1913, p. 1; S. Gale Lowrie, "Cincinnati's Charter Campaign," *National Municipal Review,* Vol. III (October 1914), pp. 730–31.

30. Ellis G. Kinkaid to Joseph B. Foraker, May 20, 1913, Foraker Papers, Box 108, CHS; *Civic News,* Vol. II (May 1913), p. 1; *Cincinnati Post,* October 17, 1913, p. 1; Marc N. Goodnow, "Motormen and Mayor in Strike Strategy," *The Survey,* Vol. XXX (July 28, 1913), pp. 432–33.

31. *Citizen's Bulletin,* August 2, 1913, p. 1.

32. *Cincinnati Post,* July 1, 1913, p. 1; July 10, 1913, p. 1; *The Chronicle,* July 5, 1913, p. 4; "Cincinnati's Ice Strike," *The Survey,* Vol. XXX (September 6, 1913), pp. 678–80; "City in the Ice Business," *The Literary Digest,* Vol. XLVII (July 19, 1913), pp. 82–83. The board of health actually seized and operated the ice plants. See Cincinnati, "Department of Health," *Annual Reports . . . 1913,* op. cit. pp. 483–84.

33. Cincinnati, "Mayor's Annual Message," *Annual Reports . . . 1913,* op. cit. p. 9.

CHAPTER 15

1. *Cincinnati Post,* January 6, 1913, p. 1.
2. Ibid. May 8, 1912, p. 1; May 10, 1912, p. 1; June 1, 1912, p. 1.
3. Charles P. Taft to William Howard Taft, June 5, 1912, Taft Papers, Presidential Series, No. 3, Box 326, Library of Congress; Thomas Pogue to William Howard Taft, June 14, 1912, ibid; *Cincinnati Post,* June 12, 1912, p. 2.
4. Ibid. March 17, 1913, p. 1; April 17, 1913, p. 3; July 16, 1913, p. 1; Judge Walter Shohl to Author, Interview, November 19, 1962. Shohl and Frank S. Dinsmore represented Cox in these cases. See *Cincinnati Post,* June 2, 1913, p. 1.
5. Ibid. November 13, 1911, p. 1; May 25, 1912, p. 1.
6. Ibid. October 30, 1912, p. 1. Also see *Citizen's Bulletin,* July 6, 1912, p. 4; William Howard Taft to Scott Small, September 18, 1912, Taft Papers, Presidential Series, No. 3, Box 523, Library of Congress.
7. James A. Green to Joseph C. Green, March 12, October 12, October 22, 1912, Green Papers, CHS; *Cincinnati Post,* October 1, 1912, p. 1; October 14, 1912, p. 2.
8. H. R. Probasco to Joseph B. Foraker, March 20, 1912, Foraker Papers, Box 105, CHS; Joseph B. Foraker to Charles Kurtz, October 24, 1912, Foraker Papers, Box 105, CHS; P. J. Brady to Carl Mahren, October 31, 1912, Foraker Papers, Box 105, CHS.
9. Joseph B. Foraker to Charles Kurtz, op. cit.; William Howard Taft to William Warrington, May 29, 1912, Taft Papers, Letterbooks, Presidential Series 8, Library of Congress.
10. Roosevelt got a total of 12,907 votes in the county and 9970 in the city, most of them in the First and Second on the Hilltops, and the Third, Sixteenth, Twentieth (Price Hill), and Twenty-third in the Zone. Eugene V. Debs had 6520, virtually all of them from Zone districts. Election returns from Hamilton County Board of Elections, "Abstract of Votes Cast . . . 1911–1914" (unpublished ms. in the offices of the Hamilton County Board of Elections, n.d.), n.p.
11. *Cincinnati Post,* November 6, 1912, p. 1; November 8, 1912, p. 1.
12. *Citizen's Bulletin,* March 8, 1913, p. 4.
13. A. Julius Freiberg, "Mayor Hunt's Administration in Cincinnati," *National Municipal Review,* Vol. III (July 1914), p. 522; *Citizen's Bulletin,* January 25, 1913, p. 6; *Cincinnati Post,* February 18, 1913, p. 7; *Cincinnati Freie Presse,* October 31, 1913, p. 2; November 2, 1913, p. 4.
14. *Citizen's Bulletin,* April 29, 1913, p. 6; June 14, 1913, p. 6; August 2, 1913, p. 4; Alexander to Author, op. cit.
15. Matthews to Author, op. cit.; *Cincinnati Post,* January 20, 1912, p. 1; May 1, 1913, p. 2; August 18, 1913, p. 5; James A. Green to

Joseph C. Green, August 16, 1913, and August 28, 1913, James A. Green Papers, CHS; *The Chronicle*, September 13, 1913, p. 4.

16. *The Chronicle*, August 30, 1912, p. 13.
17. Goldman to Author, op. cit.; *Citizen's Bulletin*, February 15, 1913, p. 6.
18. *Cincinnati Post*, May 9, 1913, p. 2; *Cincinnati Freie Presse*, November 3, 1913, p. 5.
19. *Cincinnati Post*, July 8, 1913, p. 1; *Cincinnati Freie Presse*, October 10, 1913, p. 2.
20. *Cincinnati Post*, May 29, 1913, p. 4; September 27, 1913, p. 4.
21. *Citizen's Bulletin*, September 13, 1913, pp. 4, 6; October 4, 1913, p. 5.
22. *Citizen's Bulletin*, August 9, 1913, p. 4; *Cincinnati Volksblatt*, October 14, 1913, p. 4.
23. "Annual Report Number," *The Optimist*, Vol. II (December 1913), p. 34.
24. *Catholic-Telegraph*, August 28, 1913, p. 4.
25. *Cincinnati Post*, July 16, 1912, p. 4; September 4, 1912, p. 2; September 7, 1912, p. 4; July 20, 1912, p. 7.
26. *Citizen's Bulletin*, September 14, 1912, p. 4; July 20, 1912, p. 4.
27. *Cincinnati American*, October 13, 1913, p. 3; *Cincinnati Post*, October 13, 1913, p. 3. This outburst of tribalism, like that of the 1880's and 1890's, also coincided with a period of heavy outward migration.
28. *Cincinnati Post*, October 16, 1913, p. 7; *Cincinnati American*, October 27, 1913, p. 4.
29. *Catholic-Telegraph*, November 20, 1913, p. 4; *Cincinnati Freie Presse*, October 25, 1913, p. 5. The *Catholic-Telegraph* estimated that the roster of city officials was 12 per cent Catholic while 60 per cent of the voters were members of the church. See *Catholic-Telegraph*, November 20, 1913, p. 4.
30. *Cincinnati Post*, May 26, 1913, p. 3; *Cincinnati Volksblatt*, November 1, 1913, p. 3.
31. See, e.g. *Cincinnati Volksblatt*, October 14, 1913, p. 4; *Cincinnati Freie Presse*, October 14, 1913, p. 4; James A. Green to Joseph C. Green, November 5, 1913, James A. Green Papers, CHS.
32. *Cincinnati Freie Presse*, October 12, 1913, p. 2; October 15, 1913, p. 4; October 31, 1913, p. 4; *Cincinnati Volksblatt*, October 3, 1913, p. 4; October 21, 1913, p. 4; November 3, 1913, p. 4.
33. *Cincinnati Volksblatt*, October 19, 1913, pp. 28–31; *Cincinnati Volksblatt*, October 22, 1913, p. 3; October 31, 1913, p. 4; November 3, 1913, p. 4; *Cincinnati Post*, July 23, 1913, p. 1.
34. Gotthard Deutsch to Josef Spitz, August 7, 1914, Gotthard Deutsch Correspondence, American Jewish Archives; *Cincinnati Post*, October 13, 1913, p. 4.
35. James A. Green to Joseph C. Green, October 6, 1913 and November

5, 1913, James A. Green Papers, CHS; *Cincinnati Post*, October 13, 1913, p. 4.

36. *Cincinnati Post*, September 15, 1913, pp. 1, 7; October 14, 1913, p. 10; October 11, 1913, p. 5; *Citizen's Bulletin*, October 18, 1913, pp. 1, 7; November 1, 1913, p. 2.

37. Ibid. November 1, 1913, p. 4.

38. Ibid. Hunt lost the two Hilltop wards by a total of 160 votes. He carried the First, Second, Third, Fifth, Ninth, Twelfth, Fourteenth, Seventeenth, Nineteenth, Twentieth, Twenty-first, Twenty-third, and Twenty-sixth. Thomas Hammerschmidt, the Socialist candidate for mayor, got 2746 votes. Election returns from Hamilton County Board of Elections, "Abstract of Votes Polled In the City of Cincinnati . . . on . . . The Fourth Day of November, 1913 from the Official Returns" (Cincinnati, unpublished ms. in the offices of the Hamilton County Board of Elections, 1913), pp. 2–21.

39. *Cincinnati Post*, November 12, 1913, p. 3; December 3, 1913, p. 7; *Cincinnati Times-Star*, November 5, 1913, p. 15.

40. *Citizen's Bulletin*, November 8, 1913, p. 4. Fleischmann, as we have seen, had always been something of a reformer.

CHAPTER 16

1. Cincinnati had never been organically serene. The point is that the particular situation which developed after 1880 was unique, probably exceeding both in quantity and quality the turbulence of the past, and hence delivered an intense shock to the city's social and political structure.

2. *Cincinnati Commercial-Gazette*, January 29, 1892, p. 4; *Cincinnati Post*, February 29, 1911, p. 2. Also see Zane L. Miller, intro. and ed., " 'Ruining Rudolph' [Hynicka] or 'Rud's Ready Relief,' " *Cincinnati Historical Society Bulletin*, Vol. XXIV (January 1966), pp. 41–67.

3. There were no significant differences in voting levels along Circle, Zone, and Hilltop lines. It should be noted, however, that the Circle, where one might expect to find political apathy rampant, usually had the highest marks. Indeed, in 1911, wards Six, Eight, and Eighteen scored nearly 100 per cent. These figures were computed from the election returns and federal censuses cited in the preceding chapters. All males over twenty-one, except those listed as aliens or those whose citizenship status was "unknown," were regarded as eligible voters. Others, doubtless, were not registered.

4. In the 1890's, only 20 per cent of the eligible voters were native-born whites of native parentage. In 1900, the figure stood at 23 per cent, and in 1910 at 32 per cent. Of this minority, not all, obviously, were Anglo-Saxon, old-family, or veteran urbanites. They were, however, like the majority, all strangers to the new city.

These figures and this study, in short, suggest that urbanization rather than Americanization was the central theme of all these newcomers' experience.

5. *Cincinnati Post,* May 15, 1911, pp. 1–2; *Cincinnati Times-Star,* May 21, 1911, p. 1.

Index

Adams, Henry, 53
Alter, Franklin, 48
American Civic Association, 113
American Protective Association: peak strength of, 256n24; rise of, 65–66
Ancient Order of Hibernians, 36
Anglos, Julius, 233
Annexation, 6, 26, 42, 57, 108, 109; and growth of city, 6; to 1940, 109; political importance of, 57; and population density, 26; referendum, 107–8; and taxes, 108
Anti-Saloon League, 166
Apartments, 42, 46, 49
Arnold, Bion J., 221
Associated Charities of Cincinnati, 17, 147–48; objects of, 271–72n4
Austrians, 13, 14
Avondale, 119, 165–66, 229; annexed, 107–8; anti-Semitism in, 47, 52–53; crime in, 55; described, 42; population of, 48
Avondale Presbyterian Church, pastor on religion and reform, 143

Bader, Frederich, 85, 205

Basin, 3–6, 8, 54, 221; business district, 4; exodus of industry and people, 26; housing and population in, 4; real estate values in, 4; topography, 3
Bauer, Daniel, 87, 218
Bauer, Morris, 87
Bernard, Lewis, 89, 193, 202
Berner, William, 59
Bettinger, Albert, 194, 209
Bettmann, Alfred, 214–15, 223–24
Bettmann, Bernhard, 84
Bigelow, Herbert S.: and anti-Catholicism, 234; and election of 1909, 202; and election of 1913, 237; and People's Church, 144–145; and traction, 222–23, 231
Board of Education, 153, 156; of Trade, 100
Bode, August H., 86–87
Bogen, Boris D.: on Cincinnati Jewry, 129; on Cincinnati Judaism, 132; on immigrant organizations, 21–22
Bond Hill, annexed, 177
Bond issues, 99, 108, 150, 204, 210–211, 223, 230

Urban Life and Urban Landscape Series

Zane L. Miller, General Editor

The series examines the history of urban life and the development of the
urban landscape through works that place social, economic, and political
issues in the intellectual and cultural context of their times.